Fathers, Daughters, and Slaves

Women Writers and French Colonial Slavery

T0355671

LIVERPOOL STUDIES IN INTERNATIONAL SLAVERY, ⁻

Fathers, Daughters, and Slaves

Women Writers and French Colonial Slavery

Doris Y. Kadish

Liverpool University Press

First published 2012 by
Liverpool University Press
4 Cambridge Street
Liverpool
L69 7ZU

Copyright © 2012 Doris Y. Kadish

This paperback version published 2014.

British Library Cataloguing-in-Publication data
A British Library CIP record is available

ISBN 978-1-84631-846-7 cased
ISBN 978-1-78138-113-7 paperback

Typeset by Carnegie Book Production, Lancaster
Printed and bound by CPI Group (UK) Ltd, Croydon CR0 4YY

Contents

List of Figures   vi

Acknowledgments   vii

Introduction   1

1   Patriarchy and Abolition: Germaine de Staël   31

2   Fathers and Colonization: Charlotte Dard   53

3   Daughters and Paternalism: Marceline Desbordes-Valmore   80

4   Voices of Daughters and Slaves: Claire de Duras   103

5   Uniting Black and White Families: Sophie Doin   127

Postscript   152

Bibliography   161

Index   172

List of Figures

1 Joseph Vernet, *La Mort de Virginie* (1789)   16

2 Firmin Massot, *Mme de Staël à côté du buste de son père Jacques Necker* 33

3 Western coast of Africa and islands of Senegal   55

4 Théodore Géricault, *Le Radeau de la Méduse* (1816)   65

5 *Portrait de Sophie Doin*   130

6 Guillaume Guillon-Lethière, *Serment des ancêtres* (1822)   143

7 Anne-Louis Girodet, *Portrait du citoyen Belley, ex-représentant des colonies* (1797)   153

Acknowledgments

This book represents a decade-long project that was interrupted along the way, as is often the case in the academic world, by administrative duties that I was unable to avoid. As it turns out, those interruptions were felicitous, for each time I returned to the project I saw it in a new and, it is to be hoped, more coherent and insightful way. Throughout, the University of Georgia provided me with research and travel support that I greatly appreciate. I am grateful to Liverpool University Press for encouraging me to be a part of their growing and impressive listings in Francophone and colonial studies. Anthony Cond and Charles Forsdick, whom I had the good fortune to meet on a visit to Liverpool, and Alison Welsby, with whom I have worked subsequently, made publishing this book a very positive experience.

I have lived, as it were, with the five women who are studied in this book for a long time. Not only have they been at the center of my research agenda and intellectual life, but they have become a part of me and my way of seeing their world and my own. I doubt whether I will ever cease reaching back over two centuries to once again attempt to unravel the tangled threads of their lives and works. Having the occasion to make contact in the twentieth and twenty-first centuries with persons connected to these women has been a very special experience for me. My contacts with Marc Doin considerably enriched my understanding of his progenitor Sophie Doin. Bernadette Dupont, a descendant of Charlotte Dard, kindly met with me in Paris and provided me with information and documents concerning her ancestor. Figuring out the intricacies of Dard's family life was a daunting task. I am grateful in this regard to Jean-Luc Angrand, a descendant of the African *signares* whose lives intersected with those of the Dard family, for providing me with invaluable information.

For over twenty years I have been part of the wonderful community of scholars in the Nineteenth-Century French Studies Association who meet annually at the Nineteenth-Century French Studies Colloquium. Some of the work that is included in this book was presented at those meetings where I received insightful feedback and collegial support for my research. Those whose work has been especially important to my research include Aimée Boutin, Heather Brady, Barbara Cooper, Daniel Desormeaux, Deborah Jenson, Adrianna Paliyenko, Christine Planté, and Pratima Prasad. I express my gratitude for their assistance and encouragement. Others with whom I shared ideas and discussions are too numerous to name, but I thank them all.

I wish to make special acknowledgment to scholars with whom I worked closely in the publication of material related to this book. Roger Little provided great support as the editor of the Harmattan series in which I published the volumes of Charlotte Dard's and Sophie Doin's writings. In addition, I have worked closely over the years with three collaborators— Françoise Massardier-Kenney at Kent State University, Norman R. Shapiro at Wesleyan University, and Deborah Jenson at Duke University. The professionalism, depth, and dependability of their collaborative work in writing, translating, editing, and other tasks has sustained me in what might otherwise have been an unduly lonely, arduous process.

I gratefully acknowledge the assistance of a number of other scholars. Sarga Moussa, Karyna Szmurlo, and Carol Mossman invited me to deliver papers on Staël that were occasions for me to develop further my ideas on an author whom I have admired and studied for many years and whose work figures prominently in this volume. Lisa Van Zwoll, who served as my research assistant, discovered important material that enabled me to compare several different editions of *Sarah*. At a Staël conference, I learned from Heather Belnap Jensen's paper about the portrait that appears on the cover of this book and that is analyzed in the Postscript. James Smith Allen and Denise Z. Davidson kindly agreed to read and comment on early drafts of the Introduction. Michel Hanniet provided me with information about Dard materials to which I did not have access.

I wish to acknowledge previous publication of versions or sections of the material included in this book. Part of Chapter 1 appears in Tilli Boon Cuillé and Karyna Szmurlo, eds, *Germaine de Staël: Forging a Politics of Mediation* (Oxford: Voltaire Foundation, 2011). A French version appeared in *Littérature et esclavage* (Lyon: Editions Desjonquères, 2010). A portion of Chapter 2 is published in French in my introduction to *La Chaumière africaine* (Paris: L'Harmattan 2005). Part of the analysis in Chapter 3 is found in my introduction to *Sarah* (New York: MLA, 2008) and in my article "*Sarah* and Antislavery," *L'Esprit créateur* 47, 4 (2007). Parts of the material in Chapter 4 were published in "Black Faces, White Voices in Women's Writing from the 1820s," in *Approaches to Teaching Duras's Ourika*, ed. Mary Ellen Birkett and Christopher Rivers (New York: MLA, 2008) and in "Rewriting Women's Stories: *Ourika* and *The French Lieutenant's Woman*," *South Atlantic Review* 62, 2 (1997). Chapter 5 draws in part on material in my article "Haiti and

Abolitionism in 1825," *Yale French Studies* 107 (2005). I thank the publishers for permission to reprint these items.

This book is dedicated to the late Laurence Schehr who served with me as co-president of the Nineteenth-Century French Studies Association for many years. His joyful embrace of our profession and its members, young and old, served as an inspiration to all of us laboring away daily at our computers and in libraries or classrooms.

Introduction

Pour devenir adulte, il faut accomplir deux naissances, la première bien réelle hors du ventre maternel, et l'autre plus secrète et imprévisible hors du ventre paternel. L'histoire est un piège tendu par nos pères.

(To become an adult, you must be born twice. The first birth is the real one from your mother's womb. The second, more secret and unpredictable one, is from the paternal womb. History is a trap set by our fathers.)[1]

Writing in the first decades of the early nineteenth century, a cohort of French women assumed the role of advocates of persons of African descent, the "slaves" referred to in the title of this book.[2] *Fathers, Daughters, and Slaves* looks at how these women writers pictured themselves, their biological and symbolic fathers, and the real and fictional blacks who appear in their writings. The works by these women are crucial for a full understanding of French and Atlantic history in the revolutionary and postrevolutionary years, a time when the French colonial world was menaced by the re-establishment of slave-holding authority and when class, race, and gender identities were being renegotiated. These unique contributions by women in an era of colonial nostalgia and unresolved triangular trade ambitions allow us to move beyond the traditional boundaries of exclusively male accounts by missionaries, explorers, functionaries, and military or political figures. They remind us of the imperative for ever-renewed gender and feminist research in the colonial archive.

Some of the women who told the stories considered in this book lived through the dramatic circumstances of the French or colonial revolutions and produced gripping accounts of how those events affected the lives of women and blacks.[3] Some committed themselves to the cause of enslaved Africans in exceptional and public ways that were unusual for women of their time. Those who were well-known authors include Germaine de Staël and

Claire de Duras, both of whom personally bore the effects of the harrowing events of the French Revolution, and Marceline Desbordes-Valmore, who narrowly escaped death during the slave uprisings in Guadeloupe in 1804. Two lesser-known women also demonstrated commitment to the cause of blacks in the early years of the nineteenth century. Charlotte Dard, the only woman among the survivors of the infamous wreck of the *Medusa* to have told its tale, was involved in the education of African children. Sophie Doin, a passionate defender of the downtrodden, both slaves and workers, published a series of texts about slavery and then went on to edit a journal, *Le Christianisme*, that addressed social and literary issues in the 1830s. Such different life experiences and literary achievements notwithstanding, these women all similarly helped shape the image of blacks for their contemporaries and for readers of nineteenth-century literature today.

Fathers, Daughters, and Slaves approaches these women writers from the angle of paternal authority. Admittedly, the notion of "the father" may seem somewhat anachronistic in the twenty-first century, with the increasing body of work on women's simultaneous mobility and vulnerability in colonial libertinage, queer paradigms, and recent models of economic, political, and religious globalization. But for these early nineteenth-century women, the father was the touchstone for personal and collective identity. Using the terms of the title expansively, this book dwells on the circumstances under which "daughters" in the late eighteenth and early nineteenth centuries came to call into question the oppression that "fathers"—figures of power and mastery—exercised over persons of color and over themselves and other women.[4] These women were not the "rebel daughters" of the French Revolution who openly asserted their feminine rights and even, as in the case of Olympe de Gouges, combined feminism and abolitionism.[5] Some were members of *ancien régime* aristocracy or the upper classes; others were from a younger generation that not only did not live through the upheaval of the Revolution but, under the censorship imposed during the Napoleonic era, may have had limited knowledge of France's revolutionary past. None were members of the working class, as were some of the later avatars of French revolutionary feminism, the Saint-Simonian women of the 1830s.[6] They were not overtly rebelling against the authority of their own fathers, some of whom—Staël's, Dard's, and Duras's—were abolitionists. But their fathers were for the most part either absent or diminished economically or politically as a result of the revolutionary events. Indeed, bolstering up the paternal image was one of the permutations of these writers' refashioning of the traditional daughter/father relationship. Others include following in the footsteps of substitute fathers, constructing themselves as the paternal authority, pledging allegiance to new political leaders, or denouncing illegitimate father figures. Regardless of how the centrality of the father emerges in their writings, however, it is clear that for women who came to maturity in the decades following the beheading of the nation's "legitimate" monarch, and thus at a time of weakened symbolic and political authority, the struggle to define oneself in relation to the father featured centrally in the formation of feminine identity.

Where do slaves enter the picture? The women considered here happen to have been cast in roles—either as exiles, colonists, travelers in the colonial world, or by being linked to that world through familial or political connections—that heightened their awareness of the condition of blacks. That condition triggered an emotional response that had deep-seated roots in their psychology and particular circumstances as women. That response can be designated as "empathy," a term that dates from the early twentieth century and is closely related to eighteenth-century notions of sympathy, compassion, and pity.[7] In *The Theory of Moral Sentiments*, Adam Smith speaks of "our fellow-feeling for the misery of others." He states that "it is by changing places in fancy with the sufferer, that we come either to conceive or to be affected by what he feels."[8] The nineteenth-century women who wrote about black issues arguably responded in an empathetic way that went beyond the more generalized or conventional notions of kindness and charity typically associated with and performed by women of the upper classes. Empathy suggests a more personal, visceral, spontaneous response. It entails understanding the emotions, reading the feelings, and standing in the place of those whose suffering one shares. Moreover, as Suzanne Keen explains, it is a "feeling precursor to and prerequisite for liberal aspirations to greater humanitarianism [...] empathy is associated with the moral emotion sympathy (also called empathetic concern) and thus with altruistic action."[9] I argue that many postrevolutionary women who themselves experienced estrangement, exile, loss of property, and disruption of family were able to imagine and discursively construct the emotions of blacks, to intertwine the thoughts and moods of that other disadvantaged group with their own, and to embrace the cause of the amelioration of their condition.[10] Empathy drives such antislavery sentiments as horror for the slave trade and for the inhuman treatment of slaves; recognition that blacks were feeling, thinking human beings endowed with the same moral and intellectual capacities as whites; and belief in the civilizing factors of education and religion.

The empathy that the women writers considered here displayed was grounded in the specific social conditions of their times; for, as Edward Said reminds us, authors are "very much in the history of their societies, shaping and shaped by that history and their social experience."[11] Authors are not only *shaped by* their culture but they actively contribute to *shaping* it, a fact that is often downplayed regarding nineteenth-century women writers. For if it is true that French women were denied rights of citizenship during and following the French Revolution, it is also true that these women were neither cloistered in domestic spaces nor wholly cut off from the social and cultural climate of their time. On the contrary, they performed a part in a period in French history when the status and condition of blacks was both a major political issue and a prominent literary theme. Not only were these women aware of the stakes of the system of slavery for blacks, for themselves, and for society at large, but they contributed productively to contemporary debates about that system. Empathetic French women chose to address an issue that they saw as directly affecting the lives of all subordinate members of society.

This book contends that in the postrevolutionary period women writers found themselves placed between two sharply opposed economic and social communities: white paternal authorities, whose power was real but considerably diminished, and black slaves, whose lack of power mirrored specific conditions in the experience of women and elicited their empathetic response. Clearly, these white women were not exempt from the colonialist sentiments of men whose hegemonic control of their society remained intact. Together, white men and women shared what Said calls a "structure of attitude and reference" that enabled slavery to exist as an economic system. That description refers to

> the way in which structures of location and geographical reference appear in the cultural languages of literature, history, or ethnography, sometimes allusively and sometimes carefully plotted, across several individual works that are not otherwise connected to one another or to an official ideology of 'empire.'[12]

Although it is true that these early nineteenth-century women did not challenge their society's undergirding philosophy of colonial domination and expansion, it is my contention that their responses to victims of colonial oppression differ from those written by male writers of their time: examples from the 1820s include Victor Hugo's *Bug Jargal*, Prosper Mérimée's *Tamango*, and Charles de Rémusat's *L'Habitation de Saint-Domingue*. These works by men focus on violent revolts and romantic rivalries between black and white male protagonists. They dwell on male heroes modeled after Toussaint Louverture, as would Lamartine several decades later. Like Lamartine, Rémusat was an especially empathetic writer. Indeed, he received his intellectual formation at the knees of his celebrated mother, Claire de Rémusat, and of Germaine de Staël, whose liberal, abolitionist views he emulated. Yet his treatment of blacks in *L'Habitation de Saint-Domingue* differs markedly from that found in women's works. Such is similarly the case with Bernardin de Saint-Pierre, even though he stands as the eighteenth-century model of empathetic writing about blacks for later abolitionist literary writers. As empathetic as Bernardin, Rémusat, or Lamartine may be, they do not develop such key gender-determined features as family, education, and agency for women and blacks, which are emphasized in women's abolitionist writings.

Another notion that Said illuminates has inspired the reference to the Francophone world in my title.[13] Said speaks of a contrapuntal method of analysis, "a simultaneous awareness both of the metropolitan history that is narrated and of those other histories against which (and together with which) the dominating discourse acts."[14] Although French scholars often overlook or undervalue these other stories, a certain number of them were produced in the late eighteenth and early nineteenth centuries. Others date from the twentieth century. Together, the corpus of stories produced by white and non-white writers who were schooled in the French language and imbued with French culture constitutes the set of "intertwined and overlapping histories" that Said recommends reading contrapuntally. These stories share a structure of attitude and reference to a considerable extent. At the same time, however, revealing differences are apparent. Placing writings by white women in the broader context of non-European writings by and about blacks that share the same themes and concerns enables us to draw comparisons and contrasts with respect to race, class, and gender. It permits a global perspective that avoids the narrow Eurocentric reading that nineteenth-century literature has too often received.[15] It prevents us from reading European works "stripped of their affiliations with the facts of power which informed and enabled them."[16] The point is not to attribute praise or blame. Whether male or female, white or black, writers at the time were both complicitous with and resistant toward the societal values of the world in which they lived. As Said observes, "cultures are humanly made structures of both authority and participation, benevolent in what they include, incorporate, and validate, less benevolent in what they exclude and demote."[17]

The notion of a broad cultural and ideological structure of attitude and reference, which provides a general sense of the commonality among the authors considered here, also needs to be fleshed out in very specific ways. Such detailed accounts matter greatly for women writers from the early decades of the nineteenth century. In the case of lesser-known writers, especially women, it is regrettably still necessary to make the case that women participated as equal partners in the historical and intellectual currents of their time. Specifically we need to ask where these women writers stood politically, where their writings fit into French literary history, and how their writings compare to those by other writers—white and non-white, their contemporaries and authors from the twentieth century—whose works also dwell on slavery in the Francophone world.

* * *

The women writers discussed in this book lived through the tumultuous aftermath of the French Revolution and the Napoleonic empire, which was marked by a search for legitimate and progressive figures of paternal authority. What roles could women play in such a world that denied them basic civil rights and the vote?[18] Although disenfranchised politically, these women did have increasing access in the post-Napoleonic era to information about current affairs and to the field of publishing. Moreover, although they were largely excluded from certain cultural centers of power such as universities, literary clubs, and editorial positions, they assumed prominent roles in lycées, scholarly societies, and the press.[19] Wealthy women also had access to influential political men through the culture of the salon, which assumed increasing importance during the Restoration. The fall of Napoleon—a despotic, illegitimate father in the eyes of most of these women writers—inaugurated a regime of constitutional monarchy which "made public opinion a real force in politics, created a framework for perpetual debate, and allowed party politics to spill over into le monde, as it had in the early 1790s."[20] Salons run by women became sounding boards that registered the deliberations of the Chambers. As political power shifted from the court to the Chambers, France saw the rising power of ministers, parliament, the press, and highly political ministerial salons hosted by salonnières. With the restoration of legitimate Bourbon monarchs, the place reserved for the symbolic father of the nation was ostensibly filled, but his position was far from secure. Having been forced to adopt the Charte and adhere to the principles of constitutional monarchy, Louis XVIII and his more repressive successor Charles X were painfully aware of the fact that their authority no longer derived from divine right but, under the principles of constitutional monarchy, from the will of the French people. Most of the women writers considered here, all of whom were situated on the political left or center, accepted the moderate royalism of Louis XVIII but joined the chorus of increasing resistance against the conservative measures taken by Charles X as the end of the 1820s approached.

Although some areas of women's political influence such as the salon have received considerable attention, we still do not know enough about other ways in which women functioned in the political world of their time and what impact they had. The window on to early nineteenth-century women's political opinions and activities that this book provides is that of antislavery. In *The Creation of Patriarchy*, Gerda Lerner notes the profound historical link between slavery and the subordination of women. Men's dominance over women preceded and served as a model for whites' dominance over blacks. Force, economic dependency, class privilege, notions of inferiority, control over bodies for labor and procreation: Lerner claims that all of these features of gender dominance apply to that which is based on race. She thus views the subordination of women and of blacks as inextricably connected: "As subordination of women by men provided the conceptual model for the creation of slavery as an institution, so the patriarchal family provided the structural model."[21] Asserting that "the predominant family structure in the Biblical narrative is the patriarchal family," Lerner points out that the wife called her husband master; that she was listed among his possessions along with servants and animals; and that in the early period the patriarch could sell his children.[22] When we learn that Desbordes-Valmore's father actually sold her brother as a military conscript, we should perhaps not be surprised that in her novella *Sarah* she cast herself imaginatively in the role of a slave.[23] Doris Garraway observes moreover that in early colonial history, women were so scarce that wives were indeed purchased, like slaves: "Men avid for conjugal pleasures and domestic comforts essentially purchased women as indentured servants and 'freed' them in marriage."[24]

Lerner's analysis of the workings of patriarchy also sheds light on the reasons why women's contributions to antislavery have been dismissed or undervalued. It is not that women have no history but that they have failed to gain control of the symbolic systems of society and thus have been ignored as agents of history:

> Women and men have entered historical process under different conditions and have passed through it at different rates of speed. If recording, defining, and interpreting the past marks man's entry into history, this occurred for males in the third millennium B.C. It occurred for women (and only some of them) with a few notable exceptions in the nineteenth century. Until then, all History was for women pre-History.[25]

Fathers, Daughters, and Slaves calls attention to one such instance of historical neglect: the considerable role played by French women in relation to antislavery in the postrevolutionary era.[26] Even the few literary critics who recognize women's importance at that time tend to subject them to an aestheticizing triage and to judge them in relation to male standards of literariness such as realism, which developed later in the century. Hence there is a paradox underlying such seminal literary studies as Léon-François Hoffmann's *Le Nègre romantique* (1973) and Yvan Debbasch's "Poésie et traite: l'opinion française sur le commerce négrier au début du XIXᵉ siècle" (1961). Having rescued from oblivion lesser-known works about blacks, some of which were written by women, these and other critics feel impelled to denigrate women's writing as "awkward," "inconsistent," "melodramatic," and "mediocre." These critics fail to see women writers' sensitivity to broader issues such as memory, hybridity, creolization, identity formation, and the ideological implications of pity, paternalism, and sentimental discourse.

Lerner's analysis of patriarchy also sheds light on the essential issue of co-option. This term suggests the absorbing or assimilating of members of a group into a system they serve and may even struggle against. Co-option affects privileged educated women, but also women more generally, who function under

> a form of patriarchy best described as paternalistic dominance. The term describes the relationship of a dominant group, considered superior, to a subordinate group, considered inferior, in which the dominance is mitigated by mutual obligations and reciprocal rights. The dominated exchange submission for protection, unpaid labor for maintenance.[27]

According to this analysis, the subordinate group are often unable to see their privilege. Nor are they able to see that they themselves are exploited and, indeed, perhaps also exploiters. Subordination of women continued even after the absolute legal and economic power of the male head ended in the nineteenth century with the granting of civil rights to women: "Patriarchy in its wider definition means the manifestation and institutionalization of male dominance over women and children in the family and the extension of male dominance over women in society in general."[28] But it is important to stress that subordination does not necessarily mean lack of agency: "It implies that men hold power in all the important institutions of society and that women are deprived of access to such power. It does not imply that women are either totally powerless or totally deprived of rights, influence, and resources."[29] Women's history is not just a history of oppression, nor is oppression just the work of men. Lerner's point is that women were not only objects of oppression but also participants in a power struggle in which they were assigned to subordinate positions.

Benedict Anderson's description of political agency is especially relevant for understanding how early nineteenth-century French women participated in interrogating the structures of authority in their time. Anderson speaks of an age "in which Enlightenment and Revolution were destroying the legitimacy of the divinely-ordained, hierarchical dynastic realm," in which vertical hierarchies were replaced by a notion of community, and in which, "regardless of the actual inequality and exploitation that may prevail in each, the nation is always conceived as a deep, horizontal comradeship." Community was built at this time through, among other things, literature: "fiction seeps quietly and continuously into reality, creating that remarkable confidence of community in anonymity which is the hallmark of modern nations."[30] As Anthony Appiah notes in a similar vein,

> If nationals are bound together, it is [...] by language, law, and literature, and if they share an experience of events it is [...] through their shared exposure to narrations of those events [...] they bind citizens not in a

shared relation to gods, kings, and heroes, but as fellow participants, 'equivalent persons' in a common story.[31]

If stories about blacks provided by empathetic women in the early decades of the nineteenth century could thus impact the construction of personal and national identities, why has so little attention been paid to them in accounts of French women's history? They have often remained shrouded in obscurity because, like so many other works, they have failed to be translated, anthologized, or in some way nudged into the center or at least the discernible margins of the canon. Also, they do not exactly fit comfortably within the history of feminism. These women stand in an ambiguous relation to their subordination as women. Most did not consider themselves feminists, viewing women's role in society according to notions of social complementarity or moral harmony that seem distinctly unfeminist by today's standards. Like other French women of their time, they tended to place such other concerns as the needs of members of the lower classes above their own condition as women. Only sporadically do they show an awareness of the oppressed condition of women or the movements to improve that condition that had existed earlier in France or other countries.[32]

But as James Smith Allen has shown, nineteenth-century French women forged a women's culture in their writings and their lives that is well worth our attention: they provided models for a flexible religious dogma, for greater symmetry in married life, for better education for girls, and for a more substantial public role for women. Even women who did not openly address the status of women are important for women's history because "they developed the conceptual language [...] so essential to women's historical identity, agency, and resistance. Their independence of mind, their commitment to ideals of their own, but primarily their discursive practices in common with other women like them made a difference."[33] They crafted a language to suit their needs for commitment, independence, and action; they manifested in their lives that they had some control over their world; and through writing they functioned in a space outside of the family.[34] They show how women of their time conceived matters of identity, consciousness, agency, and resistance. Although from an Anglo-American perspective we tend to define feminist foremothers in terms of a search for equality, for the French, writing was a defining factor in the formation of women's subjectivity: "*la femme auteur* represented more than the defiance of traditional notions of gender; she marked the intrusion of powerfully literate women into the politics of culture."[35]

It is also important to understand that early nineteenth-century women lived in a world in which tensions, conflicts, and rivalries between men and women existed. Their dissatisfactions and frustrations as women are not always apparent in the texts we consider here. But their silence does not obviate the fact that violence against women and gender inequalities were prevalent at the time, as they have been in other historical periods, including our own. As feminist historians remind us, it is crucial to keep in mind that "women's culture evolves amid tensions that produce symbolic equilibria, contracts and compromises of a more or less temporary nature. Specific practices as well as mere silence or absence organize these conflicts, which at times legitimize, reorient or control the logic of the powerful."[36]

One way of ferreting out issues of gender inequality is to take women writers' lives into consideration. The example of Sophie Doin, considered in Chapter 5, is illustrative. Doin was cast in a subordinate role as the wife of a Parisian doctor, Guillaume Tell Doin. Although they worked side by side as supporters of abolition and other philanthropic causes, supported throughout by Sophie's fortune, the fabric of their marriage became increasingly frayed, resulting in a legal separation and, in the final years, bitter recriminations on Sophie's part. When we read Doin's antislavery writings from the 1820s, what we see is a façade of social complementarity for both male/female and for black/white relations that seems smooth and impenetrable. Her later life raises the possibility, however, that the seeds of the later discontent had been sown in the 1820s. Guillaume Tell, not Sophie, was the member of the abolitionist Société de la morale chrétienne.[37] Since Sophie provided the financial resources for the family and actively published on the subject of slavery, she may have viewed her exclusion from that organization as an injustice that paralleled those inflicted upon her black characters. We cannot fully understand to what extent she connected the dots between the two forms of oppression. We can at least try to understand, however, the ways in which the two forms of oppression overlapped, as well as the factors that may have limited her ability to connect them.

As Said was quoted earlier as saying, "cultures are humanly made structures of both authority and participation, benevolent in what they include, incorporate, and validate, less benevolent in what they exclude and demote."[38] Doin and other early nineteenth-century women writers show the workings of such processes of inclusion and exclusion, of validation and demotion. In many ways their lives and their works exemplify what can be called "informal feminism":[39] gaining control of household finances or dowries, obtaining legal separations or rights to publish under a woman's own or her husband's name, influencing the public political positions taken by husbands and fathers, and more. But at the same time such patterns of inclusion and validation for women do not preclude other kinds of exclusions and demotions. Consider the role of the mother, who is excluded from the title *Fathers, Daughters, and Slaves* but whose presence is felt throughout this book. That the women considered here do not dwell on their roles as mothers or as daughters of mothers is not surprising in the post-Rousseauian era, when women were often relegated to an exclusively reproductive role. One form of "informal feminism" would have entailed downplaying that role. But as modern feminists remind us, to deny the mother is in one sense to deny oneself as a woman and to seek a male-oriented identity. Such is not the case with the women writers discussed here. Rather, they acknowledge the importance of motherhood indirectly, as in their writings about slaves. Through their empathetic identification with blacks, they succeed to some extent in moving outside of paternalism and establishing a connection with their own deep-seated needs as women.

* * *

Turning now to literary history, one finds a different but related story about the control of symbolic systems. Prior to the 1990s, male literary giants, especially novelists—Balzac, Flaubert, Hugo, Stendhal, Zola—enjoyed a dominance in nineteenth-century French literary studies that went largely unchallenged. Although a battle was being fought in conferences, literary journals, and classrooms to include texts by women, a thoroughgoing interrogation of the reasons for women's exclusion from the official literary canon had yet to be undertaken. An important step was taken in 1993 when Naomi Schor published *George Sand and Idealism*, which challenged the gendered aesthetic of realism against which Sand and other women writers had for so long been measured and found wanting. Schor's argument was all the more compelling in that, before the advent of an aesthetic privileging realism, Sand occupied a towering literary position worldwide. What by twentieth-century standards was considered sentimental, feminine, and inferior was by the standards of the nineteenth century viewed as politically visionary and philosophically profound. What was valued by Sand's contemporaries—"its utopian dimension, the ability of an ideal to empower and to mobilize the disenfranchised"[40]—is precisely what makes women's writings about blacks worthy of reconsideration and what explains why they too have lost favor with modern readers schooled to accept the evaluative standard of realism. Schor points the way to paying attention to literature that stands outside of the realist canon and detailing its precise political and literary characteristics. As Schor notes,

> Feminist critics or gynocritics have traditionally emphasized transhistorical, transnational, transclass, etc. specificities of women's writing, but I would argue that female specificity in writing is (also) contextual, local, a microspecificity that shifts opportunistically in response to changing macrohistorical and literary historical circumstances.[41]

Another important step in calling attention to women's exclusion from the male-centered orientation within nineteenth-century French studies was made by Margaret Cohen in *The Sentimental Education of the Novel*, published in 1999. Looking at the French novel more broadly than Schor, whose main focus is Sand, Cohen shows that a gender war of sorts was waged against women. At the center of the battle were competing aesthetic and epistemological values. In the early decades of the nineteenth century, as in the second half of the eighteenth century, the predominant mode, sentimental literature, was exemplified by women's writing. That literature can be described as follows: plots are concentrated and unspecific with respect to contemporary social events; family obstacles to marriage are central to the plot; characters are ethically driven; women's fate is emblematic of collective welfare; physical detail is minimal; material values are subordinate to moral ones. In sum, as Cohen states, "virtue is simultaneously the passive imperative to avoid fault and the active imperative to promote the moral order."[42] Citing prefaces and other nineteenth-century commentary, Cohen argues convincingly that male writers such as Stendhal and Balzac consciously chose to impose an aesthetic of realism by devaluing sentimental writing associated with women. In the new realist mode, the novel became masculinized through identification with knowledge possessed in male professions such as science. Knowledge could then be passed on to the reader, interpellated to identify with the male character of the realist *Bildungsroman*, who uses his acquired expertise to succeed in modern society and to dominate in social struggles. Subsequently, the male literary model has been handed down in male-dominated institutions of learning: for example, through an emphasis on the textual analysis of highly detailed descriptive language that is not found in women's sentimental writing.[43]

Because women's writing about blacks conforms in style and social outlook to sentimentalism, Schor's and Cohen's analyses provide a foundation for *Fathers, Daughters, and Slaves*. My approach differs from theirs by focusing more on the early decades of the century in their own right, rather than as points of comparison and contrast with the period during which realism gained literary hegemony.[44] I also emphasize women's political engagement during the Napoleonic era and the Restoration. Cohen acknowledges that the sentimental novel prior to 1830 constituted a locus for addressing the impasses of French revolutionary ideology and was thus far from apolitical.[45] But to my mind she marks too sharp a division between the early sentimental novel and what she defines as its sub-genre, the "social sentimental novel" after 1830. Cohen's dichotomy is based on what she sees as a new concern with social issues during the July Monarchy. But *Fathers, Daughters, and Slaves* shows that women writers addressed social issues during the first decades of the nineteenth century as well. "Social sentimental" writing was especially active during the 1820s, at the time of France's recognition of the independence of Haiti. The major change that took place after 1830 was that class replaced race as a major focus of women's concern with the oppressed. Among the authors considered here, several direct their attention to class issues at that time, notably Desbordes-Valmore and Doin. Cohen rightly observes regarding gender, however, that women's subordination receives increasing attention after 1830, even by women writers who refused to endorse a feminist agenda. As noted earlier, it is undoubtedly because the women writing about blacks prior to 1830 fail to fit into a progressive pattern of increased feminist consciousness that they tend to be overlooked in accounts of women's history.

If, as Schor and Cohen have shown, there is a story to be told about the sentimental novel and gender, there is a second one to be told that builds on these critics' attention to gender but does not leave race out of the picture. In that second story, fathers, daughters, and slaves play key roles. The relative lack of attention paid to race in works such as Schor's and Cohen's published in the 1990s perhaps reflects the fact that the inextricability of race, class, and gender had not gained the centrality within feminist scholarship that it has in recent years.

To retell the story of sentimental literature to include race, we must turn to the author who, as noted above, stands as the model for French colonial literature, Bernardin de Saint-Pierre.[46] Ironically, this author has always appeared prominently in standard accounts of "pre-romanticism," a literary designation that is closely tied to sentimentalism. According to those accounts, "exoticism" constitutes one of the features of the rejection of French classicism in the late eighteenth century and the establishment of romanticism in the early nineteenth century. The *locus classicus* of exoticism and pre-romanticism is Bernardin's *Paul et Virginie* (1788), a work that introduced a French reading public to stories set in precise colonial settings inhabited by both whites and blacks. It would be hard to overestimate the impact of Bernardin's work, not only at the time of its publication, but throughout the nineteenth century and up to the present time. From 1788 to 1950 there were more than 100 editions, and that number can be enlarged to nearly 400 editions if one counts translations and adaptations for the stage. The vast production of merchandise based on *Paul et Virginie* included buttons, buckles, lampshades, wallpaper, clocks, porcelain plates and cups, printed fabric, box-lids, books of paper cutouts, and embroidered suspenders.[47] The plethora of nineteenth-century dramatic and musical productions (dramas, ballets, operas, comedies, vaudeville performances) has continued into the twentieth century; it includes films, a TV series, even a song by Celine Dion. Serious literary works that interrogate the significance and implications of *Paul et Virginie*, which Chateaubriand claimed to know by heart, include Sand's *Indiana* and Baudelaire's *De L'Essence du rire*. As late as 1877, Flaubert named the two children in *Un Coeur simple* Paul and Virginie, an ironic reference to the lingering effects of romanticism in his time.

Bernardin's writings about slavery provide sentimental literature with a structure of attitude and reference that is inextricably tied to the story of fathers, daughters, and slaves, with greater emphasis placed, as one might expect, on fathers. *Voyage à l'île de France* represents one of the earliest literary works to directly address the issue of slavery. In Letter 12 of that work, the author targets "bad fathers" in denouncing the inhumane treatment to which slaves are subjected. In the author's preface to the first edition in 1773 he writes, "je croirai avoir été utile aux hommes, si le faible tableau du sort des malheureux noirs peut leur épargner un seul coup de fouet, et si les Européens, qui crient en Europe contre la tyrannie, et qui font de si beaux traités de morale, cessent d'être aux Indes des tyrans barbares" ("I hope that I can be useful to mankind if my feeble picture of the luckless blacks can save them from one single lash of a whip, and if Europeans, who cry out against tyranny in Europe, and who write such pretty treatises on morality, cease being barbarous tyrants in the Indies.")[48] The implication that certain writers represent bad figures of paternal authority is consistent throughout Bernardin's writings on slavery. Those works include the posthumously published play *Empsaël et Zoraïde ou les blancs esclaves des noirs à Maroc*, written during the French Revolution, *Voeux d'un solitaire* (1789), and *Suite des Voeux d'un solitaire* (1792). In addition to his denunciation of the mistreatment of slaves, Bernardin joined the chorus of other liberal voices such as Pierre Poivre, the governor of l'île de France, and Dupont de Nemours, a leading economist and political figure, in preferring a free indigenous or European labor force to imported African slaves.

In contrast with "bad fathers," Bernardin also paints the portrait of good representatives of male authority. A representative example is the tolerant philosopher in *La Chaumière indienne*, published in 1791. Although that work is set in India and focuses on a pariah rather than a slave, the underlying injustice to which pariahs and slaves are subjected is the same: they are condemned to live far from their native land; they are deprived of everything that is necessary and natural to their happiness; and, if they choose to flee their persecutors, they must spend their days in humble abodes hidden deep in the forest.[49] The well-intentioned philosopher is the model of the European who deplores prejudice and respects persons of other cultures, no matter how downtrodden or marginalized their condition may be. Of course, in addition to being antislavery philanthropists, most of the good male characters in Bernardin's works are Europeans involved in the colonial enterprise, which neither he nor other enlightened thinkers of his time called into question. Albert Memmi emphasizes the privileged status of Europeans in colonial settings and claims that, individual good will notwithstanding, a colonial exemplifies the exploitative economic system of which he is a part.[50] In a related vein, Jean-Paul Sartre observes that the white man has for three thousand years enjoyed the privilege of seeing without being seen.[51] This is tantamount to saying that the visual powers and privileges reserved for the European male in exotic, sentimental literature such as Bernardin's stem from their economic advantages, and that to see a foreign culture as different, picturesque, and exotic is at the same time to impose one's values on it.

Paternal authority occupies an especially salient position in the structure of reference and attitude of *Paul et Virginie*. Although women are the founders of the small community—Paul and Virginie; their mothers, Marguerite and Mme de la Tour; and their slaves, Domingue and Marie—authoritative white males provide its political and ideological foundation. An earlier settler and slave owner, Virginie's father M. de la Tour, represents those who introduced slavery on to the island. Chris Bongie observes that he "thereby turned every habitant into a tyrant" and that, following M. de la Tour's death,

> the repressed figures of the father repeatedly come back to haunt the text; most obviously embodied by the slave-owning habitant who lives on the banks of the Black River and around whom the text's first extended narrative sequence is centered, this malignant authority is that which eventually, through the dictates of the colony's governor, M. De la Bourdonnais, puts an end once and for all to Paul and Virginia's isolation.[52]

Moreover, a white male initiates the narration and assumes a validating role in relation to the stories of less privileged narrators or characters, women or slaves. This unnamed frame narrator enjoys superior historical, geographical, and linguistic mastery. His authority is then passed on to the benevolent old man who knew the protagonists of the story and who, as a stand-in for the characters' absent biological fathers, is referred to on several occasions as "father." His empathetic attitude toward slaves echoes that expressed by the real governor of île de France, Pierre Poivre, who stated, "What situation could be more delightful than that of a benevolent master, who lives among his slaves, as a father lives among his children?"[53]

Subordination does not imply a complete lack of agency, however. It is true that the outcome for all of the women in *Paul et Virginie* is tragic, with the possible exception of the phallic mother, Virginie's malevolent aristocratic aunt. But it is also true that the mothers and Virginie display certain empowered behaviors that inspired women writers in the early decades of the nineteenth century and reappear in their stories: crossing the

Figure 1.
Joseph Vernet,
*La Mort de
Virginie* (1789).
Reproduction
courtesy of
Art Resource.

ocean alone; establishing a home in an unfamiliar and undeveloped land; sustaining a community formed of other women, children, and blacks; gaining awareness of and having compassion for the condition of slaves; struggling to resist repressive forces in colonial and metropolitan society. It is not surprising then that, as an example of an eye-witness colonial account by an empathetic antislavery writer, *Paul et Virginie* stands as a foundational text for women writers, many of whom also knew about the colonies from their first-hand experience. That text furnished them with a stock of sentimental plots, characters, names, places, settings, objects, and scenes. Joseph Vernet captured salient elements in his 1789 painting *La Mort de Virginie* (Figure 1): ships arriving or departing, and beaches where blacks and whites face tragedy together. Such scenes appear in several of the works considered in this book. Other elements drawn from *Paul et Virginie* include huts in a forest inhabited by oppressed or persecuted individuals; vertical images implying moments of Christian transcendence or authority; lovers separated by prejudices of race or class; and well-meaning young people struggling to counter the cruelty exercised by older men. Such recurring intertextual components of stories about blacks by women writers provide further justification for grouping these writers' works together and including them as an early chapter in the history of nineteenth-century women and the sentimental novel.

* * *

Is it possible to envision the nineteenth-century story of slavery from below, that is, from the perspective of black agents themselves? Would their voices resound with the same paternalistic overtones as those found in a work such as *Paul et Virginie*? Would black authors assign different roles to women? These are the questions addressed by the Guadeloupian author Daniel Maximin in *L'Isolé soleil*, published in 1981. This complex, multi-generational novel includes one of the most illuminating Francophone examples of the genre of the neo-slave narrative. In that genre, practiced by Octavia Butler, Toni Morrison, Barry Unsworth, Caryl Phillips, Edward Jones, and others, contemporary authors use their imagination, oral histories, and already-existing slave narratives to construct stories about slavery. As John Erickson describes Maximin's writing, "It is a (hi)story in which poetry, song, and legend commingle, that expresses through metaphoric and connotative rather than discursive and denotative language, through exploded rather than linear narrative."[54] Neo-slave narratives such as Maximin's are especially important since no authentic slave narratives have survived in the Francophone world.[55]

Through a series of imbricated stories spanning several centuries, Maximin echoes our corpus of nineteenth-century women writers in deconstructing male ownership of the stories of slavery and abolition. By attributing decisive roles to black women characters, he shows that male heroism has assumed disproportionate significance in Caribbean history. *L'Isolé soleil* posits the existence of a slave narrative dating from the turn of the nineteenth century, the Cahier de Jonathan. Maximin then traces Jonathan's account of slavery across the multiple generation of his family. *L'Isolé soleil* thus makes the point that the rebellious spirit fostered in some blacks such as Jonathan under slavery has persisted up to the modern age, especially among women who have played a privileged role in preserving the slave legacy. As one of those women, Ti-Carole, reminds others on a number of occasions, "que ton ventre se souvienne" ("may your womb remember.")[56] Fictional feminine characters serve in Maximin's narration not only to counterbalance the overvaluation of male heroes but to propose an alternative, non-violent account of the past. Maximin embellishes the historical record by adding a poem that he attributes to a slave woman, thus calling into question the assumption that black women were merely sexual objects or mothers and giving them an empowered voice as writers. He thus echoes Staël's attribution of poetic talent to an African woman in *Mirza*.

There are a number of notable ways in which Maximin applies the principle of history "rethought by and for us" to his retelling of the story of fathers, daughters, and slaves. One is to present the agency of blacks, male and female, as consistent yet diverse. Jonathan's recourse to violence is not the only or necessarily the most significant form of agency foregrounded in *L'Isolé soleil*. Two characters—Jonathan's twin and Carole in the post-emancipation period—teach black children, as we shall see Charlotte Dard doing in our discussion of *La Chaumière africaine* in Chapter 2. Other generations respond differently. The character Marie-Gabriel in the twentieth century proposes the feminist solution that I have cited in the epigraph of this introduction, "Pour devenir adulte, il faut accomplir deux naissances, la première bien réelle hors du ventre maternel, et l'autre plus secrète et imprévisible hors du ventre paternel. L'histoire est un piège tendu par nos pères" ("To become an adult, you must be born twice. The first birth is the real one from your mother's womb. The second, more secret and unpredictable one, is from the paternal womb. History is a trap set by our fathers.") (117, 108) In other words, rethinking history entails not only rethinking the dominance of whites but of paternal authorities as well. As Marie-Gabriel writes, "tu écriras […] pour te libérer du paternalisme, de la loi du retour aux pères et des enfants prodigues, et de tout ce qui cherche à revenir au même" ("you will write […] to free yourself from paternalism, from the law of the return of the prodigal fathers and children, and from everything that tries to go back to itself"). (19, 11)

Maximin's treatment of the good abolitionist father is especially noteworthy. Like M. Primrose in Desbordes-Valmore's *Sarah*, Jean-Baptiste Alliot is an enlightened and benevolent plantation owner. He expresses his gratitude to his domestic servant Miss Béa and her sons Jonathan and Georges by emancipating them. Jonathan resents Alliot's benevolent act, considering that liberating a few slaves "était un moyen sûr de retarder la révolte qui donnerait au plus tôt la liberté à tous" ("was a sure way to slow down the revolt that would soon give freedom to all.") (33, 27) His resentment turns to rage when a group of drunken colonists rape and kill his young sister Angela, the friend and playmate of Alliot's white daughter Elisa. In retaliation, Jonathan shoots Elisa, despite his affection for her. His action is motivated by his desire to ignite rebellion among the maroon insurgents on the island with whom he joins forces. Before Alliot is executed for his abolitionist activities, he manages to document some of the tortures inflicted upon slaves "afin que la Société des amis des Noirs s'en serve pour faire progresser la cause de l'abolition" ("so that the Société des amis des Noirs could use them to further the cause of abolition.") (65, 60) Rather than forwarding Alliot's pages to the abolitionists in France, Miss Béa enters them into the Cahier de Jonathan, where they become one source and one voice among others in the multifarious account of slavery that, as Maximin would have it, whites and blacks need to construct together. Just such a construction is at the heart of Sophie Doin's writing, as we shall see in Chapter 5.

L'Isolé soleil goes to the heart of a question to which I will return repeatedly in *Fathers, Daughters, and Slaves*: to what extent and how do non-white writers differ with respect to the structure of attitude and reference that has prevailed in the Francophone world since the inception of slavery? Writing a novel that was published in 1981, Maximin seems aware of the charges of machismo that have been leveled against twentieth-century male French Caribbean writers. Choosing to write in a post-structuralist, deconstructive mode, Maximin introduces various narrative components that promote gender equality such as alternating women and men as narrators, imagining slave women as writers, and foregrounding cultural means of social change rather than only violent, military ones.[57] As one might suspect, the male nineteenth-century writers from the French colonies discussed in this book do not share Maximin's awareness about issues of gender. Most were educated in ways that prolonged the attitudes of French colonialism. But that is not to say that there is no difference between them and white writers. Non-white writers tend to understand the difference between black and white perspectives on slavery; to have had extensive first-hand experience with slavery, even if they were not slaves themselves; to emphasize black agency in its various forms; to seek to wrest control of the historical record from whites; and to focus on collective black identity rather than individual slaves. As noted earlier, each case requires careful analysis. Only through such analysis is it possible to assess the different perspectives of men and women or whites and blacks in the confusing, transitional period of the early nineteenth century.

* * *

The chapters of *Fathers, Daughters, and Slaves* draw upon the various theoretical and historiographic issues discussed in the preceding pages. Those issues include Said's notions of structures of attitude and reference as well as contrapuntal readings of European and non-European authors. The insights provided by Said and other postcolonial theorists provide a vantage point from which to assess and interrogate the ideological presuppositions inherent in writings by white authors. But as we have seen earlier, theories of race and gender do not always walk hand and hand. Postcolonial theorists often fail to illuminate, and at times even obfuscate, the gender issues involved in understanding white and black women. Hence comes the need to give serious consideration to feminist approaches to women's history and the manifestation of male dominance over women and children in the family and in society in general. A feminist historical perspective also entails acknowledging the extent to which postrevolutionary women subscribed to notions of complementary roles for men and women while at the same time grappling with tensions and conflicts between genders. Although the time was perhaps not ripe for the overt adoption of feminist positions in the early decades of the nineteenth century, the women writers considered here were aware of inequality between the sexes, as the chapters of this book will show. They participated in various forms of "informal feminism" as well as in the creation of the horizontal, non-hierarchical sense of community that both Anderson and Appiah identify as resulting from the overthrow of patriarchal structures after the Enlightenment and revolutionary eras.

Regarding its methodological approach, *Fathers, Daughters, and Slaves* maintains a consistent focus on the central issues of sentimental discursive formations, patriarchal structures, and antislavery rhetoric. The close readings provided here dissect the discourse of feeling, structures of voice and vision, codes of femininity, patterns of opposition, forms of identification, and more. Such an approach provides a way to cross generic boundaries, illuminating traditional literary forms (narrative fiction, poetry, or theater) as well as such other genres as historical accounts, memoirs, letters, and paintings. The commonality of representational modes across genres is characteristic of the early nineteenth century. As Charlotte Sussman observes about British abolitionism, literary considerations of blacks existed on a continuum with, not in opposition to, public discussions of racial issues:

Rarely has a political movement been so conscious of the cultural power of literary methods and texts as the antislavery movement was. By this I mean not only that it consistently relied on rhetorical strategies borrowed from literary discourse, both sentimental and satirical, but also that activists counted on the motivational power of the stories and poems they distributed to awaken abolitionist energy.[58]

An especially striking example is the story of Néali, the touching tale of an enslaved African girl that appeared in Mungo Park's *Travels to the Interior Districts of Africa*, published in 1799. Park presents his presumably eye-witness account in a sentimental rhetorical mode, as does Thomas Clarkson, who recounts Néali's story in *The Cries of Africa, to the Inhabitants of Europe* in 1822, and as do numerous other antislavery writers. The different versions of the Néali story make no simple demarcation between authentic experience and sentimental discourse or between fiction and non-fiction writing. In all instances, a predictable set of literary components—plot, characters, description, narrative voice, point of view, names, places, settings, objects, scenes, and more—construct blacks and their plight. The imbricated threads of that construction are what *Fathers, Daughters, and Slaves* attempts to unravel.

The organization of the book is chronological, beginning with the end of the eighteenth century and ending with 1825, the decisive year in which France recognized Haiti's independence. Chapter 1, "Patriarchy and Abolition," focuses on Germaine de Staël, née Necker, and the conflict she experienced between paternal figures of authority on the one hand and the rights of slaves and women on the other. The opposing poles of the conflict are apparent in Staël's claim to have loved, throughout her life, God, her father, and freedom. Chapter 1 questions whether Staël was able to reconcile her love of God and father with her love of freedom over the thirty years of her life as a writer. It also seeks to determine what acts of resistance and submission were entailed in reconciling those seemingly incompatible allegiances. The chapter opens with an analysis of Staël's early short stories: *Mirza*, which places a freedom-loving African heroine in a context of paternal authority and colonialism; and *Histoire de Pauline*, which recounts the tragic consequences of a young girl treated as an object of exchange by a series of men. Chapter 1 also looks at symbolic allusions to slavery in *Corinne* and, more broadly, at biographical and historical works in which Staël constructs her father, Jacques Necker, as the embodiment of benevolence and concern for the welfare of others. It examines the evolving ways in which Staël, the daughter of a powerful statesman and abolitionist, constructed herself as an advocate for victims of social injustice, including slaves and women.

Another work is introduced into this chapter that helps to interpret through comparison and contrast Staël's construction of fathers, daughters, and slaves. The second author whose story I interweave with Staël's is Isaac Louverture, the son of the Haitian hero Toussaint Louverture. Isaac is of interest because of the way in which his memoirs emphasize familial devotion, empathy for victims of oppression, and a range of other sentimental responses, in contrast with the military discourse that Toussaint Louverture himself adopts in his memoirs. Comparisons between Germaine and Isaac in relation to Napoleon and to their famous revolutionary fathers illuminate the discursive similarities and ideological differences between these white and black writers.

Chapter 2, "Fathers and Colonization," shows fathers and daughters attempting to colonize Africa in the early decades of the nineteenth century. It tells the story of Charlotte Dard, née Picard, a young girl of 18, who survived the shipwreck of the *Medusa* in 1816 that was immortalized in Gericault's painting *Le Radeau de la Méduse*. In her memoir *La Chaumière africaine*, Dard endeavored, like Germaine de Staël and Isaac Louverture, to set the record straight concerning her father's role in postrevolutionary French history. Less distinguished than Necker or Toussaint Louverture, however, her father Charles Picard apparently lacked either the bureaucratic or the agricultural talents needed to realize his various African projects. Notwithstanding his professional shortcomings, however, he appears to have been a devoted parent and the first of several benevolent fathers whose portraits will be sketched within the pages of this book. A struggling adventurer at odds with powerful forces in the colonial world, he shared his passion for Africa with his daughter and, near the end of his life, maintained contacts with another benevolent father, her husband Jean Dard, a linguist and educator. Unlike well-known male abolitionists whose politicized accounts made the *Medusa* affair a test case of colonization for the newly restored Bourbon monarchy, Charlotte Dard provides a woman's perspective on the shipwreck and a moving account of fathers and daughters struggling to survive and forming sympathetic ties to the black subjects of French colonization.

The contrapuntal issue discussed in Chapter 2 concerns the women known as *signares*, who formed relationships with European men and for a time exercised considerable power and influence among black and white populations in colonized areas of Africa. M. Picard and M. Dard were presumably involved in such relationships. One of the most famous *signares* of the late eighteenth century, Anne Pépin, was the mistress of le chevalier de Boufflers, who brought the real-life model for Claire de Duras's *Ourika* to Paris. To look at these African women from a non-hegemonic position, I will examine their depiction by male and female contemporary Francophone writers: the African poet Léopold Sédar Senghor, in his lyrical poems

"Songs for Signares"; Maryse Condé, in her saga of African history *Ségou*; and most recently Tita Mandeleau, in her historical novel *Signare Anna ou le voyage aux escales*. These authors' differing perspectives shed light on the complex interactions with Africans that marked the lives and identities of the families presented in *La Chaumière africaine*.

Chapter 3, "Daughters and Paternalism," focuses on *Sarah* and several other works about slavery by Marceline Desbordes-Valmore, née Desbordes. Although white, Sarah believes herself to be a slave and identifies with an African man, Arsène, who has served as her substitute mother. Although surprising, this identification of a young white girl with a black maternal figure assumes special meaning in relation to the circumstances of Desbordes-Valmore's life. Having traveled to Guadeloupe at the time of the slave revolts in 1804, Desbordes-Valmore found herself alone, as is Sarah, in an alien, slave-based island society following her mother's death from yellow fever. If black connotes motherhood in *Sarah*, white represents fathers. Paternal stand-ins in the novella include the kindly planter whose son she eventually marries; Sarah's benevolent biological father; and a grandfather whom Sarah has never known. This unnamed patriarch epitomizes the abuses of plantocratic society and initiates the tragic events that the story develops. Unraveling the racial and social implications of these male characters, and Sarah's relation to them, necessitates also looking at the particular circumstances of Desbordes-Valmore's own life and her relation to her father and other men. Unlike more privileged women considered elsewhere in this book, Desbordes-Valmore lived the precarious life of an actress from an early age. Standing thus on the margins of society, she felt a strong affinity for the plight of the downtrodden, including blacks, and looked to them as models of a hybrid subjectivity that was not wholly different from her own. At the same time, however, the affirmation of paternal authority in her works on slavery differs little from that found in the writings of Staël and Dard. Like them, Desbordes-Valmore is a liminal presence who stands on the border between filial duty and feminine empowerment. How she constructs and deconstructs that position is the subject of Chapter 3.

An example that illuminates Desbordes-Valmore's story and brings to the fore the dramas of white and black women's lives in colonial settings is provided by the celebrated mixed-race Saint-Dominguan actress, Minette, who, like her white counterpart Marceline, appeared on the stage as a young girl. On the basis of their connection to the world of the theater, a locus of feminine empowerment and abolitionist expression, these two women deserve to be studied and compared. Minette's story both complements and contrasts with the colonial stories recounted by Desbordes-Valmore.

Chapter 4, "Voices of Daughters and Slaves," focuses on Claire de Duras, née Kersaint, whose novella *Ourika* may arguably be the most probing work on the subject of race produced in nineteenth-century France. Fathers affect the structure of attitude and reference of daughters for Duras as much, if differently, as for Staël, Dard, and Desbordes-Valmore. Duras's own father, who perished during the Terror, was linked to the colonial world and openly professed progressive opinions about slavery. Despite the liberal political legacy that Duras inherited, however, she constructs herself and her black character Ourika in complex and at times ambiguous ways. Chapter 4 begins with a consideration of Duras herself, as a daughter linked to the colonial world. Such personal matters provide the background for a close reading of the text, which affirms forms of paternal authority (the Church, the medical profession, *ancien régime* values) while at the same time resisting and defying them. Central to the resistance and defiance that defines Duras's writing is the granting of agency: giving independent voice, vision, and choice to women and blacks. Duras thus opens a space for readers to share her identification with victims of oppression. To foreground her efforts in this regard I compare *Ourika* to the work of another woman, Henriette de La Tour du Pin, whose treatment of slaves in *Journal d'une femme de cinquante ans* differed in significant and illuminating ways from those of her friend and fellow aristocrat Duras.

Chapter 4 closes with a discussion of various twentieth-century Caribbean writers who have weighed in on Duras's depiction of an African: Aimé Césaire, Daniel Maximin, and Maryse Condé. Césaire's comments on *Ourika* in his play *La Tragédie du roi Christophe* are especially interesting because they invite comparisons between the aristocratic setting of Duras's novel and the monarchical society created by King Henry Christophe in the early years of Haiti's independence. Yet at the same time, they show little of the sympathy for Duras as a woman writer that both Maximin and Condé display. Here, as elsewhere in this book, the ideological tension between the privileging of fathers versus daughters, and race versus gender, requires careful examination.

Chapter 5, "Uniting Black and White Familes," discusses a prolific abolitionist writer who has received little critical attention until recently. Sophie Doin, née Mamy, upheld the cause of the downtrodden, including blacks, throughout her life. The theme of unity—within families, between men and women, and across racial lines—is at the heart of her writing. This harmonious theme notwithstanding, unity was more of an aspiration than a reality for Doin in her own life, as noted earlier. Like Duras, Doin strove to maintain the delicate balance between submission and resistance that is evident in her writings about fathers, daughters, and slaves. Chapter 5 considers how that balance is achieved in her autobiographical writings and within the corpus of her abolitionist works: the didactic novel *La Famille noire* as well as her short stories *Noire et blanc, Blanche et noir,* and *Le Négrier.*

The unity of families within those writings parallels and emblematizes the political situation that was uppermost in Doin's mind writing in 1825: France's public recognition of Haiti's independence and the lasting bonds of friendship, filiation, and loyalty that presumably united the two countries. Chapter 5 questions the extent to which the unified families and political solutions that Doin constructed in her fictional works are undermined by the inability to fully escape paternal authority that affected her personally. At the same time, however, Doin's imagined constructions of unified families and countries marks her as perhaps the most original French woman abolitionist of her time.

Chapter 5 also considers two contrapuntal examples. The first is the painting *Serment des ancêtres* (1822) by the Guadeloupian artist Guillaume Guillon-Lethière. This pictorial example, which depicts two leaders of the Haitian Revolution and founders of the nation—the mulatto officer Alexandre Pétion and the black slave leader Jean-Jacques Dessalines— reveals the artist's commitment to the Haitian cause and his solidarity with blacks across national lines. At the same time, however, *Oath of the Ancestors* embodies patriarchal authority in ways that illuminate through contrast the positive gender implications of Doin's treatment of Haiti. The second example, *L'Histoire de la catastrophe de Saint-Domingue*, was written by Juste Chanlatte but published under the name of the naval officer Bouvet de Cressé. In the discussion of this example, which is quoted in *La Famille noire*, I argue that Doin's willingness to rely on Chanlatte's non-white perspective on abolition parallels the uniting of blacks and whites in her works of fiction.

The book's Postscript considers Anne-Louis Girodet's *Portrait du citoyen Belley, ex-représentant des colonies*. Belley, the first black deputy to the National Convention during the French Revolution, is depicted standing alongside a bust of Guillaume-Thomas Raynal, the author of *Histoire des deux Indes*, which famously predicted that a black Spartacus would arise to avenge the rights of the oppressed. Although the painting itself and the two persons it portrays predate the period of interest in this book, the issues raised in Girodet's painting remained as urgent and timely in the first decades of the nineteenth century as at the time of its exhibition in 1797. The painting has special relevance here because of its striking similarity to *Mme de Staël à côté du buste de son père Jacques Necker*. Girodet's white-and-black dyad, upon which Staël chose to model her relationship with her father, supports this book's premise that women abolitionists held deep-seated bonds with their fathers and with people of black, mixed-race, or African descent as well.

French women writers in the first decades of the nineteenth century, the chronological framework of this book, advanced the cause of antislavery on the basis of notions of empathy for oppressed Africans. Their efforts were especially significant in the 1820s, an era of colonial nostalgia and unresolved triangular trade ambitions in France. That is not say, of course, that in this early period of abolitionist writing they fully recognized the need to bridge languages and cultures in ways that would have really shed light on the lives of Africans in the colonial world. Nor is it to say that their empathetic responses were free of "self"-oriented identification structures. Winthrop Jordan observes regarding writing in the United States that sentimentalism "overlapped and interlocked with humanitarian feeling, bringing to good-hearted benevolence a half-intended emotionalism." For French women, it was similarly the case that empathy played into such personal motivations as feelings of self-worth and the furtherance of professional or religious objectives. Such reservations notwithstanding, the women considered here made unique contributions through their empathetic impulses and strategies. Jordan rightly sums up the value of empathy when he concludes, "No matter how fluttery, sentimentality heightened empathy" and that as a mode of approach to slavery, it implied that blacks had feelings that were as legitimate as those of whites.[59]

Notes

1 Daniel Maximin, *L'Isolé soleil* (Paris: Seuil, 1981), 117; *Lone Sun* (Charlottesville: University Press of Virginia, 1989), 108.

2 In many cases the persons discussed here were not or were no longer actually "enslaved," a word that many prefer to "slave." The former connotes a condition inflicted on Africans rather than an essentialized condition.

3 Although I use lower case for the terms "black" and "white" in this book, I am aware that certain theorists prefer to capitalize them. They do so in order to emphasize the constructed nature of identities based on color. See, for example, Patricia Hill Collins, *Black Sexual Politics* (New York: Routledge, 2004), 17.

4 Susan Buck-Morss discusses the issue of categories in *Hegel, Haiti, and Universal History* (Pittsburgh: University of Pittsburgh Press, 2009), 111. Although I endorse her concept of porosity among categories (126), I consider that it is illuminating to pay attention to "fathers," "daughters," and "slaves" separately for the historical and literary reasons demonstrated in this book.

5 In *Rebel Daughters: Women and the French Revolution* (New York: Oxford University Press, 1992), Sara E. Melzer and Leslie W. Rabine use the term "rebel daughters" to designate women's rebellion against the French Revolution which rejected and excluded them. For a discussion of Gouges's abolitionism and feminism, see Marie-Pierre Le Hir, "Feminism, Theater, Race: *L'Esclavage des noirs*," in *Translating Slavery, vol. 1: Gender and Race in French Abolitionist Writing, 1780–1830*, ed. Doris Y. Kadish and Françoise Massardier-Kenney (Kent: Kent State University Press, 2009), 65–88.

6 See Claire Goldberg Moses, "'Equality' and 'Difference' in Historical Perspective," in *Feminism, Socialism, and French Romanticism*, ed. Claire Goldberg Moses and Leslie Wahl Rabine (Bloomington: Indiana University Press, 1993), 17–84. Denise

Z. Davidson mentions various class divisions identified in the early 1830s: wealthy, upper bourgeoisie, comfortable bourgeois, constrained bourgeois, comfortable workers, poor workers, and miserable workers: *France after Revolution: Urban Life, Gender, and the New Social Order* (Cambridge, MA: Harvard University Press, 2007), 13. The authors considered in this book belong to the first four categories.

7 For a discussion of the differences among these notions, see Martha C. Nussbaum, *Upheavals of Thought: The Intelligence of Emotions* (New York: Routledge, 2001), 302. Lynn Hunt discusses the centrality of empathy for the development of notions of inalienable human rights, autonomy, and individuality in *Inventing Human Rights: A History* (New York: Norton, 2007), 64–65. See also William M. Reddy for a consideration of the role of the emotions in French history from 1700–1850: *The Navigation of Feeling: A Framework for the History of Emotions* (New York: Cambridge University Press, 2001). For the critique of empathy as antithetical to action made by Hannah Arendt and others, see Catherine A. Reinhardt, *Claims to Memory: Beyond Slavery and Emancipation in the French Caribbean* (New York: Berghahn Books, 2006), 94–95.

8 Adam Smith, *The Theory of Moral Sentiments* (Cambridge: Cambridge University Press, 2002). Smith's views about empathy are compatible with his antislavery position, although the chief basis of that position is economic. In *The Wealth of Nations* (1776), Smith argued that work done by free men would be more economical than slave labor. He was, however, a gradualist who believed that through work slaves would acquire the discipline needed for emancipation.

9 Suzanne Keen, "A Theory of Narrative Empathy," *Narrative* 14, 3 (2006): 208.

10 For other, less empathetic women's attitudes and behaviors at the time, see Henri Rossi, *Mémoires aristocratiques féminins: 1789–1848* (Paris: Champion, 1998).

11 Edward W. Said, *Culture and Imperialism* (New York: Knopf, 1993), xxii.

12 Said, *Culture and Imperialism*, 52.

13 I use "Francophone" to designate the French-speaking "center" as well as the "periphery." But as postcolonial theorists point out, such a broad usage of the term is difficult to put into practice. Thus "French" often appears in this book in contexts where conventional usage dictates reference to metropolitan France, and "Francophone" in discussions of non-Europeans. See Jacques Coursil and Delphine Perret, "The Francophone Postcolonial Field," in *Postcolonial Theory and Francophone Literary Studies*, ed. H. Adlai Murdoch and Anne Donadey (Gainesville: University Press of Florida, 2005), 193–207. Chris Bongie provides further insight into current usage of the word "francophone" in *Friends and Enemies: The Scribal Politics of Post/ Colonial Literature* (Liverpool: Liverpool University Press, 2008). Among other concerns he identifies the implicit connection to France that the term entails and the temptation to use it as a code word for resistance (160, 168).

14 Said, *Culture and Imperialism*, 51.

15 In a similar vein Buck-Morss recommends reading Hegel in juxtaposition to works by Toussaint Louverture, Wordsworth, Grégoire, and Dessalines: *Hegel, Haiti, and Universal History*, 75.

16 Said, *Culture and Imperialism*, 161.

17 Said, *Culture and Imperialism*, 15.

18 Women were not alone in their exclusion from the ranks of active members of the body politic: in 1827 in France, only one person out of 360 had the vote and among

adult males about one in fifty to sixty; Sherman Kent, *The Election of 1827 in France* (Cambridge, MA: Harvard University Press, 1975), 60.

19 See Carla Hesse, *The Other Enlightenment: How French Women Became Modern* (Princeton: Princeton University Press, 2001); Alan B. Spitzer, *The French Generation of 1820* (Princeton: Princeton University Press, 1987); Elizabeth Colwill, "Epistolary Passions: Friendship and the Literary Public of Constance de Salm, 1767–1845," *Journal of Women's History* 12, 3 (2000): 39–68.

20 Steven D. Kale, *French Salons: High Society and Political Sociability from the Old Regime to the Revolution of 1848* (Baltimore: Johns Hopkins University Press, 2004), 107.

21 Gerda Lerner, *The Creation of Patriarchy* (New York: Oxford University Press, 1986), 89.

22 Lerner, *Creation of Patriarchy*, 168.

23 Francis Ambrière, *Le Siècle des Valmore: Marceline Desbordes-Valmore et les siens* (Paris: Seuil, 1987), 114–15.

24 Doris Garraway, *The Libertine Colony: Creolization in the Early French Caribbean* (Durham, NC: Duke University Press, 2005), 128.

25 Lerner, *Creation of Patriarchy*, 226.

26 For a variety of social and political reasons, French women did not participate in antislavery to the extent that their British counterparts did. For detailed historical and literary accounts of the British record, see Clare Midgley, *Women against Slavery: The British Campaigns, 1780–1870* (London: Routledge, 1992) and Moira Ferguson, *Subject to Others: British Women Writers and Colonial Slavery, 1670–1834* (New York: Routledge, 1992).

27 Lerner, *Creation of Patriarchy*, 217.

28 Ibid., 239.

29 Ibid.

30 Benedict Anderson, *Imagined Communities: Reflections on the Origin and Spread of Nationalism* (London: Verso, 1983), 16, 40.

31 Anthony Appiah, *The Ethics of Identity* (Princeton: Princeton University Press, 2005), 245.

32 For a compendium of documents that show how women and men addressed "the woman question" from the eighteenth to the twentieth century, see Susan G. Bell and Karen M. Offen, *Women, the Family, and Freedom* (Stanford: Stanford University Press, 1983).

33 James Smith Allen, *Poignant Relations: Three Modern French Women* (Baltimore: Johns Hopkins University Press, 2000), 171.

34 Allen, *Poignant Relations*, 174–80.

35 Allen, *Poignant Relations*, 180.

36 Cécile Dauphin, "Women's Culture and Women's Power: Issues in French Women's History," in *Writing Women's History: International Perspectives*, ed. Karen M. Offen, Ruth Roach Pierson, and Jane Rendall (Bloomington: Indiana University Press, 1991), 111, 113, 117.

37 The first meeting of the Société de la morale chrétienne took place on December 20, 1821. The following women members were listed: Mme la Comtesse Otto de Mosloy, Mme Treuttel, Mme Würtz, Mme Belloc (rédactrice de la Bibliothèque de Famille), and Miss Maria Gray Newbury (à Londres); *Société de la morale*

chrétienne (Paris: Crapelet, 1822). These women appear to have gained membership as exceptions based on special social or professional factors.

38 Said, *Culture and Imperialism*, 15.

39 Dauphin, "Women's Culture and Women's Power," 124.

40 Naomi Schor, *George Sand and Idealism* (New York: Columbia University Press, 1993), 14.

41 Schor, *George Sand and Idealism*, 48.

42 Margaret Cohen, *The Sentimental Education of the Novel* (Princeton: Princeton University Press, 1999), 35.

43 Cohen observes that in England, unlike France, descriptive writing "emerges in continuity" with the sentimental tradition (*Sentimental Education of the Novel*, 195). Her analysis adds important gender components to my own treatment of narrative description by French and British writers in *The Literature of Images: Narrative Landscape from Julie to Jane Eyre* (New Brunswick: Rutgers University Press, 1986).

44 See also Davidson, *France after Revolution*, 8.

45 Cohen, *Sentimental Education of the Novel*, 10.

46 Although listed in catalogues and my Bibliography as Saint-Pierre, Bernardin, I follow thoughout this book the common practice of referring to him as Bernardin.

47 Jean Fabre, *Lumières et romantisme* (Paris: Klinckseick, 1963), 170; April Alliston, "Transnational Sympathies, Imaginary Communities," in *The Literary Channel: The Inter-National Invention of the Novel*, ed. Margaret Cohen and Carolyn Dever (Princeton: Princeton University Press, 2002), 140; Kathrine Bonin, "*Paul et Virginie* in the Marketplace," paper delivered at the Nineteenth Century French Studies colloquium, Mobile, Alabama, 2007.

48 Bernardin de Saint-Pierre, *Voyage à l'île de France* (Paris: Ledentu, 1840: Gallica, texte numérisé, 17); *Voyage à l'île de France* (New York: Interlink Books, 2003), 53.

49 Staël deplores the fate of the pariah in *De L'Influence des passions*, in *Oeuvres complètes*, III (Paris: Treuttel et Wurz, 1820), 252–53.

50 Albert Memmi, *The Colonizer and the Colonized*, trans. Howard Greenfield (New York: Orion Press, 1965), 38–39.

51 Jean-Paul Sartre, "Orphée noir," in *Anthologie de la nouvelle poésie nègre et malgache de langue française*, ed. Léopold Sedar Senghor (Paris: Presses universitaires de France, 1948), ix.

52 Chris Bongie, *Islands and Exiles: The Creole Identities of Post/Colonial Literature* (Stanford: Stanford University Press, 1998), 113.

53 Jean-Charles Pajou, *Esclaves des îles françaises* (Paris: Les Editeurs libres, 2006), 39.

54 John D. Erickson, "Maximin's *L'Isolé soleil* and Caliban's Curse," *Callaloo* 15, 1 (1992): 127.

55 Deborah Jenson addresses the issue of the absence of French slave narratives in *Beyond Slave Narratives: Sex, Politics, and Manuscripts in the Haitian Revolution* (Liverpool: Liverpool University Press, 2011).

56 Maximin, *L'Isolé soleil*, 61; *Lone Sun*, 63, 59.

57 Maximin is an exception to the "disconnect" between feminist and postcolonial studies. In Francophone studies generally, as Françoise Lionnet observes, "there is no sustained engagement with feminist discourses as such, and no major attempt to investigate the new avenues opened up by transnational feminist ethics, a rubric under which much innovative 'First' and 'Third World' feminist theorizing is now being done." "Francophonie, Postcolonial Studies, and Transnational Feminisms,"

in *Postcolonial Theory and Francophone Literary Studies*, ed. H. Adlai Murdoch and Anne Donadey (Gainesville: University Press of Florida, 2005), 261.

58 Charlotte Sussman, *Consuming Anxieties: Consumer Protest, Gender, and British Slavery, 1713–1833* (Stanford: Stanford University Press, 2000), 3.

59 Winthrop D. Jordan, *White over Black: American Attitudes Toward the Negro, 1550–1812* (New York, Norton, 1977), 368–69.

1

Patriarchy and Abolition:
Germaine de Staël

This chapter looks at Germaine de Staël's complex construction of fathers in relation to slavery and abolition. Central to that construction is Staël's own father, Jacques Necker, who appears in person or in various guises in his daughter's fictional, biographical, historical, and other writings. The painting *Mme de Staël à côté du buste de son père Jacques Necker* attributed to Firmin Massot (Figure 2), which Staël commissioned shortly after Necker's death, captures the strong bond between father and daughter. Both gaze to their left in the sentimental, benevolent spirit of those devoted to the cause of freedom and the end of oppression. Despite the darkening clouds above them, both project a sense of calm fortitude. Their fates are portrayed as inextricably linked. The daughter stands proudly with her father and slightly below him, as age and sex dictate. His sole heir, Staël appears as a woman endowed with both the physical and intellectual attributes befitting the bearer of her father's familial and political legacy.[1]

I argue here that Staël's love and admiration for Necker produced a conflict between her submission to patriarchal authority on the one hand and her commitment to the rights of slaves and women on the other.[2] Consider the words she spoke at the end of her life, "J'ai toujour été la même, vive et triste. J'ai aimé Dieu, mon père et la liberté" ("I've always been the same, lively and sad. I loved God, my father and freedom.")[3] Perhaps it was the inherent incompatibility between patriarchy and freedom that fueled both Staël's passion and her unhappiness. Consider also her observation that Richardson reportedly made Clarissa suffer because he couldn't forgive her for leaving her father's house.[4] Staël stayed near her father to the end of his life, and she obeyed many of the dictates that he and the society of his time placed upon the destinies of women. Yet at the same time she actively called into question the control that society exercised over both women and slaves, two groups whose fate she often linked. As such, she prefigures modern thinkers such as Gerda Lerner, discussed in the Introduction, who states, "As subordination of women by men provided the conceptual model for the creation of slavery as an institution, so the patriarchal family provided the structural model."[5] In *De La Littérature*, Staël makes similar observations regarding the fate of women during Antiquity:

> Tout se ressentait, chez les anciens, même dans les relations de famille, de l'odieuse institution de l'esclavage. Le droit de vie et de mort souvent accordé à l'autorité paternelle [...] créait entre les humains deux classes, dont l'une ne se croyait aucun devoir envers l'autre [...] Les femmes pendant toute leur vie, les enfants pendant leur jeunesse, étaient soumis à quelques conditions de l'esclavage.

> (The odious institution of slavery affected everything in the ancient world, even relations within the family. The right of life and death that was often granted to paternal authority [...] created two classes of people, one of whom felt no obligation toward the other [...] Women throughout their life, children during their youth, were submitted to some of the conditions of slavery.)[6]

How did Germaine de Staël reconcile her love of God and father with her love of freedom over the thirty years of her life as a writer? What acts of submission or resistance did the reconciliation between those allegiances entail? Answers to these questions illuminate the antislavery legacy that stretches from her father, through her, to her son Auguste de Staël, her daughter Albertine, and Albertine's husband, le duc de Broglie.

I approach Staël's construction of fathers in relation to abolition by focusing on three phases of her work. In the first, from 1784 to 1786, Staël developed an Enlightenment outlook that resembled that of Necker, who addressed the issue of slavery in *De L'Administration des finances de la France* in 1784. That outlook endorses practices of control and exploitation, whether of slaves or at times of daughters, as long as no abuse or victimization occurs. According to that way of thinking, families, corporations, and nations need to resort to such practices in order to take advantage of commercial or other opportunities that result in increased prosperity. As an analysis of Staël's early short stories *Mirza* and *Histoire de Pauline* reveals, however, Staël is also at odds with conventional views: first, by calling attention to irresponsible fathers; and second, by attributing liberatory impulses to women and Africans. In the second phase of Staël's work, from 1802 to 1807, a more decided deconstruction of the concept of fathers occurs. Central to the shift in Staël's thinking is the persecution she endured at the hands of Napoleon who, during this era, assumed increasingly oppressive powers, including the reinstitution of slavery in the French colonies. Staël was

Figure 2. Firmin Massot, *Mme de Staël à côté du buste de son père Jacques Necker.*
Reproduction courtesy of Château de Coppet.

subjected to exile, suffering, and humiliation during this period. In *Corinne* (1807) and *Le Caractère de M. Necker* (1804) one sees a somewhat different figure of the father to the one found in her earlier works. And although in a period of censorship these works do not directly address racial issues, they do treat the relation of oppression to fathers. Finally, in the last phase of Staël's work, from 1812 to 1817, Staël directly intervened in actions related to slavery, continuing to embrace key components of Necker's antislavery views but also developing other models of paternal authority that led directly to the abolition of slavery in the decades following her death.

This chapter also broadens its focus by comparing Staël's relationship with Necker to Isaac Louverture's relationship with his abolitionist father Toussaint Louverture, the famous black leader who rallied resistance against France leading up to the independence of Haiti. Germaine and Isaac, children of famous abolitionist fathers, lived through and were witness to the major events of the Haitian Revolution. Moreover, decisions made by Napoleon determined the course of their own and their families' lives. Toussaint Louverture died after having been betrayed by Napoleon, deported to France, and left to die in a prison in Fort de Joux in 1803. This year also marks the beginning of Napoleon's persecution of Staël, who was exiled from France for a period of ten years. Necker died in 1804, the date of the declaration of Haiti's independence and the publication of *Le Caractère de M. Necker*, in which Staël tried to justify the reputation of her beloved father who had been rejected by the French and forced into exile in his native Switzerland. After the end of Napoleon's reign, Isaac Louverture wrote *Mémoires d'Isaac, fils de Toussaint Louverture*, which similarly addresses his abolitionist father's place in history. By considering Germaine and Isaac side by side I try to read metropolitan history together with and against other non-dominant histories.

* * *

It is remarkable that Staël both begins and ends her writing career with the issue of slavery. The two short stories written in 1786—*Mirza* and *Histoire de Pauline*—are set in slave-trading settings, the first in Africa and the second in Saint-Domingue. Of the two, only *Mirza* deals directly with slavery, bringing to the forefront the policies that Necker and other eighteenth-century economists at the time endorsed: notably, that Africa could be developed as an alternative source of the products such as sugar, coffee, and tobacco whose demand in Europe drove the triangular trade among Africa, France, and the Caribbean. According to Staël's proposed solution, which never proved feasible, Africans could work on their own land as free laborers, thus obviating the need for their enslavement, exportation, and abuse by European slave traders and plantation owners.[7] In contrast with *Mirza*, *Histoire de Pauline* only treats slavery obliquely, focusing on the parallel oppression of women and slaves. Both stories suggest that the fault lies not with patriarchy itself. *Mirza* suggests that fathers cannot alone address the problem of slavery and need to enlist the cooperation of women and Africans. *Histoire de Pauline* points the finger at fathers who fail to meet the high standards of a Necker, whom Staël called "le meilleur des pères" ("the best of all fathers"), and who fail to exercise their legitimate paternal authority.[8] Following in the footsteps of Rousseau in *Julie, ou la Nouvelle Héloïse*, Staël foresees a tragic outcome for households in which inattentive or absent fathers allow weak or illegitimate substitutes to assume control. Households are emblematic of other social organizations, be they colonies or nations. The two stories were written prior to the French and Haitian revolutions but published after those revolutions had occurred, precisely one year after the Convention abolished slavery in the French colonies in 1794.[9] Clearly, Staël viewed these stories as timely statements on colonial politics and not just, as a superficial reading might suggest, as love stories set in the tropics.

Fathers play dominant roles in *Mirza*. The story begins with the evocation of a European official modeled after the Senegalese governor Stanislas-Jean, chevalier de Boufflers (1738–1815), a member of Necker's social milieu who undoubtedly shared his philosophical and political views concerning slavery. The fact that it was in 1786 that Boufflers brought two young blacks to France certainly influenced Staël's choice of subject matter in *Mirza*. She wrote, "Les détails que le chevalier de Boufflers m'a contés de cette traite des nègres sont déchirants" ("The details that the chevalier de Boufflers told me about the slave trade are heartbreaking.")[10] The narrator who opens the story describes his encounter with the young African Ximéo, who has accepted the offer of the "administrateur éclairé" ("enlightened administrator") (272, 147) who helped him establish a sugar plantation, an offer rejected by other less compliant members of his race and nationality. The governor has thus provided a model to show Africans that, with European help and a willingness to apply themselves, they could be the ones to grow the crop for which their compatriots were being brutally captured and transported to the West Indies as slaves. The narrator and the governor are like fathers: they occupy important initial positions in the story as befits their dominant roles in colonial society. Their controlling and legitimizing function reflects the presumably superior racial and social status that is routinely accorded to older male Europeans in eighteenth- and nineteenth-century stories: examples include Duras's *Ourika* and Chateaubriand's *Atala*. When the narrator first approaches Ximéo's wife who, like Duras's heroine, is named Ourika, she welcomes him upon hearing that the governor sent him: "C'est le gouverneur qui l'envoie! s'écria-t-elle. Ah! qu'il entre, qu'il soit le bienvenu; tout ce que nous avons est à lui" ("The governor sends him! Let him come in, welcome! Everything we have is his.") (272, 147)

The tone of the older European is fatherly but reveals a significant denial of black agency. The narrator notes that "un seul Africain délivré de l'esclavage par la générosité du gouverneur s'était prêté à ses projets" ("One single African, freed from slavery through the generosity of the governor, had agreed to take part in his project.") (272, 147) Only Ximéo accepted the kind offer of the French to build him a home. As Ximéo explains, he alone understood that the governor was providing the solution to the problem of slavery:

> quand j'appris qu'une production de notre pays, négligée par nous, causait seule ces maux cruels aux malheureux Africains, j'acceptai l'offre que me fut faite de leur donner l'exemple de la culture. Puisse un commerce libre s'établir entre les deux parties du monde! Puissent mes infortunés compatriotes renoncer à la vie sauvage, se vouer au travail pour satisfaire vos avides désirs, et contribuer à sauver quelques-uns d'eux de la plus horrible destinée! Puissent ceux mêmes qui pourraient se flatter d'éviter un tel sort, s'occuper avec un zèle égal d'en garantir à jamais leurs semblables! (274)

> When I realized that a product of our country, neglected by us, was the sole cause of the cruel suffering endured by these unfortunate Africans, I accepted the offer to give them the example of growing sugarcane. May free trade be established between the two parts of the world! May my unfortunate compatriots renounce primitive lives, devote themselves to work in order to satisfy your greed, and help save a few of them from the most horrible destiny! May those who could flatter themselves that they had avoided slavery apply themselves with an equal zeal to protect their fellow beings from such a fate. (149)

According to this account, most blacks, having been denied an education, are like capricious, irrational children. Only colonial authority, when exercised wisely and benignly, can prevent the horrors of enslavement. At the end, when Ximéo is captured and about to be deported by evil slave traders, the governor rescues him. When Ximéo's chains are removed, he expresses his gratitude in words that question but ultimately acknowledge the control that Europeans exercise over him and his compatriots: "j'embrassai ses genoux, je bénis dans mon coeur sa bonté, comme s'il eût sacrifié des droits légitimes. Ah! les usurpateurs peuvent donc, en renonçant à leurs injustices, atteindre au rang des bienfaiteurs" ("I kissed his knees; I blessed his goodness in my heart, as if he had sacrificed his legitimate rights. Ah, usurpers may thus attain the rank of benefactors by renouncing their injustices.") (280, 155)

Staël's ambivalence is apparent: dominant colonials feel they have legitimate rights to control Africans although they are in reality "usurpers"; but they can also soften the inhuman effects of their mastery in order to "attain the rank of benefactors." That is undoubtedly how she saw benevolent pro-colonialists such as her own father. At this stage, Staël's solution to the problems of slavery is to encourage empathetic, responsible forms of paternalism, "a gentler ethos based on the sentimentalism that emerged in the late eighteenth and nineteenth centuries. It is connected to the development of a more affectionate family life, the growth of romanticism, and the increase of humanitarianism."[11]

A countervailing anti-patriarchal discourse also exists in *Mirza*, however. As noted earlier, although patriarchy may imply subordination, it does not imply lack of agency. First, Staël questions absolute paternal authority by granting Africans and women positions that command a degree of respect if not ultimate power and control. Thus the narrator tells his story to "Madame," who assumes an important role as narratee, just as Ximéo does as narrator of his own story. Such roles are possible because, although both "Madame" and Ximéo stand in the disadvantaged position of "other," it can be assumed that they both belong to a superior social class: the narrator shows respect for his narratee, as the form of address, Madame, indicates; and Ximéo legitimizes his role as narrator by highlighting his social superiority as an African: "Je suis né dans le royaume de Cayor; mon père, du sang royal, était chef de quelques tribus qui lui étaient confiés par le souverain" ("I was born in the kingdom of Cayor. My father, of royal blood, was the chief of several tribes that had been committed to his care by the monarch.") (274, 149) It is in his role as narrator that he tells the tragic story of how he loved, deceived, abandoned, and eventually contributed to the death of the inspired poet, his true love, Mirza.

The second way in which abolition emerges as an anti-patriarchal model is that concern for and commitment to freedom is attributed especially to Africans and women. In recalling Mirza's poems, Ximéo observes: "L'amour de la liberté, l'horreur de l'esclavage, étaient le sujet des nobles hymnes qui me ravirent d'admiration" ("The love of freedom, the horror of slavery were the subjects of the noble hymns that filled me with a rapturous admiration.") (274, 150) Unlike Ximéo, who is easily swayed by tribal and familial commitments, Mirza is unfettered by social obligations and freely follows the path of her inspired mind and heart. Readers familiar with Staël's novels will recognize a familiar pattern from *Delphine* and *Corinne*, both of which pit weak men bound by convention against strong women devoted to political and personal liberation. Not surprisingly, it is Mirza, the very embodiment of freedom, who offers to exchange her own freedom for Ximéo's at the end of the story, even after he has betrayed and abandoned her. It is her example that inspires the governor to order that both Ximéo and Mirza be granted their freedom: "Soyez libres tous deux ... Tant de grandeur d'âme eût fait rougir l'Européen qui vous aurait nommés ses esclaves" ("Be free, both of you ... So much nobility of soul would have shamed the European who would have called you his slaves.") (280, 155) Staël's correspondence of 1786 reveals that she was especially impressed with the moral qualities of Africans and with their commitment to family: "dès qu'ils apprennent que leur père ou leur mère sont esclaves, ils viennent s'offrir à leur place, et les barbares marchands européens obtiennent souvent deux jeunes hommes forts et robustes à la place d'un vieillard infirme, profitant des vertus de ces mêmes nègres qu'ils croient, avec raison, d'une autre nature qu'eux" ("as soon as they learn that their father or mother has been enslaved, they come forward to offer to replace them; and the barbarian European merchants often obtain two strong, robust young men instead of a sickly old man by taking advantage of the virtues possessed by the very Africans that they rightly believe to be of a different nature than themselves.")[12]

It is possible, then, to imagine close ties implicitly linking Mirza (an African embodiment of freedom and abolition within the story), Madame (a mediator between African and European culture in the frame narrative), and Staël (a European spokesperson for freedom and abolition outside the text). Sentiments such as the following articulated by Ximéo are especially close to those that Staël expressed in her later abolitionist writings: "J'avais horreur de l'esclavage, je ne pouvais concevoir le barbare dessein des hommes de votre couleur" ("I abhorred slavery; I could not understand the barbarous purpose of the men of your color.") (274, 149) *Mirza* suggests that Africans and women have a shared horror of slavery and a shared remoteness from "the barbarous purpose of the men of your color." Accordingly, Staël seems to conclude, they have a shared responsibility for saving the oppressed from "the most horrible destiny," the loss of their freedom. This responsibility transcends that which is assigned to figures of authority such as the governor.

Despite the lack of direct engagement with the subject of slavery, *Histoire de Pauline* invites an interpretation rooted in that subject: first, because its story is set in Saint-Domingue, the largest slave-holding and sugar-producing colony in the eighteenth century; and second, because it identifies slavery as the root cause of the misfortunes recounted in the story.[13] In this case, a twelve-year-old girl (Pauline de Gercourt) is given as a wife to an evil avatar of the father, the greedy M. de Valville, who only marries her to purchase more slaves. In a very real sense, then, she is traded as property in a manner not unlike that of slaves. Like them, she suffers isolation, despair, and a sense of being eternally doomed to a meaningless existence. Pauline, "orpheline et mal élevée par un tuteur ami de son époux" ("an orphan and poorly raised by a tutor who was a friend of her husband") (199), is the victim of an absent father and his replacement by illegitimate substitutes, first the tutor and then the husband. Those substitutes are followed by another, Meltin, who seduces her and then tries to lure her into marrying him after Valville's death, saying "moi seul je saurai vous conduire et vous tenir lieu de père, d'époux et d'amant" ("I alone would know how to guide you and serve as your father, husband, and lover.") (204) Pauline plays the role of a defenseless slave, passed from one dominant male to another to serve illegitimate economic interests in a colonial society. Legitimate patriarchy is not to blame; it is just absent, just as it was most often on plantations, where absentee owners were the rule, not the exception. When the elderly Mme de Verseuil enters the scene and tries to rescue Pauline, it is too late. She implores Pauline to forget the man who seduced her when she was a young girl "au nom de ce père dont la vertu t'aurait préservée des pièges tendus à ton enfance" ("in the name of the father whose virtue would have preserved you from the traps laid for you as a child.") (208) But guilt poisons Pauline's marriage to count Edouard de Cerny who, like Oswald in *Corinne*, is unable to free himself from his dead father's rigid principles.

If women are not responsible for oppression in *Histoire de Pauline*, neither can they alone constitute the solution to its continued existence. Mme de Verseuil and Pauline's father wanted to marry earlier in life, but, as for similar couples in *Julie* and *Paul et Virginie*, expectations of the appropriate selection of a spouse, whether for rank or money, prevented their union. Even in *Mirza*, we learn that Ximéo would not have been able to marry Mirza, whom he truly loved, because his father would never have allowed him to marry a Wolof. Neither young women nor young men determine their fate; fathers do, just as fathers control or are supposed to control the proper management and treatment of their property, including slaves. Mme de Verseuil, like the mother in *Julie*, is incapable of providing the moral compass that protects a young girl's virtue and her market value as a prospective spouse. Rousseau's Mme d'Etange unwisely brings a young man into her household as a preceptor while the baron d'Etange is away; he would have been more vigilant. Mme de Verseuil wrongly advises Pauline to lie to Edouard about her past. Only a wise and beneficent father like Wolmar for Julie, or Necker for Germaine, could assure that a household, like a colony or a nation, obeys the strict rules of what Hélène Cixous describes as the masculine ethic of the "propre"— what is "clean," "morally right," and "specific to the self"—which forms the conceptual common ground of both propriety and property.[14]

To summarize, both *Mirza* and *Histoire de Pauline* contain positive, if somewhat naive, depictions of the roles that fathers and daughters played in a system of slavery that had already formed deep roots in the global economy of the time. It is true, as Christopher Miller has pointed out, that Necker had ties with the Compagnie des Indes in the 1760s (a company that ended its participation in the slave trade in 1744) and that Germaine Necker's marriage contract included the transfer to Sweden, the home of M. de Staël, of the island of Saint-Barthélemy, inhabited by 400 slaves. But that does not mean that Staël was complicit in the slave trade. Miller ends up depicting Staël paradoxically as both a slave and a slave trader of sorts: "Germaine Necker was, first of all, an object of bargaining and trade, and she also was at least incidentally tied to the loss of one of France's colonial islands."[15] Notwithstanding the economic and political interests vested in this marriage by the Neckers, the royal family, and others, however, Germaine had complete free will in choosing a spouse. Indeed, despite her family's strong preference for William Pitt, whose political influence would as it turns out have been of great benefit to them in their later troubled political and literary careers, Germaine adamantly refused William and preferred to marry Eric.

As noted earlier, freedom was at the center of Staël's value system, as it was of Necker's, whose abolitionist credentials are noteworthy. Along with his wife, Suzanne Churchod Necker, he was a member of the French abolitionist society the Amis des Noirs, founded in 1788 by Pierre Brissot. In Chapter 3 of *De L'Administration des finances de la France*, published in 1784, Necker expressed outrage over the fact that 20,000 Africans were being carried away from their homeland each year and subjected to inhumane treatment during the transatlantic passage and under slavery. He deplored the hypocrisy of Europeans who scorned others on the basis of slight differences in hair or skin color. When William Wilberforce began his campaign against the slave trade in the British Parliament in 1789, he cited Necker. Admittedly Necker viewed slavery pragmatically, as an economic necessity. In 1784, and five years later in opening the Estates-General, he thus advised France to proceed with caution. He acknowledged that Africans are capable of thinking and suffering. But he cautiously went no farther than to suggest a 50 percent reduction in the official subsidy granted to slave traders.[16] Ultimately, however, Necker was on the right side of antislavery debates at the time, and concrete benefits resulted from his public interventions in the 1780s. John Isbell even suggests that *Mirza* might have influenced Necker's public stance, since Staël knew about the slaves that Boufflers brought to France before Necker's 1789 speech.[17] The chain of influence in producing social change is thus perhaps more originally feminine than many critics, and most recently Miller, have been willing to acknowledge.

* * *

Concerning issues of slavery and abolition in the second phase of Staël's writing, we can turn for direction to Staël's descendant, the comtesse Jean de Pange, who rightly situates this phase in relation to the negative representative of the father, Napoleon. Pange notes that the period in which Staël's salon became a center of liberal opposition to Napoleon coincides with the period in which the First Consul sent troops to quell revolts in Saint-Domingue and re-impose slavery on that island. Is it conceivable that such dramatic colonial events would not have been the subject of conversation in Staël's social and political circles?[18] Evidence that Saint-Domingue was on Staël's mind can be found in the letter she wrote to her father on September 27, 1803:

> Ce qui s'est passé à Saint-Domingue est horrible, et le tout pour plaire au général Leclerc, car on aurait fait avec Toussaint Louverture le traité qu'on aurait voulu, et un beaucoup plus avantageux que celui auquel on est obligé de se soumettre, aujourd'hui que les nègres sont maîtres de tout l'intérieur de l'île. Les noyades ont été exécutées là comme à Nantes. Une fois que les nègres ont attaqué le Cap, on a eu l'idée que peut-être les nègres de l'intérieur de la ville pourraient favoriser les assiégeants, et on a jeté dix-huit cents à la mer sans forme de procès. Il y a à présent aux galères de Toulon des généraux nègres en habit de généraux, et tout ce que la violence et le mépris de l'homme peuvent faire inventer de cruel a été prodigué contre ces infortunés.[19]

> What happened in Saint-Domingue is horrible, and it was all just to please General Leclerc, for the French could have made whatever treaty they wanted with Toussaint Louverture, a much more advantageous one than they are forced to accept now that the blacks are masters of the whole interior of the island. The same drownings were ordered there as in Nantes. Once the blacks attacked Le Cap, the French thought that the blacks from the interior might favor the assailants, so they threw eighteen hundred of them into the sea with no form of trial. Currently there are black generals in their military uniforms in prisons in Toulon; and whatever cruelty that violence and disregard for human beings can invent has been unleashed against these poor souls.

Staël's outrage at the cruelty and injustice concerning Napoleon's treatment of blacks is palpable. Interestingly, she is not defending Toussaint's policies in this letter; comments about Toussaint later in her life reveal that she was critical of him, perhaps for his defiant act of establishing an independent constitution in 1802 or his controversial policy of reinstituting manual labor in ways not unlike slavery itself.[20] What prompts her outrage is the way in which Napoleon treated blacks generally and the unconscionable way he treated Toussaint, a French general who entrusted his career, his life, and the education of his sons to France on the basis of promises made directly to him by Napoleon. It is the base betrayal of Toussaint, which Napoleon himself later regretted, that fueled Staël's ire.

Echoes of the events of the Haitian Revolution and the martyrdom that the celebrated hero of the Haitian republic suffered at the hands of Napoleon can be heard in two works dating from the first decade of the nineteenth century—*Corinne* (1807) and *Le Caractère de M. Necker* (1804). These echoes tell us much about Staël's views on benevolence, paternalism, and the limits of paternal authority in relation to oppression. In both works, the father and child relationship provides a model of the relationship between master and slave.

In *Corinne*, Lord Oswald Nelvil best dramatizes the fault lines inherent in patriarchal authority. Although himself neither a slave nor a master, he does face the forces of oppression and attempts, albeit unsuccessfully, to discover ways to escape from their nefarious effects. The novel begins with his self-imposed exile from his home, which is synonymous with the land of his father: "mais le souvenir de son père était si intimement uni dans sa pensée avec sa patrie, que ces deux sentiments s'accroissaient l'un par l'autre" ("but the memory of his father was so intimately linked in his mind to that of his country that as one memory grew so too did the other.")[21] Father and nation form a whole; considering himself unworthy of the former, he flees the latter. By choosing to situate Oswald's father's death in 1794, a date that almost coincides with the death of the French nation's father, the legitimate king Louis XVI, Staël invites a collective interpretation of Oswald's disarray faced with the loss of paternal authority and forgiveness. A similar disarray also comes to mind for those black generals such as Toussaint Louverture whose ties with French representatives of authority were severed at this time. A comparison between Oswald and Toussaint may seem far-fetched, but in fact a number of specific similarities exist. After initially feeling close ties with their country—England in Oswald's case, France in Toussaint's—both men experience exile: Oswald, having fled to England after his father's death; Toussaint, having been deported to France by Napoleon. The tragedy of both men derives, moreover, from their ambivalence concerning the father's authority. Oswald abandons Corinne because his father disapproves of her. Toussaint refused to resist arrest because of his loyalty to the French nation and the leader who betrayed him.

As Oswald travels through Italy, he performs a heroic act that evokes Toussaint in another context. During a fire in the Italian city of Ancône, Oswald comes to the rescue of the oppressed, gaining the name of "liberator." (36) Fires were an integral part of colonial revolts in the 1790s, with black rebels led by Toussaint choosing to burn the city of Le Cap rather than surrender control of it to the French forces led by Napoleon's brother-in-law, General Leclerc. I connect such events with the episode at Ancône because of the specific objects of Oswald's heroism. First he rescues those considered mentally defective, as blacks were by racists at the time; and next he comes to the aid of Jews, whose emancipation and recognition as French citizens enjoying full civil rights only occurred in France near the same time that blacks received their rights. Heroic rescues of innocent victims from fire or other circumstances are commonplace in writings about blacks in the early nineteenth century; such an act was actually performed by Toussaint in rescuing the white owners of the plantation on which he lived. Also integral to the historical record of slavery are acts involving water, the second instance in which Oswald appears as a "liberator." In many instances, slaves were thrown overboard to lighten a ship's load during storms or inspections, or they chose a watery death themselves over the prospect of a life of enslavement and suffering. In Staël's letter to her father she specifically states, "they threw 1800 into the sea with no trial of any kind." It is noteworthy, then, that in Book 13 Oswald rescues a dying man from the sea. Not surprisingly, when Corinne leads Oswald on a tour of Rome, he is less impressed than she is with the purely aesthetic achievements of Italian civilization. What he seeks is art with a moral purpose : "il ne voyait dans ces lieux que le luxe du maître et le sang des esclaves" ("he only saw in these places the luxury of the master and the blood of slaves.") (106)

Being a "liberator" does not mean abandoning a belief in paternal authority, however. In *Mémoires du Général Toussaint-Louverture, écrit par lui-même*, written during his imprisonment in a French jail before his death in 1803, Toussaint appeals to Napoleon as an officer and a patriot. And although the *Mémoires* is intended as a defense against Napoleon's judgments and actions, Toussaint consistently proclaims his loyalty to France and its leader.[22] Similarly Oswald, who cannot abandon his belief in fathers, speaks of "la paternité, cette noble image d'un maître souverainement bon" ("paternity, that noble image of a supremely good master.") (256) His abandonment of Corinne, his unhappy marriage to Lucile, and his unfulfilled and unhappy later life can all be attributed to his inability to transcend his father's authority. Thus although notable similarities exist between Oswald and Necker—Madelyn Gutwirth has observed that they are "reserved, Protestant, courtly, dutiful, earnest, patient, conscientious"[23]— Oswald never measures up to Staël's ideal of the beneficent father capable of freeing blacks and women from oppression. Devotion to patriarchy is the Achilles heel of both Oswald and Toussaint as "liberators."

Corinne, by contrast, is cast in Mirza's role as the victim of oppression on the one hand and an agent of resistance on the other. She is a victim because she is subject to the control not only of her father but, as a young girl, of his delegate, her rigidly conventional step-mother. After his death, although she can use her financial resources and intellectual abilities to assert an independent identity, she can only do so in Italy, a nation with no enduring ties to her father's place of birth. Having defied Lacan's "non/nom du père," she is rootless and patrilineally nameless as well. She sacrifices her social and artistic identity in part for romantic love and in part through the moral imperative to tell Oswald of his father's disapproval of her. More importantly, however, she seeks absolution for having committed the ultimate sin of leaving her father's home. She is drawn to an Englishman in the futile hope, which she shares with Pauline, that, in the absence of the legitimate father, a strong, wise, beneficent husband such as Rousseau's M. de Wolmar can take his place. Cast in the role of victim, Corinne not surprisingly speaks of herself and other Italians as slaves: "D'autres peuples, interrompit Corinne, ont supporté le joug comme nous, et ils ont du moins l'imagination qui fait rêver une autre destinée [...] *Nous sommes esclaves, mais des esclaves toujours frémissants*, dit Alfiéri, le plus fier de nos écrivains modernes" ("Other peoples have endured a yoke as we have, Corinne interjected, and they at least had the imagination to dream of a different destiny [...] *We are slaves, but always as trembling slaves*, said Alfiéri, the proudest of our modern writers.)" (97) And responding to Oswald who recognizes that he will have to return to his country, she cries : "Eh bien! s'il est ainsi, emmenez-moi comme épouse, comme esclave" ("Very well! so be it. Take me away as a wife, as a slave.") (202)

To view Corinne only as a victim or slave would of course be to seriously misread Staël's novel. As I have argued elsewhere, Corinne stands symbolically as an alternative to Napoleon: he, the oppressive patriarch of the nation, she, his beneficent, paternalistic counterpart. She is crowned, like Napoleon, at the beginning but, unlike him, she values cultural diversity and liberation from tradition: "She is a peace-loving ruler whose crown is gained for merit, not traditional privilege, whose glory is aesthetic, not military, whose freedom is gained through the powers of the mind and the pen rather than brute force and the sword."[24] She replaces paternal authority, assuming control of her own life after her father's death, and even assumes a paternal voice when she reads to Oswald his father's dying words.

Another work, *Le Caractère de M. Necker*, written following Necker's death in 1804, is especially relevant to a consideration of fathers and daughters. Although not directly about abolition, *Le Caractère de M. Necker* was published at the precise moment when Napoleon was crowned emperor and when Haitian independence was declared. Moreover, it was written when Staël, exiled like Toussaint by Napoleon, was painfully aware of issues of oppression and abuse of power. It shows a woman grappling with the issue of what her abolitionist father represented and how to make his legacy meaningful to society. When she calls Necker "the best of all fathers" she is also indirectly claiming that he was the best father the French nation ever had: his generosity to his family paralleled his loan of the major portion of his considerable fortune to the royal treasury when France was in financial crisis. And like Toussaint, Necker is a model of empathy and compassion: "il n'existe pas une injustice envers les opprimés, pas une faute en institutions politiques, qu'il n'ait pas signalée d'avance, et que l'on n'ait pas reconnue depuis" ("there is no injustice against oppressed people, no error in political institutions, that he did not call attention to before others did, and that was not acknowledged by them subsequently.)"[25] Oppressed by Napoleon, as were blacks at the time, Staël evokes the model of her own father and her undying devotion to him and his legacy. Staël is to Necker what Ximéo is to the benevolent governor whose superiority he recognizes and respects. The older man has set the course; with unwavering devotion, the women or blacks follow the wise precepts and example that the father has passed on to them. The key word of Staël's title is "character." Necker possessed what the illegitimate ruler Napoleon, who persecuted women and blacks, most lacked: the moral fiber that makes true benevolence possible and puts an end to social injustice. "Purity," "elevation," "kindness," "refinement": all of these aspects of Necker's character are the very antithesis of what Staël saw as Napoleon's crude, vulgar, cruel, and violent nature. Admittedly, the "character" of individuals, even influential ones like Necker, was not enough to bring an end to slavery as a social and economic system. Gutwirth has said regarding *Mirza* that Staël reached "the emotional impasse of wishing to represent an innovative conception of woman in a milieu wholly uncongenial to her." The same could be said for her desire twenty years later to represent her benevolent, abolitionist father. Gutwirth also observes that "Mme de Staël, when she wrote *Mirza*, could conceive of a new woman, but not of a new world."[26] It is true that Staël displays greater assertiveness in 1804 than she did in 1786. Nonetheless, *Le Caractère de M. Necker* continues to assume that benevolence as practiced by kindly, legitimate fathers would resolve social problems, including the abuses of slavery.

Curiously, Toussaint's son Isaac wrote about his famous father in ways that often bring to mind Staël's defense of Necker. Both fathers were exiled and betrayed by France; both died with a sense of rejection after having accomplished extraordinary acts of public service; both valued their honor and glory above all else; and both had children—Germaine and Isaac—who considered it their mission to set the record straight and assure their fathers' rightful place in history. Staël wrote *Le Caractère de M. Necker* at the height of Napoleon's power and at the start of the exile he imposed upon her. After the end of Napoleon's reign, Isaac Louverture wrote *Mémoires d'Isaac, fils de Toussaint Louverture*.[27] It recounts the lies, broken promises, and treacherous acts committed against Toussaint and his family and seeks to warn the French that, following Toussaint's betrayal and Napoleon's replacement by a restored Bourbon government, ultra-conservatives and former colonists were re-enacting the earlier scenario: they were machinating behind the scenes to trick the leaders of independent Haiti into believing that full international recognition required agreeing to sign away their independence. Such an agreement would have amounted to a recolonization and re-enslavement of the Haitian population. Isaac's story aims to warn well-meaning French citizens not to believe their deceitful military and political compatriots. He appeals for justice and freedom by telling the story of France's inglorious treatment of Toussaint and his family.

A striking similarity between Isaac's and Germaine's constructions of the abolitionist father lies in their similar sentimental literary practices. To tell the story of France's inglorious treatment of Toussaint and his family, Isaac intersperses Toussaint's military story with brief sentimental and familial scenes. An example occurs when Toussaint, apprised of the arrival of French forces and their precipitate military attack, arrives from Santo Domingo to take charge of the situation. Along the route, we read, "il avait compassion d'une multitude de vieillards, de femmes et d'enfants répandus sur les routes" ("He showed compassion for the throngs of old people, women, and children that lined the roads.")[28] Isaac uses a patriarchal trope in which the father is responsible for women, children, and others within his purview. In other scenes, the members of Toussaint's family are named—wife, sister, brother-in-law, nieces, uncles—with frequent mention of a "crowd" of some sort surrounding them. These scenes dramatize Toussaint's love for his family and the threat posed to them from enemy forces. The repeated detailing of family members surrounded by crowds allows the family to function as a metonymic representation of the Haitian people. As Isaac states later in the text, "Il semblait que tout eût concouru [...] pour faire voir dans un seul homme, le coeur d'un père, d'un époux et d'un guerrier défenseur des intérêts de sa patrie et de ses compagnons d'armes" ("It seemed that everything harmonized [...] enabling the people to see in this one man the heart of a father, of a husband, and of a warrior who defended the interests of his country and his fellow soldiers.") (293) Similar evocations of crowds occur in Staël's works; as Suzanne Guerlac observes, they function to represent the nation and engender a social bond among members of the nation.[29]

One scene in *Mémoires d'Isaac* is especially illustrative of the use of sentimental discourse to encourage white readers to identify with and relate to black families through such motifs as maternity, paternal authority, filial devotion, and family bonds. The scene occurs, dramatically, at night, at the paternal home, in the midst of an immense crowd.

> Il est plus facile de concevoir que de raconter ce que cette soirée eut d'attendrissant pour toute une famille, une mère, ses enfants et leur précepteur qui, comblé de remerciements et de soins, était témoin de tant de tendresse et d'amour. Toute cette famille, oubliant pour un moment,

à cause de cette réunion inattendue, le malheur de la patrie, se livrait à la joie et aux plus doux sentiments.

It is easier to conceive of than to describe what made this gathering so touching for a whole family, a mother, her children, and their preceptor, who, attentively cared for and profusely thanked, witnessed so much tenderness and love. A whole family, forgetting for a moment, because of this unexpected reunion, the country's misfortunes, gave free rein to their feelings of joy and loving sentiments. (238)

This scene, which we are called upon to "conceive of" imaginatively, clearly appeals to our emotions. We are supposed to appreciate the black family's capacity for "tenderness," "love," "misfortune," "joy," "loving sentiments." And to better enable white readers to relate to the scene, Isaac dwells here on the preceptor. Not only can this white eye-witness support the author's claim that blacks' sentimental responses are comparable to those of whites: "attentively cared for and profusely thanked," he stands as proof that blacks bear no hostility to whites.

In the posthumously published *Considérations sur la révolution française*, Staël similarly intersperses her historical account with sentimental and familial scenes. Staël describes "les transports de tout un peuple dont je venais d'être témoin, la voiture de mon père traînée par les citoyens des villes que nous traversions" ("a whole nation's strong emotions, which I witnessed; the efforts of citizens to cling on to my father's carriage in the towns we passed through.")[30] In a sentimental mode, Staël places special emphasis on "les femmes à genoux dans les campagnes quand elles le voyaient passer" ("women kneeling in the countryside when they saw him pass.") (167) And when Necker is ignobly forced to leave France and threatened with arrest on September 8, 1790, his letter of departure to the Assembly reveals, according to his daughter, that his attachment to his family and his wife's safety were his chief concerns:

Le temps ne se prêtait guère, il faut en convenir, aux affections domestiques; mais cette sensibilité, qu'un grand homme d'état n'a pu contenir dans toutes les circonstances de sa vie, était précisément la source de ses qualités distinctives, la pénétration et la bonté.

The times hardly lent themselves to domestic affection, one must admit; but this great man's sensitivity, which he could never suppress, whatever the circumstances of his life, was precisely the source of his distinctive qualities, his insight and his goodness. (232–33)

One cannot help but note in passing the emphasis Isaac places on mothers and the contrast with Staël, who virtually eclipses her own mother from the family duo of father and daughter captured in Massot's painting (Figure 2). The two women were at odds on the issue of divorce, Staël's romantic involvements, and most importantly the role of sentiment and passion in women's lives.[31] That Isaac casts his mother in a stereotypical maternal role, which Staël neither accepted nor agreed to play, points to one of the many differences between male and female writers observed within the pages of this book.

* * *

In the final phase of Staël's writing career, it is more as a mature, independent woman than as an adoring daughter that her commitment to freedom finds expression. Napoleon remains her target and the emblem of the oppression of slaves and women. Speaking of Napoleon's persecution of her in the posthumously published *Dix Années d'exil*, she states, "le plus grand grief de l'empereur Napoléon contre moi, c'est l'amour et le respect dont j'ai toujours été pénétrée pour la véritable liberté" ("the greatest reproach that the emperor Napoleon had against me was my enduring love and respect for true freedom.") (46) In the final analysis Napoleon, responsible for reinstating slavery in the French colonies, was the ultimate, abusive patriarch whom Staël viewed as the antithesis of her benevolent father. Her construction of the abolitionist father was thus part of a political struggle in which she aimed to pit good against evil, benevolence against violence. In her unwavering opposition to Napoleon, she parts company with members of the Louverture family whose agency, as black men, was expressed through military honor, notwithstanding Isaac's strategic use of sentimental writing techniques. In Toussaint Louverture's memoirs, written during his imprisonment, he maintained his loyalty to France and called Napoleon "ce grand homme dont l'équité et l'impartialité sont si bien connues" ("this great man whose fairness and impartiality are so well known"), accepting that he owed him "sa soumission et entier dévouement" ("submission and total devotion.")[32] Honor was the operative code in the Toussaint family, an invisible code during the Napoleonic period and beyond which "had a family and marital dimension" as well as "a public or political dimension."[33] To adhere to and be worthy of this noble, masculine code was the highest aspiration of talented, educated men such as Toussaint and Isaac Louverture.

Staël's outlook as a woman was far different. Although not as inclined as later feminists to reject paternal authority, Germaine de Staël unflinchingly opposed Napoleon, whom she described as "l'oppresseur qui pesait sur l'espèce humaine" ("the oppressor who lay like a pall over the human race.")[34] Staël did not directly seek to replace the father despite her imaginative configuration of a woman to take his place in *Corinne*. But after Necker's death Staël assumed a strong, proactive antislavery role in both the private and public spheres. As a strong mother, she influenced an abolitionist family that carried the concept of benevolent paternalism well into the nineteenth century. Necker stands proudly beside Staël in Massot's painting. I would like to imagine her antislavery legacy as a source of his pride. As a writer, she challenged abuses of male authority. She espoused the cause of freedom and remained unwavering in her antislavery views. In *Dix Années*, she reports countering a Russian woman's statement that serfs were happy by saying, "Heureux, c'est fort bien: mais libres! Parmi toutes les définitions de la liberté, je n'ai jamais rencontré l'esclavage" ("Happy, very well: but free? Among all the definitions of freedom I have never encountered slavery.") (270)

In 1814 Staël wrote two short abolitionist texts which reveal the more active role that she chose to play in relation to slavery near the end of her life: *Appel aux souverains* réunis à Paris pour en obtenir l'*abolition de la traite des nègres* and *Préface pour la traduction d'un ouvrage de M. Wilberforce sur la traite des nègres*.[35] The context for these works was the Congress of Vienna which began in September 1814 following Napoleon's defeat in May of that year. Among the many pressing issues that the leaders of Britain, Austria, Russia, and other countries faced was the slave trade, which the British had outlawed in 1807. It was to convince the leaders present in Vienna, and especially Czar Alexander I, that other European nations should follow Britain's example that Staël addresses them in the *Appel*, and it is to send the same message to the French public that she writes the *Préface*. Not surprisingly, the *Appel* addresses men who have the power to effect change in the public sphere. Staël never challenged the gendered rules of the game in her lifetime. What has changed by the end of her life, however, is that she has adopted a pragmatic approach that expands her father's more abstract Enlightenment views. She directly articulates abolitionist arguments—for example, that the British act in 1807 has not negatively impacted their economic prosperity—and she names the key British participants in the struggle: Pitt, Fox, Wilberforce, Clarkson, Canning, Macaulay, and others. Clearly she was abreast of all the political battles that led up to the passage of the British bill. In the *Appel*, she shows her keen awareness of the power exercised by the Russian emperor at the Congress of Vienna. She appeals to him to assume the role of savior for the African people. In addition, she implores the leaders to enact a concerted ban on the slave trade as the most fitting monument to consecrate Napoleon's downfall.

One sees the two sides of Staël at the end of her life—the woman who plays an activist role; the daughter who still adheres to a traditional outlook—in her emulation of the British abolitionist William Wilberforce, who serves as a father figure at this point in her life. Wilberforce's fervent belief in the moral significance of Christian religion for society generally and abolition in particular made him the ideal abolitionist father, who fulfilled Staël's need to reconcile the love of God and father with a love for freedom. In the *Préface* she presents Wilberforce as an "avocat de l'humanité" ("advocate of humanity") (283, 159) and describes him with the same kind of esteem she had for her father: "Orateur distingué dans la chambre des communes, remarquablement instruit sur tout ce qui tient à la littérature et à cette haute philosophie dont la religion est la base, il a consacré trente ans de sa vie à faire rougir l'Europe d'un grand attentat, et à délivrer l'Afrique d'un affreux malheur" ("This distinguished orator in the House of Commons, remarkably well-versed in everything pertaining to literature and that lofty philosophy based on religion, has devoted thirty years of his life to making Europe ashamed of a great moral outrage and to liberating Africa from a horrible misfortune.") (284, 159) Her description of the acclaim lavished on Wilberforce in *Considérations sur la révolution française* recalls her earlier description of her father: "l'homme le plus aimé et le plus considéré de toute l'Angleterre, M. Wilberforce, put à peine se faire entendre, tant les applaudissements couvraient sa voix" ("the most beloved and respected man in all of England, Mr. Wilberforce, could hardly be heard, so greatly did applause drown his voice.") (529) When he succeeded in passing the bill abolishing the slave trade in the British Parliament, she notes that, according to his fellow abolitionist Thomas Clarkson, "un rayon de soleil, comme pour célébrer une fête si touchante, sortit des nuages qui couvraient le ciel" ("a ray of sunlight broke through the clouds, as if to acknowledge so touching a celebration.)" (568) *Considérations sur la révolution française* ends with the assertion that the love of liberty is universal and resides in the souls of the greatest of men: "S'agit-il de l'abolition de la traite des nègres, de la liberté de la presse, de la tolérance religieuse, Jefferson pense comme La Fayette, La Fayette comme Wilberforce" ("Whether the issue is the abolition of the slave trade, freedom of the press, or religious tolerance, Jefferson thinks like La Fayette, La Fayette thinks like Wilberforce.") (606)

Nothing has changed with respect to Staël's views regarding the respective roles of men and women in the public arena. It is Wilberforce, as it will later be Auguste de Staël and le duc de Broglie, who visibly carries the abolitionist banner. What did change is that a mature woman and mother singled out or directly influenced the abolitionist fathers of nineteenth-century abolitionism. That woman and mother, unlike her younger, more naive and dutiful self and characters, was able to transcend her father's abstract, theoretical notions of abolition and join hands with those who could conceive, if not of a new world for women, at least of a new world without slaves.

Notes

1 Massot's painting is discussed in detail in the Postscript.

2 A version of parts of this chapter was delivered at the Staël conference at Washington University in 2009 and appears in *Germaine de Staël: Forging a Politics of Mediation*, ed. Tilli Boon Cuillé and Karyna Szmurlo (Oxford: Voltaire Foundation, 2011). A French version of some of the material appeared in *Littérature et esclavage* (Lyon: Editions Desjonquères, 2010).

3 Quoted in Charlotte Blennerhassett, *Madame de Staël: her friends and her influence in politics and literature*, vol. III (London: Chapman and Hall, 1889), 575. Translations not followed by a page number are my own. Page numbers following French and English passages refer to *Translating Slavery: Gender and Race in French Women's Writing, 1783–1823*, ed. Doris Y. Kadish and Françoise Massardier-Kenney (Kent: Kent State University Press, 1994).

4 Germaine de Staël, "Quelques Réflexions sur le but moral de *Delphine*," in *Oeuvres complètes de Mme la baronne de Staël*, vol. V (Paris: Treuttel et Wurtz, 1820), x.

5 Lerner, *Creation of Patriarchy*, 89.

6 Staël, *De la Littérature dans ses rapports avec les institutions sociales* (Paris: Garnier, 1998), 138.

7 Susan Buck-Morss relates the notion of "free labor" at the time to the defeat of the British working class, the rise of capitalism, and imperialism: *Hegel, Haiti, and Universal History*, 100.

8 Staël, *Caractère de M. Necker*, in *Oeuvres complètes*, vol. XVII, 12.

9 John Isbell questions Staël's claim that *Histoire de Pauline* was written in 1786. He argues that her breakup with Louis de Narbonne in 1794 marked a turning point in her attitudes toward sugar plantations, which his wife owned. Whereas in 1792 she had defended the Narbonnes' attempts to retain their colonial properties, in 1794 she attacked the plantocratic system: "Voices Lost? Staël and Slavery, 1786–1830," in *Slavery in the Caribbean Francophone World*, ed. Doris Y. Kadish (Athens: University of Georgia Press, 2000), 41.

10 Staël, *Correspondance générale de Madame de Staël*, ed. Béatrice Jasinski, vol. I (Paris: Jean-Jacques Pauvert, 1962), 141.

11 Philip D. Morgan, *Slave Counterpoint: Black Culture in the Eighteenth-Century Chesapeake and Lowcountry* (Chapel Hill: University of North Carolina Press, 1998), 259

12 Staël, *Correspondance générale*, vol. V, 141.

13 Citations from *Pauline* are from Staël, *Oeuvres de jeunesse*, ed. John Isbell and Simone Balayé (Paris: Desjonquiers, 1997).

14 Hélène Cixous and Annette Kuhn, "Castration or Decapitation?" *Signs* 7, 1 (1981): 48, 50.

15 Christopher Miller, *The French Atlantic Triangle: Literature and Culture of the Slave Trade* (Durham, NC: Duke University Press, 2008), 143. I address Miller's critique in *Translating Slavery, vol. 1: Gender and Race in French Abolitionist Writing, 1780–1830*, ed. Doris Y. Kadish and Françoise Massardier-Kenney (Kent: Kent State University Press, 2009), x–xi.

16 Alfred Berchtold, "Sismondi et le groupe de Coppet face à l'esclavage et au colonialisme," in *Sismondi Européen*, ed. Sven Stelling-Michaud (Geneva: Slatkine, 1976), 172.

17 Isbell, "Voices Lost?" 40.

18 Comtesse Jean de Pange, "Madame de Staël et les nègres," *Revue de France* 5 (1934): 426–27.

19 Staël, *Correspondance générale*, vol. V, 23–25.

20 Staël, *Dix Années d'exil* (Paris: Fayard, 1996), 115.

21 Staël, *Corinne, ou, l'Italie* (Paris: Gallimard, 1985), 161.

22 I am grateful to Deborah Jenson for pointing out to me that the critical spirit of the *Mémoires* is the reason why Napoleon refused to allow Toussaint to keep sending his writings to him.

23 Madelyn Gutwirth, *Madame De Staël, Novelist* (Urbana: University of Illinois Press, 1978), 232.

24 Doris Y. Kadish, "Narrating the French Revolution: The Example of Corinne," in *Germaine De Staël: Crossing the Borders*, ed. Madelyn Gutwirth (New Brunswick: Rutgers University Press, 1991), 119.

25 Staël, *Caractère de M. Necker*, 68.

26 Gutwirth, *Madame De Staël, Novelist*, 72.

27 Isaac Louverture, *Histoire de l'expédition des Français à Saint-Domingue*, ed. Antoine Marie Thérèse Métral (Paris: Fanjat aîné, 1825). The relation between Isaac's text and Métral's is ambiguous. Isaac's text appears as an appendix to Métral's and is less clearly abolitionist. For more about Isaac Louverture, see Jenson, *Beyond Slave Narratives*, 206–12.

28 Louverture, *Histoire de l'expédition des Français à Saint-Domingue*, 234.

29 Suzanne Guerlac, "Writing the Nation (Mme de Staël)," *French Forum* 30, 3 (2005): 43–56.

30 Staël, *Considerations sur la révolution française* (Paris: Tallendier, 2000), 529.

31 Catherine Dubeau, "The Mother, the Daughter, and the Passions," in the forthcoming volume *Sensibility, Society, and the Sister Arts: Germaine de Staël's Historical Revisionism*, ed. Tili Boon Cuillé and Karyna Szmurlo.

32 Toussaint Louverture, *Mémoires du Général Toussaint Louverture écrits par lui-même*, ed. Joseph Saint-Rémy (Paris: Pagnerre, 1853), 48, 63.

33 Reddy, *Navigation of Feeling*, xi.

34 Kadish and Massardier-Kenney, eds, *Translating Slavery: Gender and Race in French Women's Writing*, 282, 158.

35 Subsequent references to these texts are to the original and translated versions in Kadish and Massardier-Kenney, eds, *Translating Slavery: Gender and Race in French Women's Writing*, 281–87, 157–62.

2

Fathers and Colonization:
Charlotte Dard

The name of Charlotte Dard, née Picard, would have remained buried in obscurity were it not for the notorious shipwreck of the *Medusa* in 1816. That event set off one of the great scandals of the Restoration and provided the impetus for the renewal of French efforts to enforce the abolition of the slave trade. *La Chaumière africaine*, Dard's account of the shipwreck and her life in Africa from 1816 to 1820, published in 1824, provides the basis of this chapter's analysis of fathers, daughters, and slaves. It tells two different stories. The story of an early colonizer, Charles Picard, whose reputation his daughter attempted to rehabilitate, is the first. Her efforts mirror those of Germaine de Staël and Isaac Louverture discussed in Chapter 1. Dard's defense of her father, although clearly not unbiased, is supported by material found in the extensive archival records of the shipwreck of the *Medusa*. Dard's own unique story of a woman who survived a shipwreck and put her experiences in written form is the second. It details her struggle to stay alive in early nineteenth-century Africa, living in wild and deserted places, enduring poverty and illness, and witnessing the demise of her parents and siblings. The Scottish translator of *La Chaumière africaine*, Patrick Maxwell, wrote in 1827, "There is not, on the records of misery, an instance of more severe and protracted suffering; and I trust there is not, nor ever will be any, where human nature was more foully outraged and disgraced."[1] Yet Dard's story, like that of the other women discussed in this book, is also one of empowerment. A traveler as a young girl and an educator later in life, she tells a tale of discovery: not in the sense of conquest or exploration, but rather in the sense of learning something new. Charlotte Dard discovered in Africa what it meant for a young woman and for blacks, with whom she lived and worked, to possess an independent subjectivity.

A brief summary of the complex facts of the shipwreck and its aftermath can serve as an introduction. On June 17, 1816, the *Medusa* and three smaller ships set sail for Senegal, which had been returned to the French by the convention of November 20, 1815. The *Medusa*'s 250 passengers—officers, sailors, military personnel, colonizers, family members—were all connected in some capacity with the plans for the resumption of French commerce in Africa, interrupted in 1809 when the English took possession of Senegal. Most had little knowledge of their destination or the treacherous waters they would cross to reach it. Nautical incompetence was especially egregious in the case of the commander of the ship, Hugues Duroy de Chaumareys, an *ancien régime* officer who had not commanded a ship for twenty-four years. In contrast, Charlotte's father, Charles-Marie César Picard, had extensive experience with travel to and residence in Africa. Born in Paris in 1769, Picard was an educated French explorer and functionary who spent the years from 1799 to 1801 and from 1802 to 1809 in Senegal until the British gained control of the colony.[2] Senegal was returned to France in 1814 with the fall of Napoleon; at that time, Picard would have returned to Africa if the Hundred Days had not produced a hiatus in the resumption of French colonial expeditions. Only in 1816, with the *Medusa* expedition, was he able to resume his colonial career. Calling attention to the fact that naval officers refused to listen to Picard's warnings or to acknowledge his superior knowledge of the region is one of Charlotte's many justifications on behalf of her father in *La Chaumière africaine*. Defending her father is the reason why Dard wrote the memoir.

The *Medusa* ran aground on the shelf of the Arguin embankment off the coast of Africa on July 2 (see Figure 3). Lifeboats accommodated only some passengers of note. One hundred and fifty other persons, mostly lower-rank soldiers and sailors, were relegated to a hastily constructed raft. After thirteen days with almost no food or water, only fifteen of those on the raft survived, of whom five died shortly after their rescue. Seventeen others were left on the ship for fifty-two days. An eye-witness account of the events appeared almost immediately. The navy surgeon Jean-Baptiste Savigny wrote a report which appeared in the *Journal des débats* on September 13, 1816. A year later, the engineer and geographer Alexandre Corréard, another survivor of the raft, collaborated with Savigny to co-author *Le Radeau de la Méduse*, an expanded version of Savigny's earlier report, and in 1818 and 1819, second and third editions were published. In the preface to *La Chaumière africaine*, Charlotte explains that refuting certain inaccuracies in those accounts is one of her motivations in writing her memoir. Those book-length accounts went much farther than the initial report, targeting naval officers, the minister of the navy, and the Restoration government, which the authors held responsible for appointing Chaumareys as commander of the ship. The scandal intensified with the exhibition of Théodore Géricault's *Le Radeau de la Méduse*, based on Savigny and Corréard's account, at the Salon

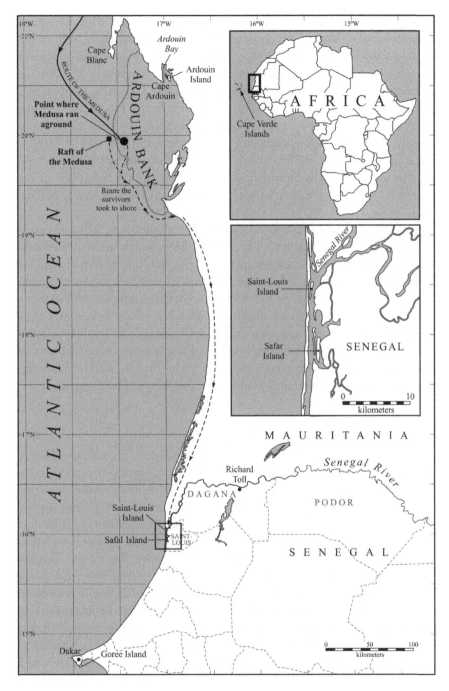

Figure 3. Western coast of Africa and islands of Senegal.
Original map by Mary Lee Eggart.

of 1819. What historian Philippe Masson has called "the Medusa Affair" comprises these basic facts about the disaster and rescue as well as the survivors' subsequent experiences in Africa, the judicial proceedings against Chaumareys, and the political implications of the events. The *Medusa* affair afforded liberal abolitionist sympathizers like Corréard, Savigny, and Géricault the occasion to highlight the French failure to comply with the international ban on the slave trade instituted at the Congress of Vienna in 1814. Although no slave traders were among the passengers on the *Medusa*, the attention focused on the African coast by the shipwreck brought to light the ongoing practice of French slave trading. As a result, the failure of the Bourbon regime to punish violators of the ban on the slave trade entered public discussion.[3]

This summary of the events raises a number of questions. To what extent did the fathers in Charlotte's life and in the colonial world depicted in *La Chaumière africaine* conform to the patriarchal model? What resistant strategies did Charlotte as a daughter devise in order to survive and gain some measure of control of her life? How did she interact with African natives and the abolitionist debates surrounding the *Medusa* affair? A final question can be answered through the contrapuntal method adopted in this book. How do twentieth-century Francophone representations of the African women with whom the men in the Picard and Dard families interracted in early nineteenth-century Africa relate to Dard's story?

* * *

The first father to appear in Dard's story is her maternal grandfather, Claude Miroufle. The rosy picture that Dard paints of him signals the glorification of paternal figures in her writing. She makes no mention of the economic difficulties in her early life with him, claiming instead that "nos années s'écoulaient dans une parfaite tranquillité" ("our years glided on in perfect tranquility.")[4] She praises her grandfather for playing the role of both father and mother to her and her younger sister Caroline during the roughly ten-year period when her father was in Africa. She confesses that when M. Picard returned from Africa in 1809, the two girls initially refused to recognize him as their father, "tant nos jeunes âmes s'étaient habituées à ne voir et à n'aimer, dans le monde, que le respectable vieillard qui avait pris soin de notre enfance" (6) ("so much were our young minds habituated to see and love but one in the world—the worthy old man who had watched over our infancy)." (20) Archival records indicate that in fact Miroufle was burdened by the care of Charlotte, born in 1798, and Caroline, born two years later. After the death in 1807 of Charlotte's mother, Marie Françoise Geneviève, who had struggled to get by during her husband's absences in

Africa, Miroufle relied on the money that M. Picard sent from Senegal to support the children. When that money stopped coming, Miroufle registered complaints with the authorities: in 1808 he states that his daughter has "just succumbed to a long and cruel illness and left two young children that my position unfortunately does not allow me to support" and that, having for the past thirteen months received nothing from their father, "this poor sixty-year-old has had to sustain them by his own work." Other documents confirm the family's straitened financial circumstances. An appeal addressed to the Ministre de la Marine regarding Miroufle refers to "the destitution in which I have found him for the last eighteen months." A letter from Miroufle suggests that the grandfather feared that Picard might abandon his children.[5]

The chief focus of Charlotte's familial attachment as a teenage girl and young woman is her father. After having assumed responsibility for his children, Picard formed a union with Marie-Antoinette Fleury, widow of Simon Giraut, whom Charlotte calls her "second mother" although there is reason to believe that she and Picard were not legally married.[6] Picard resembles other needy, at times impoverished, fathers, such as the father of Marceline Desbordes-Valmore discussed in Chapter 3, struggling to survive in the tumultuous world of postrevolutionary France. His colonial career, like the artistic and theatrical career of Marceline's father, placed him on the margins of society, barely able to provide for his family. Such fathers tend to fall into the category of benevolent figures who are pitied, beloved, and cared for by their daughters.

As Dard explains, Picard specifically directed her before he died to clear up the misunderstandings that surrounded his activities in Africa: "Il me témoigna en expirant le désir que nos malheurs ne demeurassent pas inconnus; c'est donc pour moi un devoir, et un devoir sacré de les publier. Je goûte en le remplissant la consolation de penser [...] que nos persécuteurs éprouveront au moins quelque regret" (3) ("On his deathbed, he expressed to me the desire that our misfortunes should not remain unknown. It then became my sacred duty to publish them. In fulfilling his wish, I feel the consolation of knowing [...] that those who persecuted us will at least experience some regret.") (19) The extent to which Picard may have influenced the writing of the memoir is unclear. Michel Hanniet has seen an early version of the manuscript that is in the possession of an heir of the Picard family and concludes that Picard may have seen Charlotte's account prior to his death in 1819. Hanniet notes a number of differences between that manuscript and the 1824 memoir.[7]

Dard depicts her father as a colonialist of modest means and social standing who pursued a series of unsuccessful entrepreneurial, bureaucratic, and agricultural endeavors. It would appear that Picard's inability to adapt to the changing conditions of the colonial world as well as his poor judgment were largely to blame for the misfortunes that he and his family endured. His daughter sees matters differently, however. She places the blame for his failures on those within the colonial system who possessed the privilege and power that Picard lacked. She identifies them as her fathers' "persecutors." She sees them in relation to Picard much as Staël viewed Napoleon in relation to Necker. Uncouth, ignorant, and unfeeling, they are the antithesis of the benevolent father beloved and glorified by his daughter.

The first of the persecutors is the captain of the *Medusa*, Hugues Duroy de Chaumareys, who embodies aristocratic privilege. Arrogant toward others, including his own officers, he went so far as to make it known that "having been named by the king, it was the king himself who was on board and who spoke through his mouth."[8] This statement reveals the sharp division between Picard's enemies and himself. Situated on a lower rung on the social and economic ladder, Picard was anti-monarchist, as were a considerable number of the officers, sailors, and military personnel sent to establish the settlement in Africa. Abolitionism tended to emanate from such social ranks, not from the ranks of monarchists who, in many cases, supported the restoration of property they had lost in the Haitian Revolution and the reimposition of slavery. In contrast, Chaumareys had followed the monarchy into exile during the Revolution and the Empire. As reward for his loyalty he was named ship's captain, despite his patent inability to fulfill the functions of that position. Indeed, blame for the shipwreck can be attributed to such failures on his part as his unwillingness to acknowledge the danger presented by the change of color of the water as the ship approached the notoriously dangerous Arguin embarkment. On March 3, 1817, a naval military council declared him guilty of not having taken sufficient measures to avoid the shipwreck of the *Medusa* and of not having been the last to abandon the ship, as was required by military protocol. He was condemned to three years in prison.

The second persecutor in Dard's account is Julien-Désiré Schmaltz, governor of Senegal from 1816 to 1820. He too had gained favor with the royalist government. His sense of privilege and social superiority is the chief basis of Dard's enmity toward him. As others, including Charlotte's family, sought desperately to find places on the lifeboats after the shipwreck, she describes Schmaltz who "se faisait descendre mollement dans un fauteuil, d'où il arriva par une *ascension inverse* au grand canot, où se trouvaient déjà plusieurs grandes caisses, toutes sortes de provisions, ses plus chers amis, sa fille et son épouse" (29–30) ("descended comfortably in an armchair into the barge, where there were already various large chests, all kinds of provisions, his dearest friends, his daughter and his wife.") (45) Charlotte alleges that when she begged for her family to be allowed to join the Schmaltz family on their boat, she learned that Mme Schmaltz and her daughter, "qui s'étaient embarquées dans le plus grand *incognito* [...] n'avait pas envie de 's'embarrasser' de notre malheureuse famille" (30–31) ("who had embarked in a mysterious *incognito* [...] had no intention of encumbering themselves with our family.") (46–47)[9]

Picard's resentment toward colonial authorities such as Schmaltz had various causes. Class differences played a part. Moreover, Picard was witnessing a new wave of colonists who were profiting from a colonization project that he had initiated. Charlotte maintains that in 1815 her father had been promised the rank of captain and commander of a settlement in Senegal, which he would have received if the political events of the Hundred Days had not occurred: "Il avait le premier donné les renseignements sur les contrées où l'on pouvait fonder des établissements de culture en Afrique, et proposé des plans qui furent accueillis dans le temps, par le Président du conseil d'État et par le Ministre de la marine, pour la colonisation du Sénégal" (97) ("He was the first to provide information concerning the countries where they were to found the agricultural establishments in Africa, and had proposed plans which were accepted at the time by the President of the Council of State, and by the Minister of Marine, for the colonization of Senegal.") (114) Having spent four years in Africa prior to 1816, Picard knew about Senegal—its geography, its agriculture, its people, its economy—in contrast with uninformed newcomers in the country such as Schmaltz. Despite his many shortcomings, Picard bears a similarity to the committed, informed colonizer that Staël presents in the opening pages of *Mirza* and whose involvement in Africa was promoted by liberals such as Boufflers, Necker, and La Fayette.[10] Firmly opposed to slavery, Picard envisioned developing sustainable agriculture in Africa to meet the needs of blacks as well as less privileged whites such as himself.

The French colonial government also plays the role of persecutor because of its unwillingness to meet the family's needs and demands once they arrived in Senegal, despite Picard's repeated attempts to enlist its support. In contrast, Dard emphasizes the willingness of other national groups to come to their aid: for example, Arabs and "ces bons maures" ("those good Moors") (70, 84), who showed compassion and hospitality as the Picards made their arduous passage through the desert. Dard also dwells on the assistance afforded by an Englishman, M. Carnet, as well as the warm welcome she and her sister received upon their arrival in Saint-Louis from M. and Mme Kingsley and the empathy of the English officers who were eager to hear their story. Although the identity of the translator of *The Sufferings of the Picard Family* is unclear, there was a Major Maxwell who played a role in the British administration of Senegal before it was turned over to the French and who appears to have been a lieutenant-governor of the settlement of Senegal.[11] Dard's favorable comments about Englishmen fit with the esteem in which her father and other abolitionists held the English. Not surprisingly, in the introduction to his translation Maxwell expresses pride that "there are some pleasing traits of character in the story" and that "some of the brightest of them belong to our own nation." (xviii)

Charlotte's depiction of Picard's victimization in the second half of the memoir focuses less on individuals than on economic and political systems in French colonial Africa. According to the Traités de Paris of 1814 and 1815, France was allowed to take possession of settlements on the western coast of Africa that it had held on January 1, 1792, and that, since 1809, had been in the possession of the English. Although settlements had been established on the coast of Africa as early as 1630, and French commercial activity flourished on the Senegalese island of Saint-Louis, the interior of Africa was unknown until its exploration by Mungo Park in 1793. Relying on the new knowledge that Park and other explorers provided, French colonizers like Picard who returned to Senegal in the 1790s sought to develop commerce and agriculture in new ways. French plans consisted specifically of shifting power away from the northern Moors, gaining control of the highly profitable trade in gum arabic, employing free labor by blacks, and cultivating markets in the interior of Africa.[12] African workers would produce at low cost and learn to consume products that were popular in Europe, such as cotton, indigo, sugar, and tobacco. Ultimately such efforts were in vain, not only during the governorship of Schmaltz but during that of Baron Roger from 1821 to 1827.[13]

Picard's inability or unwillingness to adapt to colonial authority during his third and last residence in Senegal, from 1816 to 1819, was ultimately as tragic and dramatic for his family as the disaster of the shipwreck. Matters were complicated by the size and complexity of his family. To summarize briefly a puzzling family story, Dard states that nine members undertook the voyage on the *Medusa* in 1816 (31, 148) although the number and identities of those individuals vary within the text itself and in secondary texts that refer to it.[14] In addition to Picard, Marie-Antoinette Fleury, Charlotte, and Caroline, Dard states that there were four children. Dard presents them as the offspring of her father and his second wife, although we shall have occasion to discuss later the possibility that at least one may have been the mixed-race offspring from Picard's earlier trips in Senegal.[15] Two others are mentioned, both of whom were undoubtedly related to Marie-Antoinette Fleury. Antoinette Louise Gillet, identified as a cousin Charlotte's age, traveled as her companion; she returned to France during the family's stay in Africa. Alphonse Fleury is called a cousin whom her father had always treated as a son near the end of *La Chaumière africaine* (148) although he was not counted as one of the nine persons who left on the *Medusa* at the beginning of the memoir.[16] Speculation exists that he was the son of Picard and Marie-Antoinette.[17] At the end of the memoir we are told that only three members of the family survived: Charlotte, Caroline, and Alphonse Fleury.

In addition to the social and financial issues attached to such a large and diverse family, Picard proved to be a dissatisfied employee of the French government, convinced that his rank and compensation did not match his abilities and experience. Complaints and requests for greater privileges were constant. Georges Bordonove describes him as "the embodiment of the average resentful Frenchman, a good soul but excessively inclined to criticism, highly acerbic and, moreover, totally convinced that as the father of a large family society owed him special rights and privileges."[18] Schmaltz ignored his incessant appeals, which Dard interprets in her father's typical paranoid way: "s'étant laissé circonvenir par certaines personnes auxquelles mon père avait peut-être dit de trop grandes vérités, il ne pensa plus à lui, et nous fûmes même en butte à toutes sortes de vexations" (192) ("but he allowed himself to be circumvented by certain people, to whom my father had perhaps spoken too much truth. He thought no more of him, and we were set up as a mark of every kind of persecution.") (115) In 1818, Picard was officially fired, accused of gross incompetence and a performance deemed "scandalous." After that time, Picard and his family had no source of income other than cultivating cotton on the island of Safal, one of the numerous islands in the Senegal River near Saint-Louis. Picard had been granted rights to this island in 1807 during his second stay in Senegal.[19]

* * *

To shift emphasis from fathers to daughters is to move from Picard's story of persecution to Dard's story of resourcefulness. In *Silencing the Past*, Michel-Rolph Trouillot identifies three ways in which persons denied power have managed to play a role in history: as agents, in categories such as workers, slaves, or family members; as actors, called upon to play roles in specific historical situations; and as subjects, who act purposefully and are aware of their own voices.[20] Charlotte Dard functioned in all of these ways to survive and gain some measure of control of her life. Regrettably, Dard has been overshadowed by missionaries, explorers, adventurers, functionaries, and other men in the early colonization of Africa. Typically, her narrative only furnishes touches of human interest, femininity, or sentimentalism into the *Medusa* story. Hanniet begins *La Véridique histoire des naufragés de la Méduse* with Dard's story, which he embellishes with conjectural descriptions: "We can imagine that without being pretty Charlotte has an agreeable face framed by brown hair and that she exudes a sense of gentleness and sensitivity."[21] In other cases Dard is not taken seriously. Roger Mercier admits that "Mme

Dard made a contribution to the anti-slavery campaign," and he notes "her interest in blacks, the description of their life and their feelings." But he also reminds readers that "unfortunately Mme Dard lacks literary talent" and that "the sincerity in expressing feelings is somewhat marred by the use of the literary artifices popular at the time."[22] Similarly, although Léon Fanoudh-Siefer notes her pathbreaking role in describing Africa, he calls attention to "her melodramatic awkwardness," "her exceedingly mediocre literary qualities," and "her insipid complaints." Using the condescending tone often reserved for women writers, Fanoudh-Siefer characterizes what he calls Dard's hyperbolic presentation of events as stemming from "the feminine sensitivity of the author, always emotional, always rushing to act for the most trivial reasons, and always dramatizing everything."[23]

A close examination of *La Chaumière africaine* reveals a very different picture. Dard was both an agent and an actor within the family. True, the family appears at first glance to be the traditional male-centered unit in which the father exercised absolute authority and others followed his orders. Upon closer consideration, however, it becomes apparent that the Picard family was far from traditionally authoritarian or patriarchal. As noted above, M. Picard struggled for years to keep his head above water financially. Although knowledgeable about Africa, he fails to measure up as a hero or strong leader. On the ship, he often retreats to his cabin when a crisis arises, as he did at the time of the shipwreck. Overwhelmed by the potential dangers, he acts more like a sentimental heroine than a hero:

> L'idée des pertes que notre naufrage vient de lui causer et le danger où se trouve ce qui lui reste de plus cher au monde le plongent dans un profond évanouissement. La tendresse prête à son épouse et à ses enfants des forces pour tâcher de le tirer de cet état. Il revient à la vie, mais hélas! c'est pour mieux déplorer l'infortune et l'horrible position de sa famille. (47)

> (The idea of the loss which the shipwreck had occasioned to him, and the danger which still menaced all he held dearest in the world, plunged him into a deep swoon. The tenderness of his wife and children recovered him; but alas! his recovery was still more bitterly to deplore the wretched situation of his family.) (63)

In this scene and others, Dard herself assumes the competence and fortitude of the traditional male provider. She cares for her siblings, attends to domestic duties, and sustains her father's flagging morale. Without her agency it is doubtful whether she or her sister would have survived.

Dard also functions as a subject who, as Trouillot puts it, acts purposefully and is aware of her own voice. In one striking example, she uses her narrative voice to correct the sexist portrayal of her by the other survivors of the shipwreck. Refuting Savigny and Corréard's account, she refers to a scene in which a Moor approached her in the middle of the night.

> Croyant sans doute le rendre plus intéressant ou plus amusant, ils disent qu'un Maure [...] soit par curiosité, soit par tout autre sentiment, s'approche de l'aînée des demoiselles Picard pendant qu'elle dormait, et qu'après avoir examiné ses formes, il souleva le voile qui couvrait sa poitrine, y fixa attentivement ses regards, resta pendant quelques instants comme un homme vivement étonné, s'en approcha ensuite de très près, mais n'osa cependant pas y toucher; qu'après l'avoir bien observée, il laissa tomber le voile et revint à sa place, où, tout joyeux, il raconta à ses camarades ce qu'il venait de voir. (75)

> (Believing doubtless to make it more interesting or amusing, they say that one of the Moors [...] either through curiosity or a stronger sentiment approached Miss Picard while asleep, and, after having examined her form, raised the covering which concealed her bosom, gazing awhile like one astonished, at length drew nearer, but dared not touch her. Then, after having looked a long while like one astonished, he replaced the covering; and, returning to his companions, related in a joyous manner what he had seen.) (90)

What really happened, she informs us, was quite different:

> Ma cousine et moi, nous allâmes nous coucher auprès d'une petite élévation, où nous nous fîmes un ombrage avec quelques mauvaises hardes qu'on nous avait prêtées. Ma cousine portait un habit d'uniforme dont les galons plurent singulièrement aux Maures de M. Carnet; à peine fûmes-nous couchées que l'un d'eux, croyant nous trouver endormies, vint pour tâcher de les arracher; mais voyant que nous ne dormions pas, il se contenta de les examiner fort attentivement. (74–75)

> (My cousin and I went to stretch ourselves upon a small rising ground, where we were shaded with some old clothes which we had with us. My cousin was clad in an officer's uniform, the gold braid of which strongly attracted the eyes of Mr. Carnet's Moors. Scarcely had we lain down, when one of them, thinking we were asleep, came to endeavor to steal it; but seeing we were awake, contented himself by looking at us very steadfastly.) (89)

Savigny and Corréard transformed an innocent scene into an erotic episode, a sort of visual rape of the two girls. Dard uses her voice as a woman to rectify the inaccuracy of their account, thereby calling into question the seemingly transparent, objective nature of the male narrative.

In addition, Dard calls attention to the potentially racist implications of

Savigny and Corréard's account. She refuses to demonize the curious Moor and resists the temptation to create an "us" and "them" polarity. Savigny and Corréard stigmatize individuals along class and race lines and consistently vilify Moors and other persons of color. The lower-class soldiers on the raft are not only portrayed as "the debris of all kinds of countries" and "the elite of the prisons from which they had dredged up this impure trash" but as "miserable creatures [...] whose moral fiber has been destroyed or eternally compressed under the weight of the indelible shame that makes them foreigners in the country." The depiction of the soldiers as distinctly non-French is reinforced by their portrayal as non-white. Their leader is termed an "Asian": "A colossal man, short hair, an extremely wide nose, an enormous mouth, and swarthy skin, gave him a hideous aspect."[24] This "Asian," who is racialized but not as African, stands in contrast to the sub-Saharan blacks described elsewhere who would presumably welcome the French colonizers as liberators wresting them from the clutches of corrupt Africans working in tandem with European slave traders. According to this scenario, blacks must be rescued by compassionate Frenchmen like Corréard and Savigny. Such abolitionist ideas are of course not unique to Corréard and Savigny. Ultimately their antislavery views and Dard's are similar: indignation at certain inhuman practices by Moors, calls to abolish the slave trade, visions of a peaceful exploitation of Africa with the cooperation of the native people. Dard does not, however, adopt Corréard and Savigny's bifurcating approach to race. Rather, she constructs her own subjectivity by highlighting overlapping and interdependent traits among persons of different races and ethnicities.

Another illustrative contrast can be drawn by comparing *La Chaumière africaine* with Théodore Géricault's celebrated painting *Le Radeau de la Méduse* (Figure 4). Unlike Corréard and Savigny, who dichotomize races, Géricault is more like Dard in emphasizing social cohesion. Not only does he include black bodies as equal members of the suffering society depicted on the raft, he also chooses to focus on a black man waving to the rescuers at the summit of the painting's triangular structure. Albert Boime sums up the abolitionist thrust of this decision as follows:

> Progress [...] requires the emancipation of the most oppressed member of society removed from the bottom of the social pyramid and installed on the summit [...] French society is synecdochally represented by the shipwrecked crew on a broken-down raft, who must give their support to the black member who alone can save them.[25]

Moreover, Géricault muddies the difference between the two racial groups. Darcy Grimaldo Grigsby points out that reviewers of *Le Radeau* complained that the whites and blacks in the painting seem to be "uniformly colored."[26]

Figure 4.
Théodore
Géricault, *Le
Radeau de la
Méduse* (1816).
Reproduction
courtesy of
Art Resource.

By blurring racial categories, *Le Radeau* makes the point that regardless of class or race, all persons on the raft were victims.

Similarities exist between *La Chaumière africaine* and *Le Radeau de la Méduse* with respect to race.[27] However, Dard and Géricault differ significantly regarding gender. No women appear in the painting, although in a preliminary study the family on the raft included a father, mother, and child. For the final version, the painter presents a masculine, motherless group. Why did Géricault choose thus to de-emphasize femininity in *Le Radeau*? Linda Nochlin argues that the feminine is displaced, not dismissed. Since women are traditionally positioned as victims, Géricault's use of the mass of nearly nude men on the raft as objects of pity has the result of feminizing them. The raft is peopled by pitiful, suffering bodies who, in addition to being neither clearly white nor black, are symbolically not wholly male or female either.[28] As with race, so too with gender, clear-cut distinctions cease to obtain in the leveling process of human disaster. Blurring allows Géricault to produce a visual image of a heterogeneous collectivity. It enables him to depict the universalized humanity that is at the heart of liberal, abolitionist thought. In colonizing Africa, the painting suggests, collective humanity will form a new society unmarked by hierarchies of class, race, and gender. Dard was not a universalist in the sense that Géricault and other abolitionists such as Grégoire were.[29] Her goal was less philosophical and more pragmatic. Instead of considering that all races were equal, provided that they were "regenerated," she viewed Africans as having a different but valuable culture and as being different from but also compatible with whites.

La Chaumière africaine contrasts with other representations of shipwrecks in its creation of a feminine subjectivity and its rejection of women as victims. The example of *Paul et Virginie* immediately comes to mind (Figure 1). Because of her unparalleled modesty, Virginie ultimately drowns in a shipwreck when sailors demand that she disrobe. Charlotte is no Virginie. She thinks nothing of a woman wearing men's clothing when necessary and seems indifferent to gender expectations. In addition to eschewing Virginie's stereotypical modest femininity, she actively constructs herself as a force for the betterment of Africans, unlike Virginie who passively returns the runaway slaves to their master with an ineffectual plea for compassion. Dard held Bernardin in high regard as an author known to be sympathetic to blacks. But she chose to depict herself as a strong woman who lived and worked among Africans, not as the submissive, doomed European daughter from *Paul et Virginie*.

Dard's creation of a feminine subjectivity is also linked to Bernardin through the title of her memoir, *La Chaumière africaine*, an obvious reference to his philosopical tale *La Chaumière indienne*, published in 1790. In that story, a beneficent traveler discovers a family—an Indian pariah, his Brahmin wife, and their child—rejected by society and deprived of all material posessions, living in the forest. The link between the pariah and the slave, developed by Corréard and Savigny as well, is apparent. As victims of injustice, pariahs and slaves are similarly condemned to live far from their native land and deprived of all that is necessary and natural for human happiness. The metonymic link between the hut, a humble dwelling in a primitive natural setting, and blacks, inhabitants of such dwellings, undoubtedly explains the reference to Bernardin in Dard's title.

Dard's allusions to *La Chaumière indienne* contrast sharply with Corréard and Savigny's, however. Having described a young black mother living in the hollow of an enormous baobab tree, they exclaim, "Who is the man, standing before this charming spectacle, who would not be transported by indignation if he saw ferocious Moors violate this peaceful asylum and take away members of this family to be sold as slaves? To suitably paint such a picture one would need the brush of the author of *La Chaumière indienne*." (297) Again the woman is depicted as the potential victim and the Moors as the bad, racialized Other. In contrast, Dard's reference to Bernardin's story in her title refers to her own forest retreat and to a life that overlaps with the one that Africans lead in their huts: the very life that the slave trade disturbs and destroys. Instead of looking at the black person from the outside, like Corréard and Savigny, Dard constructs an image of herself as the captured slave. Hence the quotation that appears on the title page of *La Chaumière africaine*—"Heureux! oui, mille fois heureux, celui qui jamais ne porta ses pas sur une terre étrangère!" ("Happy! yes, a thousand times happy he who never stepped foot on a foreign land!")—which echoes the words that the beneficent visitor addresses to the pariah in *La Chaumière indienne*: "je n'ai trouvé la vérité et le bonheur que dans votre cabane" ("I have found truth and happiness only in your hut.")[30] Not merely an expression of regrets about the *Medusa* disaster, these words suggest Dard's overlapping identity as a French traveler and a resident of Africa. In wishing to have never left her native land she empathizes with slaves who have similar feelings of nostalgia for their home. Charlotte's entire story can indeed be related to the slave's trajectory: peaceful life, nightmarish crossing on the ship, arduous crossing of the Saharan desert, arrival on the other side of the Atlantic. Charlotte simply reversed this pattern by beginning in Europe instead of Africa before ending up in her "chaumière africaine."

Dard's commitment to the construction of overlapping European and African identities is especially salient in the chapters that treat the Picard family's life in Africa.[31] At the end of Chapter 11 Charlotte is sent to the island of Safal with her two younger brothers to farm cotton, which her father envisions as the hope for their economic survival. She is assisted there by the trusted older black worker Etienne. In Chapter 12, she describes how she picked cotton with the hired slaves—"nègres cultivateurs" ("black farmers")—under horrific conditions: heat, fatigue, hunger, illness, insects, and wild animals. In many ways Charlotte was herself a "nègre cultivateur," sharing their meager food and struggling to survive. Charlotte almost loses her identity as a white colonizer. Near the end of her African stay, when she and her sister return to Senegal, they find the world there to be totally alien:

> L'isolement dans lequel nous avions vécu et les malheurs que nous avions essuyés, ne contribuaient pas peu à nous donner un air sauvage et embarrassé [...] N'ayant pour toute coiffure que nos cheveux, pour vêtements qu'une robe de grosse toile mi-usée, sans bas et sans chaussures, il nous était très pénible de paraître ainsi accoutrées au milieu d'un monde où jadis nous avions tenu un certain rang [...] Nous apprîmes alors qu'on nous désignait au Sénégal sous différents noms, les uns nous appelaient "les solitaires de l'île de Safal," les autres, "les éxilés en Afrique." (134–35)

> (The isolated manner in which we had lived, and the misfortunes we had endured, contributed in no small degree to give us a savage and embarrassed appearance [...] Having no cap but our hair, no clothes but a half-worn robe of coarse silk, without stockings or shoes, we felt very distressed in appearing thus habited before a society among which we had formerly held a certain rank [...] We learned that we were known at Senegal by different names, some calling us "the hermits of the isle of Safal," others "the exiles in Africa.") (152)

Not only does Dard share the life of a slave, but she empathizes with their condition in a true abolitionist spirit. When Picard returns to Safal and the family is reunited, they are joined by twelve rented slaves, including women and children. Together they form the plantation community which Dard calls "notre petite république" ("our little republic.") When some of the slaves desert, Dard views the situation with empathy and the conviction that the desire for freedom pertains to all races: "Je dois avouer ici, que, quoique je fusse profondément affectée de la désertion de ces esclaves qui nous étaient nécessaires pour réaliser nos projets de culture, mon coeur ne put blâmer des malheureux qui cherchaient à recouvrer la liberté qu'on leur avait ravie" (114) ("I confess, though I was deeply distressed at the desertion of these slaves, who were so necessary to us for realizing our agricultural projects, my heart could not blame these unfortunate creatures, who only sought to recover that freedom from which they had been torn.") (132) Picard is also sympathetic, listening attentively to the reasoning of a slave who had tried to escape earlier: "nous ne sommes pas dans notre pays; nos parents et nos amis sont éloignés de nous; on nous a ravi notre liberté" (131) ("we are not in our native country; our parents and friends are far from us. We have been deprived of our liberty.") (149) Picard is "attendri jusqu'aux larmes par ces paroles" (132) ("melted to tears with this speech.") (149) Instead of forcing the unhappy blacks to remain in his employ, Picard allows them to leave. In reporting this scene, Dard even makes an effort to give voice to the slaves with whom she worked:

> "Toi Picard, mon maître, si l'on t'arrêtait lorsque tu cultives ton champ, et qu'on t'emmenât bien loin de ta famille, ne ferais-tu pas tous les efforts pour la rejoindre, et pour recouvrer ta liberté ?" Mon père ne sachant pas trop que répondre, lui dit: "Oui je le ferais." "*Nakamou* (eh bien), répartit le nègre, je suis dans le même cas; comme toi, je suis père d'une nombreuse famille; j'ai encore ma mère, des oncles; j'aime ma femme, mes enfants, et tu trouves extraordinaire que je veuille aller les rejoindre?" (131–32)

> ("If you, Picard, my master, were arrested when cultivating your fields, and carried far, far from your family, would you not endeavor to rejoin them, and recover your liberty?" My father promptly replied, "I would!" "Very well," continued Nakamou, "I am in the same situation as you, I am the father of a numerous family; I have yet a mother, some uncles; I love my wife, my children; and do you think it surprising that I should wish to rejoin them?") (149)

Admittedly, this dialogue entails considerable revoicing if not invention of the African worker's actual words. But it should not be confused with what Peter Kitson calls the "sentimental ventriloquism" found in abolitionist texts by late eighteenth-century British writers such as Hannah Moore and William Cooper.[32] Dard at least tries to recognize native culture by introducing an African word, which Maxwell curiously mistranslates. The phrase "*Nakamou* (eh bien), répartit le nègre" becomes "'very well,' continued Nakamou." Maxwell thus presumes, wrongly, that the African word is the name of Picard's interlocutor. By the inclusion of African language, Dard attempts to give a voice to slaves. She also suggests her understanding of what the process of colonizing Africa meant for blacks, including the erasure of their native language. She cites Mungo Park in *La Chaumière africaine*, indicating that she knew the importance Park attributed to first-hand testimony about slavery's impact on the individual lives of Africans.

Dard's life in Africa, living in the "little republic" of Safal, sheds further light on her awareness of both European and African subjectivities. Dard states that she was charged with providing the instruction "de mes jeunes frères et soeurs et des petits nègres de l'habitation" (110) ("of my young brothers and sisters and the young negroes of the plantation.") (128) The distinction between the two groups may not have been absolute.[33] Jore and Debien allege that the children who traveled on the *Medusa* with Picard were from what they call "various women of color" with whom Picard had had relations in Senegal and whom he had brought to France.[34] If their allegation is true, the blurring of racial and ethnic boundaries was not just an empty concept for Charlotte, but was the lived reality of the African contact zone in which races and cultures intermingled routinely. The blurring occurred in her own family. After her father's death, she married Jean Dard who had fathered a son, Théodore, with an African woman, Marie Laisné. That child "was never kept apart from the family" and corresponded with Charlotte Dard.[35] An educator and linguist, Jean Dard instructed African children based on the British system of mutual education, in which the most talented students were used to instruct their classmates. Jean and Charlotte were committed to educating black children and to living among Africans. In 1832, Jean returned to Senegal where he died a year later. Charlotte received her certification as a teacher and bore three children.[36] She returned several times to Africa, where she died in 1862. Before her death she composed a series of poems entitled "Heures du soir, poésies d'Afrique" (Evening Hours, African poems).[37] These poems written on African soil reflect her nostalgia for her native French family and landscape. Although her nostalgia focuses on her grandfather and her sister Caroline,[38] there is no mention of her father. The emotional attachment to other family members that is apparent later in Dard's life may well be the "non-dit" ("unspoken truth") beneath the dutiful daughter's defense of her father in *La Chaumière africaine*. In the first two paragraphs of *La Chaumière africaine* Charlotte refers to the mother she lost as a child: nursing the baby Caroline, suffering from her husband's absence, falling into a listless state, and dying after five years of suffering. Even in a story about fathers, mothers never disappear entirely from their daughters' lives.

Were Charles Picard, Charlotte Dard, and Jean Dard abolitionists?[39] They were active participants in the process of colonizing Africa who held enlightened, liberal views. True, they stood apart from such political issues associated with abolition as discrediting the restored monarchy following the shipwreck or implicating the French government in the slave trade. Their abolitionism was deep-seated and sincere nonetheless. In 1814 Picard submitted a report entitled *Considérations sur les possessions françaises en Afrique*, advocating the end of the slave trade and alternative labor solutions for colonized regions.[40] In *La Chaumière africaine*, Charlotte unequivocally expresses her empathy for blacks and her antipathy toward subjecting them to enforced labor. Through Jean, Charlotte was undoubtedly familiar with the work of the abolitionist Société de la morale chrétienne and its Committee on the Abolition of the Slave Trade. In 1826 Jean Dard published *Grammaire wolof, ou Méthode pour étudier la langue des noirs*. In this work and *Dictionnaire Français-Wolof et Français-Bambara*, published a year earlier, he acknowledges the sponsorship of the Société and thanks its members for having chosen him "to sow the first seeds of instruction on the distant shores of Senegal."[41] Speaking of French schools in Senegal, Jean Dard speaks out against the slave trade, asserting that education is the best weapon against slavery: "it is no longer possible on the face of the earth to have nations treated as savages or slaves because it has been shown to be possible to communicate with them and to civilize them by writing their spoken language."[42]

As noted earlier, the Dards were not universalists in the same way that Grégoire and other abolitionists were. True, they believed that blacks needed to be "lifted up" and educated, as did all nineteenth-century thinkers, blacks and whites. However, they did not share the views of Hegel, who dismissed sub-Saharan Africa as a world of barbarity which held no importance for world history because of the intellectual deficiencies of Africans.[43] They did not believe in erasing African culture, as Grégoire did with respect not only to blacks but Jews and peasants. Grégoire aggressively proposed and implemented policies eliminating the use of regional languages within France. Such a view contrasts starkly with Jean Dard's conviction as a linguist and an educator that a thorough understanding of indigenous language by colonists was necessary to educate Africans. He believed that African language and culture were inherently valuable. He emphasized that Africans have preserved intellectual attributes over the centuries. Using the Africans' own words he mentions, for example, their love of truth—"amänä bénne yalla dale (il n'y a qu'un seul Dieu)"—and their filial respect—"Itta ma wandez boul saga säma baye (frappe-moi mais n'insulte pas mon père)."[44] Another acknowledgement of African subjectivity concerns the production of narratives:

> On a prétendu que les noirs n'avaient point de contes pour charmer leurs loisirs, ni de jeux récréatifs. C'est encore une de ces erreurs où sont tombés ceux qui veulent écrire l'histoire d'Afrique, sans avoir visité ses diverses peuplades. Les nègres sont passionnés pour les contes, les proverbes et les fables; et ils possèdent deux jeux fameux dans toutes l'Afrique, le *oury* et le *yotey*.[45]

> (It has been said that blacks had neither recreational games nor stories from which to derive enjoyment in their leisure hours. This is another of those mistakes made by people who want to write the history of Africa without having ever visited its diverse populations. Blacks are passionate about stories, proverbs, and fables; and they have games—*oury* and *yotey*— that are famous throughout Africa.)

Without a doubt, Jean Dard had great respect for Africans, as his tracing their achievements back to Antiquity reveals.

L'Egypte, dont les habitants, au rapport d'Hérodote, avaient l'épiderme noir et les cheveux crépus, l'Egypte a été le berceau et la première patrie des connaissances humaines [...] il est certain que les Grecs ont dû leurs lumières moins à leurs progrès intérieurs et à leurs facultés intellectuelles, qu'à leurs communications avec les peuples de l'ancienne Egypte.[46] (vi)

(Egypt, whose inhabitants had black skin and kinky hair according to Herodotus, was the cradle and first homeland of human knowledge [...] There is no question that the Greeks owed their enlightenment less to their internal progress and their intellectual faculties than to their communication with the peoples of ancient Egypt.)

Such a statement is so surprisingly modern that Robert Cornevin calls Jean Dard a true precursor of the twentieth-century notion of *négritude*.[47]

* * *

We now turn to reading *La Chaumière africaine* together with, and against, relevant instances of non-European history: in this case, the African society in which the Picard and Dard families lived in the early years of the nineteenth century. Said's concept of "intertwined and overlapping histories" has special relevance for these families in which intimate personal and commercial interactions between fathers and the property-owning African women called *signares* were a fact of life. What were the "facts of power" that informed and enabled these relationships in the colonial society of the time? What gendered interpretations of the *signares* have been articulated by non-white writers in the twentieth century? In light of those interpretations, what conclusions can be drawn about Dard within the colonial world and about *La Chaumière africaine*?

The boundaries between blacks and whites on the African coast during the period described in *La Chaumière africaine* were porous. Interactions between the races were commonplace, for reasons that were both sexual and commercial. As William B. Cohen explains, the small white population in Senegal had to accommodate themselves to the African environment. They had to rely on the good will of the non-white population, especially the mulatto *signares*, to mediate between European and African languages and cultures.[48] Moreover, the *signares* played a vital role in providing contacts for conducting business. White men used those contacts to acquire the precious commodities of gold and gum arabic, which they transported illegally on slave ships in order to acquire the goods to trade with Africans. Merchants, soldiers, government officials, and other white men routinely engaged in arrangements in which local women—either African or Eurafrican—served as mistresses, concubines, or wives. If a marriage took place, it followed the practice known as marriage "à la mode du pays," that is, marrying for the duration of the colonist's stay in Africa.[49] The practice was not considered degrading to white men. Between 1802 and 1807, governor Blanchot had a Senegalese wife. Children born of interracial unions were often sent to Europe for an education and took on their fathers' names. "Such recognitions created less embarassment than in the Antilles, where white fathers, whose families were with them, did not want to recognize publicly the offspring of an illegitimate connection."[50]

An illustrative case is the celebrated *signare* Anne Pépin. Her brother, Nicolas Pépin, was an educated mulatto who served as spokesperson for his social group known as "habitants." From 1785 to 1787, Stanislas-Jean, chevalier de Boufflers, the last royal governor of Senegal, maintained a personal and commercial partnership with Anne Pépin. Their relationship presumably did not interfere with the one he had had since 1780 with la comtesse de Sabran, whom he later married. The attitudes toward slavery held by Boufflers and Pépin differed little from those held by members of the Picard and Dard families. It is true that Boufflers used his influence to favor the Compagnie de la Guyane that in 1787 added the slave trade to its other commercial enterprises. It also the case that Pépin, like other wealthy *signares*, owned slaves, who were mainly used to meet their personal, domestic needs but were also hired out to European and Eurafrican traders. Both Boufflers and Pépin responded empathetically to blacks, however. He was an enlightened thinker and writer who expressed sympathy for Africans and sought to increase knowledge about their culture in France. He expressed pity for the oppressed and showed compassion for black children, sending one of them to the duchesse d'Orléans and rescuing the young girl named Ourika discussed in Chapter 4.[51] Pépin and other *signares* also went out of their way to help other Africans escape the dreaded fate of the transatlantic passage and enslavement in the French colonies.[52]

Like Dard, the *signares* experienced a complex blend of empowerment and disempowerment. Just as Charlotte was stronger and more effective in many ways than her father, the *signares* were more knowledgeable and experienced in conducting the business of colonial life than the white men with whom they formed alliances. These women had the power to help colonists survive the hardships of African life and prosper economically. But the *signares* were also hybrids who, despite their elevated economic and social status, stood uneasily between African and European cultures. They and their children were dependent on white men for their existence, and they were held apart from Wolof society.[53] By the time the Picards and Dards lived in Africa, the fortunes of the *signares* had begun to decline due to the suppression of the slave trade after 1807 and British control of the Senegalese settlements.

If we turn now to the twentieth century, we find treatments of the *signares* which double and shed light on Charlotte Dard's African experiences. An early instance is "Songs for Signares" by the celebrated poet and statesman Léopold Sédar Senghor. Unlike the Picard and Dard families, for whom Africa and the *signares* were occasions for economic and personal survival, Senghor sees the mixed-race women of an earlier era as sensual, alluring symbols of the poet's desire to return to his native Africa: "Quand m'assiérai-je de nouveau à la table de ton sein sombre?" ("When will I sit again at the table of your dark breasts?"); "O mon amie couleur d'Afrique" ("O my love, the color of Africa.")[54] One is reminded of Savigny and Corréard's sexualization of Charlotte's nighttime encounter with the Moor. The difference between nineteenth- and twentieth-century perspectives is less apparent, however, with respect to cultural integration. The *signares* are important to Senghor because their mixed race emblematizes the merging of cultures that, as an African educated in France, he embraced. Such integration was prefigured by the outlook and activities of Charles Picard as well as Charlotte and Jean Dard. Senghor's vision of the coming together of African and European cultures as a hope for the future of Africa was theirs as well.

Writing some thirty years after Senghor, Maryse Condé incorporates the *signares* briefly into her African saga *Ségou* (1984) but with a far greater awareness of the economic and feminist issues that *La Chaumière africaine* raises. Condé puts a spotlight on Anne Pépin during the early years of the nineteenth century, the period during which Dard lived in Africa and the transitional period when the power of the *signare* culture was approaching its end. Ageing, losing her beauty, left behind by Boufflers with no prospect for the future, Anne Pépin is depicted as representing the fate of African women dependent on powerful men in the colonial world. But Pépin's commercial acumen is also highlighted. She talks of cultivating the surrounding areas, as the Picard family attempted to do, and of creating an experimental agricultural outpost, as Charlotte's brother-in-law Richard and the governor Baron Roger did.

Condé refuses to remain silent about the fact that Africans sold, owned, or profited from slaves. On one hand, then, Anne Pépin was an oppressor. But on the other hand, she was an object of oppression, caught up in a colonial system over which she had limited control and which put both black and white women at a disadvantage. Condé observes that the rules in French settlements forbade the presence of the wives of married personnel. Thus women such as Mme Sabran or Charlotte's mother stayed behind while their partners enjoyed the comforts and pleasures afforded by the *signares*. The colonial system protected those men, who went on to acquire power or respectability elsewhere. Although Condé depicts Anne Pépin as a greedy, selfish woman, she also shows how much more vulnerable she was than her white male counterparts in the colonial world.

Another treatment of the *signares* occurs in *Signare Anna ou le voyage aux escales* by Tita Mandeleau, an African woman writer born in Martinique, which was published in 1991. Mandeleau's novel, which is set before the period of Dard's time in Africa, focuses on the British takeover of the French Senegalese settlements in 1758. This historical moment enables Mandeleau, like Condé, to focus on the *signares'* empowerment while also delving into the causes and effects of their economic decline. Like Dard, Mandeleau provides insight into women's lived experiences, rather than men's desires or ideologies. In addition to a wealth of information concerning the economic, political, and social conditions of the *signares'* lives, Mandeleau delves into their psychological responses to social status and the management of households inhabited by slaves and various legitimate and illegitimate children. *Signare Anna* thus provides a twentieth-century doubling of issues raised in *La Chaumière africaine*. In both cases, the *signares* exist as women in their own right, not just as symbolic inspiration for men.

These diverse viewpoints of non-white writers in the twentieth century can set the stage for concluding speculations about what the *signares* represented to Dard. As noted earlier, Charlotte and Jean accepted into the family Théodore, the son of Jean and a *signare*. True, Dard does not mention this son in her memoir. That is understandable since the memoir is about her father, not her or her husband. Also, as someone well acquainted with the practices of colonial life at the time, she may have considered interracial relationships within her family to be a fact of life. There is no reason to believe that Dard was uncomfortable with blacks, either within or outside of her family.

There remains, however, a puzzling story of fathers, daughters, and slaves which does raise questions about her attitudes toward race. Four children—Charles César Picard, Laure Marie Picard, César Alphonse Picard, and Gustave Picard—are listed on the *Medusa*'s passenger list as having been born in Paris between 1810 and 1815.[55] As noted earlier, Jore and Debien maintain that there were mixed-race offspring from Picard's years in Senegal. Hanniet refutes their allegations based on birth certificates in the possession of the Picard family: in point of fact, a descendant of Alphonse Fleury, whose connection to the family seems to have been tenuous.[56] Matters are complicated by what seems to have been an intentional omission from Dard's account of one of the surviving members of this group of children. She states at the end of the memoir that the only survivors were herself, her sister, and Alphonse Fleury (148) and specifically records the deaths of Gustave and Laure. (137–39, 147–48) It appears, however, that Charles César Picard survived. I derive this information from Jean-Luc Angrand, the author of *Céleste ou le temps des signares* and a descendant of Anne Pépin. He documents the birth of a son to Charles Picard and princess Fatime

Yamar Comba Diara in 1803. This birth would have taken place during one of Picard's earlier visits to Africa. Angrand cites as his source the abbé Boilat, the first mulatto priest in nineteenth-century Africa and recipient of the prize of the Institut de France in 1853 for his *Esquisses sénégalaises*, which has been described as the first book written by an African.[57] Boilat refers to "the mulatto branch of the Picards" and to "M. Charles Picard, prince du sang royal," whose aunt was the queen Ndeté-Yalla.[58]

Did Dard want to erase the Picard mixed-race progeny from the family record? Or did her father, who according to Hanniet's account saw an earlier version of the memoir, desire this erasure? Concluding that her father may have modified her more straightforward, objective account of the events, Hanniet warns: "Don't attribute to Charlotte what unquestionably derives from her father's feelings of persecution."[59] Ultimately, Charlotte undoubtedly found herself in the same problematic position as all of the women considered in this book. On one hand, she obeyed her father and strove valiantly in her writing to defend him. On the other, she possessed her own voice and her own attitudes toward fathers, daughters, and slaves. What counts is that both voices, and the enlightened attitude toward slaves in the Picard and Dard families, survived.

Notes

1 Charlotte Dard, *The Sufferings of the Picard Family after the Shipwreck of the Medusa in the Year 1816*, trans. Patrick Maxwell (Edinburgh: Constable, 1827), xvii.

2 That he was educated and of bourgeois origins can be inferred from a report that he sent to authorities as a government official, in which he quotes in Latin and mentions Plutarch: Archives Nationales, Section Outre-Mer, EE 1546, Dossier de Charles Picard, document 131.

3 Philippe Masson, *L'Affaire de la Méduse* (Paris: Tallendier, 1989).

4 Charlotte Dard, *La Chaumière africaine, ou histoire d'une famille française jetée sur la Côte occidentale de l'Afrique à la suite du naufrage de la frégate La Méduse*, ed. Doris Y. Kadish (Paris: L'Harmattan, 2005), 6; *Sufferings of the Picard Family*, 20. On occasion I have made minor modifications to this translation.

5 Archives Nationales, Section Outre-Mer, EE 1546, Dossier de Charles Picard, documents 178, 213, 218.

6 Léonce Jore and Gabriel Debien, "Autour de *La Chaumière africaine*," *Bulletin de l'Institut français d'Afrique noire* 27, 1–1 (1965): 298–99. They note that the name Picard does not appear on her death certificate.

7 Michel Hanniet, *La Vérédique Histoire des naufragés de la Méduse* (Paris: Actes Sud, 1991), 18, 20; Charlotte Adélaïde Dard, *La Chaumière africaine, ou histoire d'une famille française jetée sur la Côte occidentale de l'Afrique à la suite du naufrage de la frégate La Méduse* (Dijon: Noellat, 1824).

8 George Bordonove, *Le Naufrage de la Méduse* (Paris: Laffont, 1973), 49–50.

9 Hanniet observes that the early version of the published memoir did not contain such allegations; *La Vérédique Histoire*, 171.

10 See Miller, *French Atlantic Triangle*, 248–50.

11 Jean-Yves Blot, *La Méduse, chronique d'un naufrage ordinaire* (Paris: Arthaud, 1982), 79, 394.

12 See George E. Brooks, "Artists' depictions of Senegalese signares: insights concerning French racist and sexist attitudes in the nineteenth century," *Genève-Afrique* 18, 1 (1980): 75–89. Gum arabic, made from the hardened sap of the acacia tree, is a basic commodity harvested in Senegal.

13 See Miller, *French Atlantic Triangle*, Chapter 10.

14 In *L'Affaire de la Méduse*, Masson misidentifies Caroline as the future Mme Dard (42). In *Le Naufrage de la Méduse*, Georges Bordonove states that there were eight family members (64) as does Darcy Grimaldo Grigsby in *Extremities: Painting Empire in Post-Revolutionary France* (New Haven: Yale University Press, 2002), 171.

15 Jore and Debien, "Autour de *La Chaumière africaine*," 298–99.

16 In emails sent to me on April 16 and 20, 2007, Hanniet notes that Antoinette was not mentioned in the early unpublished edition of the text and that confusion surrounds the exact familial ties of both of these individuals to the Picard family.

17 Jore and Debien, "Autour de *La Chaumière africaine*," 298–99.

18 Bordonove, *Le Naufrage de la Méduse*, 63.

19 Jean-Marie Volet takes issue with my interpretation of Picard in "Mme Dard, le naufrage de la Méduse en 1816 et le début de l'expansion coloniale au Sénégal. Africa and Women Writers" (2007), http://aflit.arts.uwa.edu.au/colonie_19e_dard_fr.html (accessed May 1, 2011).

20 Michel-Rolph Trouillot, *Silencing the Past: Power and the Production of History* (Boston: Beacon Press, 1995), 24.

21 Hanniet, *La Vérédique Histoire*, 17. In Hanniet's *Le Naufrage de la Méduse, Paroles de rescapés* (Louviers: Franck Martin, 2006) he refers to Dard in a similar manner.

22 Roger Mercier, "Le Naufrage de 'La Méduse': réalité et imagination romanesque," *Revue des sciences humaines* 125 (1967): 60–61.

23 Léon Fanoudh-Siefer, *Le Mythe du nègre et de l'Afrique noire dans la littérature française* (Paris: Klincksieck, 1968), 20, 21, 22, 25.

24 Alexandre Corréard and Jean-Baptise Henri Savigny, *Le Naufrage de la frégate la Méduse* (Paris: Eymery, 1818), 96.

25 Albert Boime, *The Art of Exclusion: Representing Blacks in the Nineteenth Century* (Washington, DC: Smithsonian Institution Press, 1990), 53.

26 Grigsby, *Extremities*, 220, 223.

27 Contemporary critics did not perceive or comment on any issues of race or abolition in their reviews of the painting, however, as noted by Maureen Ryan, "Liberal Ironies, Colonial Narratives and the Rhetoric of Art: Reconsidering Géricault's *Radeau de la Méduse*," in *Théodore Géricault: The Alien Body: Tradition in Chaos*, ed. Serge Guilbaut, Maureen Ryan, and Scott Watson (Vancouver: University of British Columbia, 1997), 32.

28 Linda Nochlin, "Géricault, or the Absence of Woman," in *Géricault, Louvre conférences et colloques*, I, ed. Michel Régis (Paris: La Documentation française, 1996), 405–09.

29 For Grégoire, see Alyssa Sepinwall, *Abbé Grégoire and the French Revolution* (Berkeley: University of California Press, 2005). For the notion of universal humanity and abolition, see Buck-Morss, *Hegel, Haiti, and Universal History*.

30 Bernardin de Saint-Pierre, "La Chaumière indienne," in *Oeuvres choisies* (Paris: Firmin-Didot, 1848), 161. The title page of *La Chaumière africaine* on which this quotation appears is not reproduced in the L'Harmattan edition of the novel.

31 Volet criticizes my use of the word "utopian" to describe race relations in the "little republic" of Safal. Although I continue to find the fictionalized version of African life presented in Chapter 12 of *La Chaumière africaine* to be embellished and to sidestep substantive issues of social inequality, I agree with Volet's overall assessment that Dard "anticipated a development of Saint-Louis based on freedom of the individual and solidarity among people" and that her writing is "an illustration of the human empathy and trust that was guiding the family's interrelations with 'others'." Volet, "Mme Dard."

32 Peter J. Kitson, "'Bales of Living Anguish': Representations of Race and the Slave in Romantic Writing," *English Literary History* 67, 2 (2000): 522.

33 Revealingly perhaps, Maxwell chooses to translate "des petits nègres de l'habitation" as "the young negroes of the family."

34 Jore and Debien, "Autour de *La Chaumière africaine*," 298.

35 Joseph Gaucher, *Les Débuts de l'enseignement en Afrique francophone: Jean Dard et l'école mutuelle Saint-Louis du Sénégal* (Paris: Le Livre africain, 1968), 70.

36 The birth certificates located in Bligny-les-Beaune, M. Dard's home town, document the births of Anne-Reine-Adèle, December 6, 1822; Charles Michel Alexandre, October 28, 1825; and Jean Baptiste Léon, December 6, 1827.

37 I am indebted to Dard's descendant, Bernadette Dupont, for having provided me with the poems.

38 Caroline married the botanist Jean-Michel-Claude Richard in 1820. He created the agricultural center Richard Toll (from "toll," meaning garden), now a city on the Senegal River that contains a reminder of his name.

39 I discuss the abolitionist context of Dard's writing in my introduction to *La Chaumière africaine* (L'Harmattan, 2005), xx–xxvii.

40 Archives Nationales, Section Outre-Mer, FM/SEN/II/1.

41 Jean Dard, *Grammaire wolof ou Méthode pour étudier la langue des noirs* (Paris: Imprimerie Royale, 1826), i. Although Jean Dard's name has largely disappeared from mainstream historical accounts, it is not forgotten in Senegal. An article about him published in the Senegalese newspaper *Dakar-Matin* in 1967 pays tribute to him as the first French teacher officially sent by the French government to Africa, where he arrived in Gorée on October 9, 1816. At that time, the only education in largely islamized Africa was provided in Koranic schools.

42 Dard, *Grammaire wolof*, viii.

43 Buck-Morss, *Hegel, Haiti, and Universal History*, 68. Buck-Morss clarifies, "Hegel was perhaps always a cultural racist if not a biological one," 74.

44 Dard, *Grammaire wolof*, vii.

45 Dard, *Grammaire wolof*, xi.

46 Dard, *Grammaire wolof*, vi.

47 Robert Cornevin, "Précurseurs de la négritude au XIXe siècle: Edward W. Blyden ou Jean Dard?" *Journal of African History* 9, 2 (1968): 315–17.

48 William B. Cohen, *The French Encounter with Africans: White Response to Blacks, 1530–1880* (Bloomington: Indiana University Press, 2003), 121–26.

49 "Marriage à la mode du pays" included "paying a dowry to the woman's parents, supplying a wedding feast, providing the woman with a dwelling, and adhering

to accepted norms of marital practices, including sexual fidelity": Brooks, "Artists' depictions of Senegalese signares," 78.

50 Cohen, *French Encounter with Africans*, 125.

51 Roger Mercier, *L'Afrique noire dans la littérature française; les premières images, XVIIe–XVIIIe siècles* (Dakar: Université de Dakar, 1962), 162–65.

52 Jean-Luc Angrand, *Céleste ou le temps des signares* (Sarcelles: Edition Anne Pépin, 2006), 13, 89.

53 George E. Brooks, "The *Signares* of Saint-Louis and Gorée: Women Entrepreneurs in Eighteenth-Century Senegal," in *Women in Africa: Studies in Social and Economic Change* (Stanford: Stanford University Press, 1976), 23.

54 From *Nocturnes* (1961), included in Léopold Sédar Senghor, *The Collected Poetry* (Charlottesville: University Press of Virginia, 1991), 412, 121; 416, 125. *Nocturnes* contains a revision of *Chants pour Naëtt* (1949), retitled *Chants pour Signares*.

55 Archives Nationales, Section Outre-Mer, F5/B9.

56 Jore and Debien, "Autour de *La Chaumière africaine*," 298–99 ; Hanniet, *La Vérédique Histoire*, 23. Hanniet graciously provided information about the birth of these children in emails sent to me dated April 16 and 20, 2007. He points out that there are three different passenger lists with conflicting information. Accordingly, the birth dates of the children from 1810 and 1815 noted above may not be accurate.

57 Angrand, *Céleste*, 204–05. Angrand also supplied me with archival references in electronic correspondence dated September 29, 2011.

58 David Boilat, *Esquisses sénégalaises, Atlas* (Paris: P. Bertand, 1853). I am grateful to Jean-Luc Angrand who helped me track down this reference which appears not in the volume of the *Esquisses sénégalaises* but in the *Atlas* which was printed separately. Boilat refers to the education of a Charles Picard in 1844. One can speculate that if Charles César Picard was born in 1803, the student in question might be his son, as might also be the case with regard to a Charles Picard's marriage to Marie Wynh, a *signare* from Gambia, in 1853. Angrand states that a daughter born to Charles Picard and Marie Wynh in 1856 was named Charlotte Félicité Picard. Angrand's documentation is the marriage license signed on May 21, 1854, by Fatime Yamar granting permission for her daughter's marriage.

59 Hanniet, *La Vérédique Histoire*, 171.

3

Daughters and Paternalism:
Marceline Desbordes-Valmore

The life of Marceline Desbordes-Valmore provides a striking instance of the congruence of fathers, daughters, and slaves. After having been placed on the stage at age twelve, Desbordes-Valmore accompanied her financially strapped mother to Guadeloupe four years later. There Mme Desbordes either hoped to find work in the French colonial theater or to make contact with wealthy relatives.[1] Marceline was thus abruptly separated from her father and siblings at a young age. The arrival of mother and daughter in Guadeloupe in 1802 coincided with the outbreak of both slave revolts and yellow fever, to which Mme Desbordes succumbed, leaving her bereft and motherless daughter forced to cross the Atlantic alone to rejoin her family. While in the French colonies, Marceline witnessed slavery. That she did so under the traumatic circumstances of slave uprisings undoubtedly explains the sensitivity to the plight of slaves that is evident in her writings. What is more, the early separation from her father, which coincided with her contact with Africans, may explain the association she makes between paternal figures and slaves, also torn away from their families and ancestral homes. Although Antoine-Félix Desbordes was by all accounts a pretentious and irresponsible man, Marceline loved him. As her biographer Francis Ambrière states, "no one ever felt more deeply than she the force of what in astrology is called the sun of the father"; "Marceline's whole life bears witness to her having nourished a veritable cult for her father"; and in her own words, "I loved my father like God himself."[2] How that cult found expression in Desbordes-Valmore's writings about slavery, and how these writings bear the imprint of the non-patriarchal model that she constructed of fathers based on his example, are the questions addressed in this chapter. The chapter closes by viewing Desbordes-Valmore's writings in relation to colonial theater and racial politics in the years leading up to the Haitian Revolution.

The consideration of Desbordes-Valmore here focuses on the novella *Sarah* along with a small body of other texts that bear a direct relationship to slavery and colonialism. Most of these texts date from the 1820s when the recognition of Haitian independence and the abolition of the slave trade gained considerable public attention. In addition to *Sarah*, first published in 1821, several poems—"Le Réveil créole" (Creole Awakening), 1819; "L'Esclave" (The Slave), 1821; "Chant d'une jeune esclave" (A Young Slave's Song), 1821; "La Veillée du nègre" (Black Man's Vigil), 1824; and "La Jeune esclave" (The Young Slave Girl), 1828—also recall Desbordes-Valmore's Caribbean experience.[3] Other evidence that slavery was very much on Desbordes-Valmore's mind in the 1820s exists in unpublished materials such as a copy of an advertisement for a runaway slave from a Charleston paper in 1827 and a drawing of a slave for one of her poems that she presumably requested of her uncle, the artist Constant Desbordes.[4] In addition, Marceline mentions the voyage to Guadeloupe in her semi-autobiographical narrative portrayal of her relationship with her uncle, *L'Atelier d'un peintre*, written in 1828 and published in 1833. In the chapter entitled "Le Nid d'hirondelles" ("The Swallows' Nest"), Marceline's fictional double Ondine states:

> Peu de temps après, je naviguais avec ma mère—seulement ma mère,—vers l'Amérique—où personne ne nous attendait. Nous nous regardions avec épouvante, comme si nous ne nous reconnaissions plus; elle me serrait le bras, elle me collait contre elle à chaque roulis de cette maison mouvante, fragile et inconnue, dont les mouvements la faisaient malade à la mort.

> (Shortly thereafter I traveled with my mother—only my mother—toward America—where no one awaited us. We looked at each other with fear, as if we no longer recognized each other. She grasped my arm, clinging to me with each lurch of the fragile and unfamiliar seafaring edifice whose movements made her deathly ill.)[5]

After the 1820s, very little in Desbordes-Valmore's *oeuvre* relates to the subject of slavery. A short children's story entitled "La Jambe de Damis" was published in 1834, around the time of the publication of *L'Atelier d'un peintre*. A revised edition of *Sarah* in a volume entitled *Huit Femmes* was published in 1845, shortly before the abolition of slavery in the French colonies.

* * *

The men who most profoundly affected the conception of fathers found in Desbordes-Valmore's literary works are her own father, Antoine-Félix Desbordes, and his younger brother, Constant, whom Marceline also viewed as a father of sorts. As the result of a deathbed quarrel between Marceline's grandfather Edme-Antoine and his eldest son Nicolas-Louis, Antoine-Félix, the middle son, was entrusted with the family's inheritance and instructed to further the promising artistic career of the youngest son, Constant. Antoine-Félix and Constant were thus freed from the nineteenth-century patriarchal pattern whereby the eldest brother replaced the father and controlled younger members of the family. Moreover, the men in the Desbordes family worked in artisanal professions related to the theater. Accordingly, they lived in a less hierarchally defined social world than more standard bourgeois spheres. The traditional hierarchy that placed men in control of women was also diminished in Marceline's upbringing. Because Mme Desbordes married an unreliable wage earner, whose fortunes waxed and waned, she came to bear greater responsibility and to acquire greater economic empowerment than had traditionally been the case for women. Entering the theatrical world by making costumes and placing her young daughter Marceline on the stage enabled her to assume the role of breadwinner in times of crisis. She thus set an example that her daughter often assumed later, at times supporting her father, her husband, and others.

Desbordes-Valmore could draw on her father in constructing the good, non-patriarchal father or master because she viewed him not as victimizer but as himself a victim. Although up to the age of forty he had maintained a comfortable and even luxurious lifestyle, due in part to the family inheritance that favored him and Constant over his older brother, by the time of Marceline's birth in 1786 his fortunes were in a state of flux. For one thing, although he continued to paint theatrical sets, the antireligious policies of the French Revolution reduced his commissions to paint altars and ornate church interiors.[6] For another, his flawed judgment led him to engage in a variety of risky and unsuccessful enterprises. His repeated failures notwithstanding, his daughter continued to love, pity, and provide for him when needed. Indeed, it was because of his poverty and vulnerability that she identified with him, as she did with other victims of life's misfortunes. They included her mother, who came from the peasant class and was illiterate when she married Antoine-Félix. Her mother's humble origins and her father's reduced financial circumstances heightened Desbordes-Valmore's sensitivity to social disparity, inequality, and suffering. As Marc Bertrand states, "She was born on the side of the people. If her inclinations ultimately were with the people, it is because she saw in them the distress of those who were banished, massacred, and impoverished. By inclination and her own experience, she belonged to the clan of victims."[7] Standing on the margin of society, and viewing her father in that position as well, she associated him not with the class of masters, but with those who feel sympathy for the downtrodden, including blacks.

Another basis for Marceline's feelings of pity for her father—and another association among father, daughter, and slaves—concerns the fact that preceding the trip to Guadeloupe, at a time when the Desbordes's marriage was troubled and the family's finances were especially precarious, Marceline's mother deserted the family home, running off with a lover and taking Marceline with her.[8] "Le Nid d'hirondelles" shows that Marceline viewed the family's dissolution from her father's viewpoint. Before evoking the fear that she and her mother experienced on board the ship taking them to Guadeloupe, Ondine tells the story of a family of birds that once emblematized happiness and good luck for her family. She calls the story of the birds "une des images restées le plus au fond de mon souvenir de ce temps-là" ("one of the most deeply felt recollections I have of that period of my life.")[9] The story focuses on a father bird whose mate, perched on a nearby rooftop, has abandoned the nest and the four helpless hatchlings it contains. The father makes five or six frantic attempts to bring back the mother, "la fugitive" ("the fugitive") (75) but to no avail. Her behavior remains a mystery to all concerned.[10] The male bird shows tremendous concern for his brood, covering the little birds with his outspread wings. Finally, in a last desperate, heartwrenching act, having torn his own feathers from his breast, he throws the newborn birds from the nest, one at a time, watching their tiny bodies fall to their death on the pavement. The horrific sound of the female bird's "cris de mère" ("mother's cries") (77) is followed by the frenetic departure of the two quarreling birds and the sound of thunder in the distance. It is a story of a family's destruction in which the mother bird inexplicably refuses to remain with her mate and children, and in which the drama is viewed directly by Marceline's father, who had poetically named the birds' nest their "palladium tremblant" ("their home's fluttering safe haven.") (74)[11]

As victims—both the sacrificed children and the grieving father—the birds emblematize the disintegration of Marceline's family. Their grief is that of abandonment, which Ondine shares with her father and Marceline shares with slaves, who are torn away from their beloved country and family. It is a sentimental response that Desbordes-Valmore often attributes to what might be called maternal men, those who nurture children in the absence of mothers. *Sarah*, as we shall see, is about several such men. These men, who blur traditional gender roles, date back to Rousseau's Saint-Preux, the prototype of a man who stands outside of dichotomized representations of male and female identity and who prefigures the sentimental males found throughout French romantic literature. But the suffering experienced by Desbordes-Valmore's sentimental father is far more acute; like that of the father bird, it resembles the suffering endured by slaves, who often resorted to the horrific act of killing their offspring in order to spare them a life of enslavement. Reference to such practices remains a thematic constant in slave and neo-slave narratives up to the present time: the beginning of

Toni Morrison's *Beloved* is one of the most unforgettable examples. That Desbordes-Valmore consistently associated birds and slaves is evident in a letter she wrote to her friend Pauline Duchambge in which she states, "It is hard to understand the blacks when one first arrives in the colonies, but their voices resemble the breath of a bird."[12]

In an interesting contrast, the poem "La Jeune Esclave," written at the same time as "Le Nid d'hirondelles," focuses on a slave mother who suffers a lifetime of regret for having sold her own daughter to slave traders. Again, the imagery of birds appears. The poem begins with the poignant question, "Jamais voyez-vous la colombe livrer ses petits au vautour" ("Does the dove ever yield up her young unto the vulture, willingly?")[13] Although the answer is yes, the reason is never provided. All we know is that, as in the case of the mother swallow, the dove emits despairing cries as her hatchling falls to its death. Yet her conduct evokes sympathy not blame from the first-person narrator of the poem. Although she wrongly placed her own pleasure in life above that of her youngest child—"Le luxe affreux qui m'environne" ("Vile, my luxurious habitat!")—the fact that she has never been able to forget her heinous act evokes the reader's compassion. The poem ends with an evocation in her own voice of unending remorse and of an earlier, innocent time before slavery.

In addition to Antoine-Félix, other men served Desbordes-Valmore as model fathers. One was her uncle, Constant Desbordes, who is fictionalized as Constant Léonard in *L'Atelier d'un peintre*. Indeed, she was prompted to write *L'Atelier* as a result of the death of this beloved uncle, whom she saw as a second father.[14] One will recall that Necker's death was a similar catalyst for Staël's decision to write *Le Caractère de M. Necker*. Disguised fictionally in *L'Atelier* as the aspiring female painter Ondine, the name of Desbordes-Valmore's daughter, Marceline places herself in her uncle's world of the atelier, a world she imagines as transcending the hierarchy between master and student. She thus constructs her uncle as embodying a "master" who combined authority with compassion, a combination that is a thematic constant of her sentimental worldview. Old and young, rich and poor, male and female in this world all share the fate of the suffering, misunderstood, impoverished artist:

> A cette humble école, les riches ne payaient pas plus que les pauvres; c'est-à-dire qu'ils ne payaient pas du tout. Par cela même, il y régnait un ton de concorde et d'égalité qui se tournait en respect pour le maître [...] dans ce coin obscur du monde, on ne respirait que l'amitié, le désintéressement et l'enthousiasme.

> (In this humble school, the rich paid no more than the poor, that is, they paid nothing at all. As a result, a sense of harmony and equality prevailed

which led to respect for the master [...] In this obscure corner of the world, one breathed an air of friendship, disinterest, and enthusiasm.) (28)

M. Léonard gladly gives everything away to those in need: his moral principle is to always give to the poor. Moreover, he harbors no feelings of male superiority. Following the example of his revolutionary-era model, Jacques-Louis David, Léonard admits women into the atelier and actively develops their talents as painters. Such an example of fatherly love unquestionably inspired and motivated Desbordes-Valmore, providing her with the encouragement and recognition that she needed to flourish as a young woman poet.

An additional father figure exists whose influence was no less considerable for having been less direct than that of actual family members: Bernardin de Saint-Pierre, the author of *Paul et Virginie*, who is mentioned in *L'Atelier*. When the health of a priest persecuted during the Terror is failing, Constant reports that the priest finds comfort in reading the Bible and "quelques pages pures de Bernardin" ("a few pure pages by Bernardin.") (268) On another occasion, Constant compares one of his young women students to Bernardin's heroine Virginie, who represents for him the perfect combination of virtue, resignation, and courage. He refers to the shipwreck in the closing pages of Bernardin's novel, famously depicted in Vernet's painting *La Mort de Virginie* (Figure 1), in which Virginie dies rather than remove her clothing. Constant conjures up this scene as a sentimental image of ideal femininity: "Placez ce personnage dans un naufrage: vous la verrez disparaître, comme cette douce et gracieuse Virginie, qui se laisse glisser dans l'eau, plutôt que d'alarmer un moment la craintive pudeur" ("Put this person in a shipwreck: you will see her disappear, like that sweet and gracious Virginie, who let herself slide away into the water rather than disturb modesty's delicate sensibility for even a moment.") (87) As noted earlier, scenes of beaches and shipwrecks are recurrent thematic elements in the corpus of texts considered in this book.

Virginie also stood as a model for less "pure" women, however. Virginie may have remained a virgin, as her name suggests, but it was Bernardin's emphasis on her sensitivity, courage, and resignation, not just her virtue, that would have inspired Desbordes-Valmore and other women in her family, whose precarious circumstances did not afford them the luxury of eschewing extramarital affairs, illegitimate children, or other "impure" forms of feminine conduct. Virginie may be known in literary history for her unwillingness to disrobe, but her story is one of feminine victimization by social and economic forces beyond her control: an aristocratic aunt forced the governor of the island to send Virginie away from her native island; transport her across the ocean against her will, like a slave; and finally, send her back heartlessly to the island where the shipwreck occurred. Like the poor hatchlings whose mother could not or would not protect them from death, Virginie was doomed. Yet by choosing her death rather than submitting to it, she demonstrated the strength and dignity that Desbordes-Valmore attributes to her feminine characters who are often modeled in one fashion or another after Virginie. Their virtue, like Virginie's, depends less on chastity than on moral qualities such as benevolence, compassion, forbearance, pity, and determination to survive.

Following in the tradition of Rousseau, Bernardin also depicts the kind of good and bad fathers that recur in Desbordes-Valmore's writing. Bad fathers separate young lovers, as does Rousseau's M. d'Etange, who prevents Julie from marrying Saint-Preux because of his inferior social station. In *Sarah*, separations of lovers based on class disparities are central to the plot. A variation on this story occurs in another novella in *Les Veillées des Antilles* entitled *Marie*. In this case, the lovers are free to wed. But in addition to feeling unworthy of the wealthy shepherdess Marie, the young shepherd Olivier is haunted by his father's dying wish that he put his fate in the hands of an elderly pastor, whom Olivier comes to recognize as "l'ombre chérie de mon père" ("the cherished shadow of my father.")[15] As the story draws to a happy conclusion, the pastor, who assumes the name of "father," endows Olivier with the financial resources necessary to marry Marie as an equal. The old pastor is the good father, like Sarah's. The authority of the father, or in this case his designated substitute, is pre-eminent. But his intentions and his respect for the wishes of those over whom he has authority, whether children or slaves, is benevolent. The pastor can be compared to the old man who narrates *Paul et Virginie*. The traveler meets him upon arriving on the island and addresses him as "my father" in asking him to tell the tale of the inhabitants of the deserted huts he observes. The old man functions as a benevolent father, an important role since both children are raised by women: a widow and an unwed mother. Like Edwin's father, who welcomes Sarah into his home, the narrator of *Paul et Virginie* lovingly agrees to befriend the two mothers. He similarly extends a fatherly hand to others on the island, including blacks. Were it not for nefarious forces exercised from afar—the aristocratic aunt and the *ancien régime* values and power she represents—all would have ended happily for Paul and Virginie. Bernardin's old man promotes tolerance, acceptance, and compassion. In this, he follows Rousseau's Wolmar in *Julie*. Men must exercise authority but in a kindly and benevolent manner.

Although Desbordes-Valmore does not specifically mention *La Chaumière indienne*, that work may have also inspired her, as it did Staël and Dard. It provides another example of a kindly, enlightened voyager who encounters the nefarious effects of class and race prejudice. The pariah and his family experience the "social death" experienced by slaves.[16] Bernardin, like

Desbordes-Valmore, opposes tyranny, whether it is the product of slavery or the Indian caste system. But women, often themselves victims of tyrants, cannot thwart it; good fathers must do so. Elderly, paternalistic men must stand up for defenseless girls and slaves. A good father—Wolmar in *Julie* or the fathers depicted in *Sarah*—has the economic means and wisdom to create a benevolent society.

* * *

Uniquely among the writings of Marceline Desbordes-Valmore, the novella *Sarah*, first published as part of *Les Veillées des Antilles* in 1821, dwells at length on the topic of slavery.[17] Its main protagonists are Arsène, an African who has painfully endured the indignities of capture, transport, and sale; Silvain, an overseer who selfishly practices abusive methods of control; Mr. Primrose, an owner who irresponsibly ignores the conditions on his plantation; and Sarah and Edwin, children who observe and try to respond to the injustices of colonial life. It is a story about four fathers. Two have set events in motion before the story begins: Mr. Primrose's father and Sarah's paternal grandfather. Both embody traditional patriarchs. They resemble Julie's father, M. d'Etange, whose concern for class superiority outweighs his interest in the happiness of his child. The two other fathers—Edwin's father, Mr. Primrose, and Sarah's unnamed father who appears at the end of the story—are benevolent and paternalistic, but in different ways and with different degrees of effectiveness. How *Sarah* functions to intertwine the fates of daughters and slaves and how the story relates the conduct of fathers to the system of slavery are the questions that the following analysis attempts to answer.

Daughters and slaves are linked in Desbordes-Valmore's work according to the conventions of the prevalent genre of nineteenth-century French sentimental writing, a mode that often included sympathy for blacks.[18] The discourse of feeling encompasses narratives of misfortune that portray the humanity of suffering heroes and heroines. By propelling the downtrodden to center stage, sentimental narratives celebrate their humanity. Sentimentalism also foregrounds the importance of the voice of the heart and natural goodness, illustrating how feeling and virtue transcend social hierarchies. By offering a popular audience unreceptive to Enlightenment discourse examples of suffering humanity, it brings readers into the text. By inspiring pity for characters suffering from misfortune, it provides a model with which readers can identify. Sentimental narratives highlight the misfortune that occurs when a villain causes harm to a member of the family and disrupts a previous state of happiness. They pit virtue against villainy; they oppose innocence and persecution; and they end with a leveling of social classes:

"one of the structural requirements of the process of sentimentalization is a more or less explicit denial of the importance of social hierarchy. It is where social barriers are transgressed, when some kind of *déclassement* occurs, when a shift down the social ladder takes place, that true sentimental epiphany is provoked."[19]

The characters in *Sarah* conform well to the model of the sentimental narrative. Arsène stands out as the quintessential member of the excluded class who is propelled to center stage and whose humanity is celebrated.[20] He rescues Sarah, sacrifices his freedom for hers, and serves as her substitute mother. By setting a virtuous example that readers are invited to follow, he transcends social hierarchies. Although placed on the lowest rung of society, he ascends morally to its summit. Interestingly, through a number of small but revealing changes in Arsène's presentation in the 1845 edition, his moral exemplarity takes on more overt antislavery meaning.[21] When Arsène first appears at the Primrose plantation with Sarah, in the second version he bears "l'acte de son affranchissement" (39) ("the papers attesting to his emancipation") (12), whereas the 1821 edition indicates the less specific "gage de sa liberté" (10) ("guarantee of his freedom.") He is less hopeful in the later edition, pausing at one point to "respirer" ("breathe") rather than to "rêver" ("dream") and to breathe "un soupir de regret et d'adieu" (46) ("a sigh of regret and farewell") (17), rather than "un soupir de regret et d'espoir" (15) ("a sigh of regret and hope.")

In sharp contrast to Arsène, Silvain functions as a villain. Through his greed and resentment, he introduces misfortune into the peaceful world of the Primrose plantation. He causes harm to Edwin, whose love for Sarah he threatens, and to Mr. Primrose, whose fortune he appropriates. In the years preceding emancipation in 1848, more attention was drawn to the cruelty of overseers who acted with impunity when employers such as Mr. Primrose abdicated their responsibility to supervise their properties. Not surprisingly, then, the 1845 edition depicts Silvain as even more harsh and frightening than he is in the 1821 version. For example, sentences added in the later version reinforce and clarify his evil nature and intentions: "On peut juger de l'affreux sourir que cette idée parvient à faire naître sur ses lèvres qui tremblent" (72–73) ("One can imagine from the atrocious smile that this idea caused to spread across his trembling lips") (29); "Il croit soupirer, il rugit; il essaie de flatter son maître, quand il voudrait le déchirer dans son fils" (73) ("Believing he merely sighed, he roared. He tried to flatter his master, even though he yearned to rip his master apart by tearing his son limb from limb.") (29–30)[22] And whereas in 1821 Primrose is described as "insouciant sur sa fortune et ses propriétés" (13) ("careless about his fortune and his properties") for relying unduly on Silvain, the *Huit Femmes* edition calls him the victim of Silvain's "intelligence mercenaire" (43) ("mercenary ambitions.") (14)

In short, Sarah, the abandoned, disenfranchised daughter, is placed within a structure where she stands on the side of slaves, not fathers. That structure pits black against white, good against evil, sacrifice against selfishness, African against colonial, devotion against ingratitude. Desbordes-Valmore's use of such oppositions, grounded in the logic of the sentimental narrative, takes on a distinctively antislavery meaning which is present in 1821 and further accentuated in 1845. By attributing the positive moral and spiritual attributes traditionally reserved for whites to the black man who has been a mother to Sarah, and by placing Africa above the degraded colonial world, Desbordes-Valmore uses the sentimental genre to evoke abolitionist notions and deepen the ties between daughters and slaves.

The narrative structure of *Sarah* also establishes the commonality between Sarah and Arsène and their shared capacity to achieve moral superiority. *Huit Femmes* opens with a prefatory section entitled "Mon Retour en Europe" in which an unnamed frame narrator recounts how her mother died in the Caribbean islands, how the narrator lived among natives of the colonies, how she listened to (or, she suggests, may have just imagined) their stories, and how she ultimately returned with difficulty to Europe. One of them is the story of Sarah.[23] The frame narrator in "Mon Retour en Europe" describes herself in a way that points toward the "real" author. By thus providing personal information in literary form, Desbordes-Valmore deepens her connection with the story and renders it more compelling as a slave narrative. Both the frame narrator and the author were in the same place (Pointe-à-Pitre, Guadeloupe), at the same time (1802), under the same circumstances: "après la révolte et mon deuil," (2) ("since the slave revolt and my mother's death.") (3) Sarah's story is recounted by the frame narrator's companion, a young girl named Eugénie, who inhabits the island of Saint-Barthélemy where the story is set. A multipartite narrative and authorial pattern is thus set in place. It reaches from the "real" author through the semi-autobiographical frame narrator to the fictional embedded narrator Eugénie. Inaugurating the novel with this series of young girls, Desbordes-Valmore places authority firmly in feminine hands, as opposed, for example, to *Ourika*, which in a more traditional way invests authority in a male frame narrator. The multipartite narrative structure in *Sarah* prepares the way for the reader to see the central character Sarah as an extension of the series of feminine figures in the frame. It also problematizes the authority of fathers.

Within the novel, another narrative participant emerges: the former slave, Arsène, serves as the narrator of his and Sarah's past lives. The thematic bonds among the frame narrator, Sarah, and Arsène are strong. All three have lost their mothers, and that loss is the primary cause of the alienation and estrangement from which they suffer. Displaced geographically at a young age, the three are forced to adapt to life among strangers. Their stories place them on or near water: the frame narrator en route to Guadeloupe, Sarah on the boat that brings her to the Primrose plantation, Arsène transported from Africa. The result of these thematic bonds is again that meaning passes along a narrative chain; and, through association, all of the narrative participants are linked to each other and to Arsène's condition as a former slave. Revealingly, the frame narrator compares herself to a black in describing her desire to flee the colonies immediately after her mother's death: "j'aurais tenté ce qu'un petit nègre de la maison voulait entreprendre pour me suivre: je me serais jetée à la mer, croyant, comme lui, trouver dans mes bras la force de nager jusqu'en France" (4) ("I would have tried what a black boy from the house wanted to do in order to accompany me: throw myself into the sea, believing, as he did, that my arms would find the strength to transport me to France.") (4) In addition to such associations with slavery, antislavery positions are developed through and in some cases directly by Arsène. Reflections such as the following, assumed to derive from his status as an eye-witness to the horrors of slavery, present the kind of testimony that abolitionists sought to provide to the public:

Ses souvenirs couraient dans sa mémoire; ils réveillaient en lui ce qui n'est jamais qu'endormi dans le coeur, l'amour d'une patrie, le besoin de la liberté. Du haut de la montagne, il plongeait ses regards dans l'île où les Blancs s'enferment avec tant de soin pour éviter les rayons perçants du jour. Ses yeux erraient sur les bords de la mer, où quelque nègre, traînant un fardeau à l'ardeur du soleil paraissait y succomber comme lui, et comme lui, peut-être, envoyer à sa patrie absente un soupir de regret et d'adieu. Il plaignait l'esclave, tous les esclaves. (45–46)

(Reminiscences unfurled in his memory and reawakened what remains dormant in all men's hearts: love of the native land, the need for freedom. From high on the lofty mountainside, his eyes settled upon the village below where white inhabitants so intently sought shelter from the sun's ardent rays. His eyes wandered along the seashore where some black man, weighed down by a heavy burden in the burning heat of the day, seemed, like himself, to send a sigh of regret and farewell to his homeland as he succumbed to his fate. He pitied this slave, all slaves.) (15–16)

Emphasizing love of country, the need for freedom, and solidarity with other blacks through their common oppression are important elements in an African perspective on slavery. And associating that perspective with the viewpoints of the frame narrator and Sarah gives added weight and authority to the slave's testimony, just as American slave narratives were typically endorsed and authorized by white sympathizers and sponsors.

Sarah and Arsène only have first names, a further link between them. That is understandable in the case of Arsène, who was once a real slave, since slaves were stripped of their African names upon arrival in the colonies and forbidden to bear the family name of their owners. But Sarah's first-name-only status indicates her social disenfranchisement. Her father, who appears at the end of the novel, and who was subjected to the harsh rule of his father, remains unnamed altogether. As Arsène explains to Sarah about her father's ill-fated love for her mother, Narcisse, "Dès qu'il eut avoué qu'il la voulait pour femme et ne voulait qu'elle, son père le traita sans pitié, comme il traitait les nègres"; "Il eut, peu de jours après, la barbarie de faire conduire son fils sur un vaisseau destiné pour l'Europe, et le fit si bien garder jusque là qu'il ne semblait pas moins esclave que nous" (119, 121) ("As soon as my master had admitted that he wanted her and no other to be his wife, his father began to treat him as pitilessly as the slaves" (52); "A few days later my master's father was so barbarous as to have his son placed aboard a ship headed for Europe: a ship so well-guarded that he seemed no less a slave than are we.") (53)

Other characters' identities are also linked to their names. Sarah's mother Narcisse lacks a family name, symbolically associating her with slaves while ironically signaling, through the name of a white flower, that social status in the colonies was a function of both race and class. The name Sarah is a variant of "Sahara." In a series of poems entitled "Mila" by the Haitian writer Coriolan Ardouin, one reads "La vie est le Sarah, l'amour, c'est l'oasis" ("Life—the Sahara; love—the desert spring.")[24] Sarah, the emblematic slave, is thus associated metonymically with the land of the Sahara, Africa, the place from which slaves originated. Another possible association is with the Hottentot Venus, Saartje Baartman, often referred to as Sara. This woman was taken from southern Africa, exhibited as a freak across Britain in the first decade of the nineteenth century, and taken to France in 1814 as the object of scientific research on black female anatomy.[25] Although Desbordes-Valmore's knowledge of Baartman is not documented, the name was widely recognized and could have been intended to reinforce the protagonist's association with slavery and Africa. As for Sarah's benefactor, Mr. Primrose, his name recalls a protagonist in Oliver Goldsmith's *The Vicar of Wakefield*, published in 1766. Desbordes-Valmore's use of a British name metonymically associates Sarah with British abolitionism. Significantly, Primrose provides Sarah with the education that beneficent owners often gave to talented slaves on plantations. Moreover, Goldsmith's novel, which also contains a character named Edwin, tells a tale of misplaced trust, resulting in the loss of the protagonist's wealth and property; it too ends with the villain discovered and the family restored to financial health and happiness. "Vilain" ("villain") itself resonates as an anagram of sorts for Silvain's name. And as a final onomastic observation, the contrast between Arsène and Silvain is underlined by the opposing associations of their names: Arsenius was a saint of Egyptian origin; Silvain connotes the forest and its fauna. The symbolic meanings of their names suggest on one side that which is good, spiritual, and African; on the other, the uncontrolled forces of nature, materiality, and bestiality in the colonies.

In addition to intertwining the fates of daughters and slaves, *Sarah* relates the conduct of fathers to the patriarchical and paternalistic underpinnings of the system of slavery. As Philip Morgan observes, patriarchy can be understood as an *ancien régime* mode of control built on "obedience, discipline, and severity."[26] Although in principle patriarchal rule carried with it obligations of protection and guardianship, in practice, especially on plantations, it led to egregious acts of injustice and abuse. Sarah's paternal grandfather illustrates the vulnerability of women and slaves under patriarchy. Although we learn little directly about the abusive acts he performed toward his slaves, we can surmise how he dealt with them from his heartless treatment of his son. Desbordes-Valmore chooses, significantly, to recount the sad story of Sarah's father and his beloved Narcisse from the perspective of Arsène, a slave on the grandfather's property until Sarah's father frees him from bondage. By recounting the tragic consequences of tyranny from a slave's viewpoint, Desbordes-Valmore reveals both her antislavery sentiments and her general political outlook. Marc Bertrand finds it amazing that "such a young girl so clearly conceived [...] an exact historical vision of the sources of colonialism"; and he explains this vision of colonialism by observing that "she was [...] always suspicious of 'kings,' whether in the strict sense of sovereigns or, more figuratively, absolute power, tyranny with its repressive entourage."[27]

Desbordes-Valmore also attributes an outlook of empathetic paternalism to Mr. Primrose, an Englishman, which is not surprising since England served as a model for French liberals and abolitionists at the time. When Arsène arrives with Sarah and offers to surrender his freedom to secure her safety and future happiness, Mr. Primrose responds in a way that not only shows respect for Arsène's status as a freedman but extends that respect to all blacks on his plantation: "Sois au nombre de mes serviteurs; je ne les appelle pas mes esclaves; j'ai besoin d'en être aimé" (40) ("join the ranks of my servants; I refuse to call them slaves; I need to be loved by them.") (13) His devotion to his son parallels the concern that he professes for his workers; and the enduring love he feels for his deceased wife Jenny illustrates his capacity for profound sentimental attachment.

But *Sarah* seems concerned to convey a message regarding the right and wrong practices of well-intentioned fathers. Sarah's fate hinges on the conflict within Mr. Primrose between the forces of paternalism, which correspond to his true nature, and those of patriarchy, which he feels bound by tradition to obey. Aimée Boutin observes that Sarah is reduced to the status of a non-person, owing both Arsène and Mr. Primrose "a blind obedience which is an affront to her humanity and her individuality."[28] Mr. Primrose also errs by allowing Silvain to usurp his paternal role, thereby abrogating the responsibilities that form the foundation of plantocratic societies. He thus joins the ranks of the numerous plantation owners in the colonies, especially absentee proprietors, who failed to administer their land holdings and watch over the well-being of their black workers. Other planters professed enlightened views but failed to reconcile those views with the harsh reality of plantation life.[29]

That the need for responsible paternalism mattered to Desbordes-Valmore is apparent in her short story "La Jambe de Damis," which appeared in the 1834 edition *Le Livre des petits enfants*. In that story, a spoiled white child, Damis, demands capriciously to throw a little slave boy out the window. His mother, like Mr. Primrose, declines to exercise the necessary parental authority: "Jetez, ami, dit la mère indolente en le regardant faire" ("Throw him out, my child, said the lazy mother who was watching the act.")[30] However, his father intervenes: "'Va panser ton esclave!' dit ce singulier philanthrope, en le lançant par le même chemin" ("'Go take care of your slave!' the remarkable philanthropist said, chasing the boy off on the same road as the slave.") (71) The contrite child is saved from becoming a tyrant. His father emancipates the slave and sends the two children to receive an education in France. The end of the story affirms the author's faith in the paternal exercise of authority and benevolence: "Damis, guéri et grandi, s'appela un jour le Sauveur des blancs. Le jeune planteur, préservé de l'influence fatale d'une mère trop faible et d'un père trop violent, fut depuis estimé sous le nom d'un philanthrope" ("Damis, reformed and grown up, was one day called he who saved the whites. Preserved from the fatal influence of a weak mother and an excessively violent father, the young planter was subsequently respected as a philanthropist.") (72) Paternalistic authority here coincides with the principles that antislavery advocates promoted: compassion, just exercise of authority, education, and belief in the future happiness of both blacks and whites.

Sarah's father provides the same model of colonial benevolence as Damis's father. I would call this model "maternalistic": not in the patronizing sense of benevolent white women helping powerless, victimized blacks, but in an empowering sense of combining a "maternal" ethic of caring with paternal authority.[31] Hélène Cixous pits that maternal ethic against the masculine ethic of the "propre," which forms the conceptual common ground of both propriety and property:

> everything that supports society and its properties, everything that is the basis of its laws and codes. Its whole political economy, in fact, like

its whole psychic economy, depends on conventions that require distinguishing yours from mine, the self from the non-self, true from false, the
"propre" from the "non-propre."[32]

Desbordes-Valmore rejects the "propre," relegating the notions of ownership
that underlie possessing slaves to the villain, Silvain. In contrast, Arsène
functions as Sarah's substitute mother, embodying a feminine ethic of caring
which ultimately prevails over Silvain's masculine ethic of proprietariness.
Similarly Sarah's father has no desire to possess either land or the labor that
is needed to farm it. Giving his property to his daughter is not a masculinist
gift of reciprocity but a feminist gift of generosity, confidence, love, and
commitment.[33] That Sarah's father lacks a "proper" name takes on additional
symbolic meaning in this context. As Boutin explains, Desbordes-Valmore
rejected "the permanence of the proper name, as well as the inheritance,
even the unified identity, it promised." To indicate how little she valued her
name, and the fame that attached to it, she expressed the wish to give it to
a pauper, "a 'disinherited' individual like herself."[34] It is true that at the end
of the novel Sarah will marry Edwin, whose father bears a "proper name."
But that name has been stripped of the "property" that formerly legitimized
its privilege. With the inheritance of her nameless father, who has disavowed
his own lineage and privileged social status, and with the nurturing that the
slave "mother" Arsène has provided, Sarah and Edwin face their future as
members of a new benevolent and just colonial class.

* * *

Marceline Desbordes-Valmore—the young actress who traveled to the
French colonies at the time of the slave uprisings in the early nineteenth
century and the author of *Sarah*, which reflects her colonial experience—has
been viewed in literary history from a predominantly French perspective
as one of the first writers of romantic poetry. Yet her background did not
preclude significant commonalities with those living on the margins of
society: socially, economically, even linguistically. She was born and raised
in Douai, which although incorporated into France since 1667, was the
capital of Flemish-speaking Flanders. Despite her French background,
Desbordes-Valmore remained nostalgically attached to Flemish customs
and language. Also, when stranded in Saint-Barthélemy, she learned what
she called a "patois créole," which she mastered sufficiently to be able to
publish two poems in that language.[35] Desbordes-Valmore's life and works
are broadened when they are viewed through the prism of Said's notion of
"intertwined and overlapping histories" that share a "structure of attitude
and reference."

The relevant perspective in Desbordes-Valmore's case is the world of late eighteenth-century and early nineteenth-century theater in which her literary formation and her career began. That world was not limited to France. Theater flourished in Saint-Domingue up to the time of the Haitian Revolution in the 1790s, and after the French Revolution it was sufficiently vigorous to motivate persons in search of theatrical employment, like Marceline's mother, to travel to that region. Throughout the Francophone world actors and actresses performed the same repertoire by well-known playwrights such as Voltaire and Rousseau, along with plays by writers who are lesser known today such as Jean-François Marmontel and Charles Simon Favart. In addition to the same theatrical works, similar conditions existed for actors of various social and racial conditions. Only in 1791 did actors obtain recognition of their civil rights, at the same time as Jews and non-whites.[36] Poor women such as those in Desbordes-Valmore's family faced obstacles and struggles for survival that were similar to those encountered by non-whites. One example is the actress and singer Minette, a star of Saint-Dominguan theater a generation before Marceline appeared on the stage. Both the notable similarities and the significant differences between these two young women illuminate "the facts of power" of the colonial world.

One such fact is that the male dominance depicted in sentimental narrative fiction like *Sarah* or *Paul et Virginie* was less extensive in the unconventional arena of the theater. Women often empowered other women. Marceline's mother Catherine was illiterate when she married Antoine-Félix in 1776 but learned to read, assisted in her self-education by her sister-in-law, Thérèse Sagé, and other educated women. Catherine came to love literature and made it a part of her children's upbringing. Thérèse also provided instruction to Cécile Desbordes, who in turn taught Marceline to read. At a time when education was neither free nor available to girls, women teaching other women could be a ticket out of impoverishment and oppression, as it was for blacks who received instruction from whites and from educated peers. Without that education, learning the parts for theatrical performances would have been impossible. Later in her life, Marceline, the godmother of her sister Eugénie's daughter Camille, encouraged her niece's education, advising her to learn to spell by copying great works, as she herself had done. Haitian historian Jean Fouchard tells us that Minette's mother secretly hired a tutor to provide her two daughters, Minette and Lise, with an education, which at the time was denied to persons of color.[37] Education for girls is thus an important point of intersection between daughters and slaves. For both it provided a form of liberation and empowerment.

Another fact of power concerns the similar ways in which white and black daughters pursued artistic careers. In Marceline's case, her mother chose, out of economic necessity, to put her on the stage at a young age.

And although Marceline's theatrical success never equalled Minette's, her early exposure to the world of literature and art through the theater was a dominant influence in her later success as a writer. Minette also had women to thank for her rise to fame as an actress and singer. Women were powerful in Saint-Dominguan theater at the time, not only as actresses but as theatrical directors as well. Madame Acquaire took Minette under her wing and helped promote her career. She also helped her to negotiate the racial obstacles that might have precluded Minette, the daughter of a former slave, from appearing on stage in colonial Saint-Domingue.[38] Fortunately for Minette, the director of the Comédie française of Port-au-Prince, Monsieur Saint-Martin, rejected racial divisions and had a mulatto mistress.[39] Like the African world in which Charlotte Dard was placed, the world of theater did not obey rigid plantocratic standards of conduct.

Can a line of influence be drawn between the two young actresses? It seems unlikely that Marceline and others around her would have been unaware of the notable facts of colonial theater such as Minette's success. Many indications in *Sarah* suggest that Desbordes-Valmore was familiar with the theatrical world in which Minette lived and worked. Sarah, like Minette, does not have a family name: as noted earlier, the absence of a patronym is consistent with Sarah's proximity and resemblance to slaves throughout the story. Women like Minette's mother were forbidden from having a last name: "For having been born in chains, once liberated she only had the right to bear the first name that the master gave her."[40] Her daughters, Minette and Lise, similarly had only first names: indeed, until Minette had achieved considerable success as an actress, she was only referred to in the press as "la jeune personne" ("the young person") before being designated as "la demoiselle Minette" ("Miss Minette").[41]

Sarah also features the themes and the names of the main characters from the popular dramas and operas in which Minette and other actresses of her time starred. The most important was Charles Simon Favart's *La Belle Arsène*. As Fouchard observes,

> How many times did theaters in the Cap and Port-au-Prince present Favart's "comédie-féérie" *La Belle Arsène* which had been launched at Fontainebleau on November 6, 1773 and performed in Paris on August 14, 1775? No play achieved such a brilliant and lasting career in Saint-Domingue as this one did. No play foregrounded better the talent of star actresses such as Minette or Madame Marsan; indeed, a ship was named "La Belle Arsène."[42]

To give the slave who serves as a mother of sorts to Sarah a well-recognized and admired name that was associated with Minette is significant. So is the thematic importance of slavery in Favart's opera. Although chattel slavery is not mentioned, slavery for women in love and marriage is a leitmotif. In Act I, Arsène protests:

> Non, non, j'ai trop de fierté
> Pour me soumettre à l'esclavage;
> Dans les liens du mariage …
> Je chéris ma liberté,
> Je prétends en faire usage
> Ma règle est ma volonté.
> On perd son autorité,
> Dès l'instant qu'on la partage.

> (No, no, I am too proud
> To submit to slavery;
> In the ties of matrimony …
> I cherish my freedom,
> I intend to make use of it
> My rule is my will.
> We lose our authority,
> As soon as we share it.)[43]

Although ultimately Arsène unites with Alcindor, who has resorted to various ruses to win her love, a woman's desire to control her own fate resurfaces frequently in Favart's work. A message about feminine power would have been especially relevant for women like Minette and Marceline, struggling to survive in the theatrical world.

The name of another principal protagonist in *Sarah*, Silvain, is also drawn from a popular dramatic work in which Minette performed: Marmontel's *Silvain* (1770). Desbordes-Valmore may have wished to draw on the popularity of the name Silvain despite the fact that Marmontel's Silvain— the embodiment of humility, generosity, and genuine affection for others—is the direct antithesis of the character who bears that name in *Sarah*. The plot of *Silvain* revolves around marriage across class lines, as does *Sarah*; and the nefarious results of paternal class prejudice are common to the two works. As Silvain explains to his morally exemplary wife Hélène after many happy years together and when their two daughters are about to be married, "Je te donnai ma foi sans l'aveu de mon père: voilà ma seule faute" ("I pledged myself to you without my father's permission: that is my only fault.")[44] After he fled his father's home, control of the family property devolved to Silvain's mean-spirited younger brother, who threatened the livelihood of Silvain and other peasants by refusing them access to the surrounding fields. All ends well when the father recognizes that Hélène is in fact "une femme bien née" ("a well-bred woman"), and he accepts his formerly banished oldest son's whole family. He also recognizes the right of one of the daughters to marry the peasant she loves, stating that "il est bon de montrer quelquefois que la simple vertu tient lieu de la naissance" ("Sometimes it is good to show that simple virtue takes the place of birth.") (700) Ultimately, however, patriarchy remains intact: the oldest son is returned to his rightful place in the family; and the play concludes with an elegy to fathers, "Rien de plus tendre qu'un bon père [...] Une âme tendre, un coeur de père est du ciel le plus heureux don" ("Nothing is kinder than a good father [...] A kind soul, a father's heart is the greatest gift that heaven can bestow.") (700)

A third play that has strong resonance with *Sarah*, Jean-Baptiste Collet de Messine's *Sara, ou la fermière écossaise*, published in 1774, is inspired by Saint-Lambert's *Le Roman de Miss Sara* (1765). As with *La Belle Arsène*, no direct mention of slavery occurs; however, Sara's husband Phillips—like Silvain, the ideal model of benevolent fatherhood—is called "master" by the peasants whose land he controls and whose fate he both shares and endeavors to improve. Thematically, then, it contains the same notion of benevolent control found in *Sarah*. And as in Desbordes-Valmore's work, control does not pass through conventional lines. Phillips has married above his station: revealingly, he and his father Peterson have only one name, whereas his socially superior wife, Sara Thompson, has retained a patronym. However, Sara does not seek to pass on to her daughters any part of the legacy to which she was entitled when her parents died. It is enough that their death gave her the authority to decide her own fate. The family heritage that she renounced in order to marry Phillips has devolved to her long-lost cousin Clarens (an obvious reference to Rousseau's *Julie*, in which Clarens is the name of the family home). Through his choice of marrying Sara's daughter, Clarens returns the fortune that Sara refused to claim to its rightful heir; yet while entering the family as her daughter's husband, he also keeps the fortune in well-born male hands. Revealingly, when Clarens seeks to obtain permission for the marriage, he turns to Sara, not Phillips. Ultimately all matters are happily resolved. Class boundaries are crossed, but without threatening the traditional foundations of society.

Having seen some of the ways in which Minette's story may have wound itself into Marceline's colonial memory, thus producing what Said calls "intertwined and overlapping histories," we should note differences between the two young actresses which reflect "the facts of power" of the colonial world. Poor and abandoned as Marceline may have been when her mother died in 1802, she was white and was accordingly afforded certain forms of respect and aid that enabled her to return to France. In contrast, when the Haitian Revolution occurred, Minette seems to have disappeared. In fact, the fires that were lit in Port-au-Prince were blamed on slave women and women of color, many of whom were arrested at the time.[45]

Minette may have harbored feelings of resentment toward the white establishment and may even have participated in the uprisings, as she and others of her color and class were accused of doing. Expressing feelings of hatred toward white oppressors is the ending to Minette's story imagined by the twentieth-century Haitian writer Marie Chauvet in *La Danse sur le volcan*. Constructing Minette as a heroic model of feminine resistance, Chauvet gives a voice to women who were silenced in the historical record of the fight for Haitian independence. Chauvet's Minette never forgets her mother's experiences as a slave. On her first appearance on stage, she conjures up images of women's backs marked with scars from the whippings they received; and as a girl, her naive goal is "acheter tous les esclaves du pays pour les libérer ensuite" ("buy all the slaves in the colony in order to free them immediately after.") [46]

The real Minette may have been more like Desbordes-Valmore in being concerned with survival and her own career. Her mother's slave past may have less consciously preoccupied her than it does Chauvet's Minette, although unquestionably that past would have weighed on the daughter both psychologically and socially. Fouchard tells us that Minette consistently aspired to elevated theatrical parts and refused to play roles that cast her as a black person. Such black roles did exist: even Rousseau's enormously popular *Le Devin du village* was played in a "negro" version that starred Lise, who ranked lower than her sister in the hierarchy of successful actresses.[47] Bernard Camier quotes Minette herself as having referred to certain productions of strictly local interest that degrade ("abâtardissent") lyric opera.[48] In a curious twist of history, it was Desbordes-Valmore who wrote poems in Creole, whereas Minette adamantly refused to use that language on the stage: "This language signified degradation to her. She shared a complex common among the Haitian elite. It affected Minette as well as many blacks and free mulattoes who considered French, the language of the master, the symbol of good taste, distinction, and elegance."[49] One sees again that power took many forms in the colonial world, including the politics of language; and that daughters and slaves both resisted and complied with that power in diverse, complex, and at times even contradictory ways.

Notes

1 Although correspondence by Marceline's family members suggests both possibilities, neither has been confirmed: Ambrière, *Le Siècle des Valmore*.

2 Ambrière, *Le Siècle des Valmore*, 26; Aimée Boutin, "Introduction," in Marceline Desbordes-Valmore, *Les Veillées des Antilles*, ed. Aimée Boutin (Paris: L'Harmattan, 2006), 213.

3 The poems as well as their translations by Norman R. Shapiro appear in Kadish and Massardier-Kenney, eds, *Translating Slavery, vol. 1: Gender and Race in French Abolitionist Writing*. "L'Esclave," which appears within the pages of *Sarah*, was also

published on four other occasions. Shapiro's rhymed version in *Translating Slavery*, *vol. 1* (222) differs from the more literal translation in Marceline Desbordes-Valmore, *Sarah: An English Translation*, ed. Deborah Jenson and Doris Y. Kadish (New York: MLA, 2008), 16.

4 Boutin, "Introduction," xviii–xxi.

5 Marceline Desbordes-Valmore, *La Jeunesse de Marceline ou l'Atelier d'un peintre*, ed. Auguste Jean Boyer d'Agen (Paris: Editions de la Nouvelle Revue Française, 1922), 78. Unless otherwise indicated with references to specific published material, all translations are my own. Alexandria Wettlaufer notes that in this edition, Boyer d'Agen cuts nearly a third of *L'Atelier d'un peintre* and recasts it as an autobiography; *Portraits of the Artist as a Young Woman: Painting and the Novel in France and Britain, 1800–1860* (Columbus: Ohio State University Press, 2011), 278.

6 Ambrière, *Le Siècle des Valmore*, 28.

7 Marc Bertrand, "Introduction," in *Les Oeuvres poétiques de Marceline Desbordes-Valmore*, ed. Marc Bertrand (Grenoble: Presses universitaires de Grenoble, 1973), 8.

8 Ambrière notes that it may have been because Marceline (who was blond, like her mother and unlike the other Desbordes children) was illegitimate that she alone was taken on the colonial voyage with her mother.

9 Desbordes-Valmore, *La Jeunesse de Marceline*, 73.

10 Biographical facts suggest that M. Desbordes's illegitimate child triggered her mother's flight from the family; Ambrière, *Le Siècle des Valmore*, 51.

11 The use of "palladium" as a concrete or abstract entity safeguarding a collectivity, an institution, or a value, is now considered archaic. I thank Aimée Boutin for help in interpreting this term.

12 Quoted in Aimée Boutin, "Colonial Memory, Narrative, and Sentimentalism in Desbordes-Valmore's *Les Veillées Des Antilles*," *L'Esprit créateur* 47, 4 (2007): 63. In a poem entitled "L'Esclave et l'oiseau," Desbordes-Valmore dwells on the intertwined motifs of birds and love, casting herself—"l'oiseau sans ailes" ("the wingless bird")—as the one who frees a love-sick bird. Bertrand (ed.), *Les Oeuvres poétiques de Marceline Desbordes-Valmore*, 514

13 Kadish and Massardier-Kenney (eds), *Translating Slavery, vol. 1: Gender and Race in French Abolitionist Writing*, 219–23. The French poems appear in the Appendix of that volume, 269–73.

14 Boyer d'Agen, "Préface," in Desbordes-Valmore, *La Jeunesse de Marceline*, viii.

15 Boutin, "Introduction," xxxiii.

16 Orlando Patterson, *Slavery and Social Death: A Comparative Study* (Cambridge, MA: Harvard University Press, 1982).

17 Desbordes-Valmore published *Sarah* in 1821 as part of *Les Veillées des Antilles* (Paris: Chez François Louis, 1821). She later republished the same work in 1845 as part of *Huit Femmes*. Volume II of this 1845 edition contains the section "Mon Retour en Europe," which is not part of *Les Veillées des Antilles*. The 1845 version is a rare edition found in the collection of Harvard University and not available in the Bibliothèque nationale de France. The edition of *Huit Femmes* edited by Marc Bertrand in 1999 is presumably based on the 1845 edition, but differs from the Harvard edition in a number of ways. Differences between the 1821 and 1845 editions highlighted in the following analysis of the novel are not always apparent in the Bertrand edition.

18 This analysis of *Sarah* develops the analysis found in the introduction to the MLA edition of *Sarah* (*Sarah: The Original French Text*, ed. Deborah Jenson and

Doris Y. Kadish [New York: MLA, 2008]) and in Doris Y. Kadish, *"Sarah* and Antislavery," *L'Esprit créateur* 47, 4 (2007): 93–104.

19 David J. Denby, *Sentimental Narrative and the Social Order in France, 1760–1820* (Cambridge: Cambridge University Press, 1994), 2–16, 72–81, 90–96.

20 Michelle Cheyne identifies Jean Piraquemon as a possible model for Desbordes-Valmore's black protagonist; "Introduction," in Jacques-Louis Lacour, *Pyracmond, ou les Créoles* (Paris: L'Harmattan, 2012), xxviii–xxx.

21 Page numbers for French passages drawn from the 1845 edition refer to *Sarah: The Original French Text*, ed. Jenson and Kadish. Page numbers for passages in English refer to *Sarah: An English Translation*, ed. Jenson and Kadish. Page numbers for the 1821 edition refer to *Les Veillées des Antilles* (Chez François Louis, 1821). English translations from this edition are my own.

22 The preceding translations are amended slightly from the version published in *Sarah: An English Translation*, ed. Jenson and Kadish.

23 The MLA editions of *Sarah* place "Mon Retour en Europe" at the beginning of Sarah's story. However, as an explanatory note on p. xxxvii of the French MLA edition explains, "Mon Retour" is in fact the beginning of the two-volume 1845 edition of *Huit Femmes. Sarah* is found in chapters 26 to 33 of volume II of the 1845 edition.

24 Coriolan Ardouin, *Poésies* (Port-au-Prince: R. Ethéart, 1881), 74. Translation by Norman R. Shapiro.

25 See T. Denean Sharpley-Whiting, *Black Venus: Sexualized Savages, Primal Fears, and Primitive Narratives in French* (Durham, NC: Duke University Press, 1999). Abdel Kechiche directed a film entitled *Vénus noire* in 2010.

26 Morgan, *Slave Counterpoint*, 258–59.

27 Marc Bertrand, *Une Femme à l'écoute de son temps* (Lyon: La Cicogne, 1997), 101, 114. Aimée Boutin also notes that "an antipatriarchal spirit was appealing in an historical period inaugurated by parricide and repeatedly faced with the prospect of failed fatherhood"; *Maternal Echoes: The Poetry of Marceline Desbordes-Valmore and Alphonse de Lamartine* (Newark: University of Delaware Press, 2001), 14.

28 Boutin, "Introduction," xxx.

29 A critique of the disparity between word and deed among plantation owners is provided in Charles Rémusat's 1825 play *L'Habitation de Saint-Domingue* (Baton Rouge: Louisiana State University Press, 2008).

30 Marceline Desbordes-Valmore, "La Jambe de Damis," in *Contes*, ed. Marc Bertrand (Lyon: Presses Universitaires de Lyon, 1989), 71. This short story is included in *Les Veillées des Antilles*, ed. Boutin.

31 For benevolent white women, see Midgley, *Women against Slavery*, 102; for a maternal ethic, see Boutin, *Maternal Echoes*, 80.

32 Hélène Cixous, *Prénoms de personne* (Paris: Seuil, 1974), 53.

33 Cixous and Kuhn, "Castration or Decapitation?", 48, 50. For a discussion of the traditional social implications of the gift and its relation to colonialism, see Françoise Vergès, *Monsters and Revolutionaries, Colonial Family Romance and Métissage* (Durham, NC: Duke University Press, 1999), 6–7.

34 Boutin, *Maternal Echoes*, 90–92. The sentiment expressed in these words was presumably intended to be her epitaph.

35 See Jenson, *Beyond Slave Narratives*, 266–67.

36 David Geggus, "Racial Equality, Slavery, and Colonial Secession during the

Constituent Assembly," *American Historical Review* 94, 5 (1990): 1303. Although Masonic lodges routinely allowed membership from all ranks, trades, and religions, the lodge in Bordeaux excluded Jews and actors in the 1770s; Buck-Morss, *Hegel, Haiti, and Universal History*, 63, fn 123.

37 Jean Fouchard, *Le Théâtre à Saint-Domingue* (Port-au-Prince: H. Deschamps, 1988), 304. Bernard Camier's archival research identifies Minette as Louise Alexandrine Elizabeth Minette Ferrand, who was born in 1767 in Port-au-Prince and died in 1807 in New Orleans; "Musique coloniale et sociale à Saint-Domingue dans la seconde moitié du 18e siècle," unpublished dissertation, Université des Antille et de la Guyane, 2004, 272–74.

38 For obstacles to the representation of mulattos on the stage in France during the Restoration, see Michelle Cheyne, "Pyracmond, ou les Créoles: L'Articulation d'une hiérarchie des rôles raciaux sur la scène française sous la Restauration," *French Colonial History* 6 (2005): 79–102.

39 Fouchard, *Le Théâtre à Saint-Domingue*, 308.

40 Fouchard, *Le Théâtre à Saint-Domingue*, 304.

41 Fouchard, *Le Théâtre à Saint-Domingue*, 346.

42 Fouchard, *Le Théâtre à Saint-Domingue*, 224. Camier observes that Minette played in *La Belle Arsène* in 1775 and 1787, and that this lyric opera was performed 30 times between 1778 and 1791; "Musique coloniale et sociale à Saint-Domingue," 270.

43 Charles Simon Favart and Pierre-Alexandre Monsigny, *La Belle Arsène* (1775), 216–17.

44 Jean-François Marmontel, "Silvain," in *Oeuvres Complètes*, vol. V (Geneva: Slatkine Reprints, 1968), 678–700

45 Fouchard, *Le Théâtre à Saint-Domingue*, 343.

46 Marie Chauvet, *La Danse sur le volcan* (Paris: Plon, 1957), 57; Marie Chauvet, *Dance on the Volcano*, trans. Salvator Attanasio (New York: William Sloane, 1959), 67.

47 Fouchard, *Le Théâtre à Saint-Domingue*, 281.

48 Camier, "Musique coloniale et sociale à Saint-Domingue," 270.

49 Fouchard, *Le Théâtre à Saint-Domingue*, 323.

4

Voices of Daughters and Slaves:
Claire de Duras

Claire de Duras's haunting portrayal of the young African woman Ourika grew out of experiences with dramatic revolutionary and postrevolutionary events linked to slavery. Her father, Admiral Armand-Guy-Simon de Coëtnempren, comte de Kersaint, was a liberal Breton aristocrat. He played an active role in the legislative arena at a time when colonial issues were pressing objects of discussion, publishing *Moyens proposés à l'Assemblée nationale pour rétablir la paix et l'ordre dans les colonies* followed by *Suite des Moyens*. The two works were written in 1791, before the slave insurrections in Saint-Domingue occurred, and published in 1792.[1] As a distinguished naval officer, Kersaint had extensive and deep-seated connections to the colonial world. A liberal presence throughout the various stages of the French Revolution, he ultimately sided with the Girondins in voting against the death penalty in the trial of King Louis XVI. Having denounced Marat and other revolutionaries during the Terror, Kersaint was sentenced to death and guillotined on December 5, 1793. Claire was sixteen at the time. On the maternal side, Duras's mother, Claire-Louise-Françoise de Paul d'Alesso d'Eragny, was born in Martinique into a wealthy, influential family. She was the first cousin of comte d'Ennery, governor of the French Antillean islands. To rescue the colonial fortune of her ailing mother, Duras left France in 1793 from Bordeaux. It was there that she heard the news of her father's death.[2]

Fathers, daughters, and slaves were thus linked in especially painful ways for Duras, as for other women considered in this book. Like Desbordes-Valmore, she traveled to the Americas as a young girl, suffered the loss of a parent during her travels, and was required to act with an exceptional degree of independence and responsibility for a person of her age. Duras's story also brings Staël's to mind. In fact, the two women had much in common socially, personally, and politically. They knew, respected, and admired each other, and Duras included the abolitionist duc de Broglie, Staël's son-in-law, in her exclusive social circle. Most importantly for our discussion here, Staël's and Duras's devotion to their distinguished fathers was similarly profound and enduring. Gabriel Pailhès observes, "Claire adored her father. She mourned him. She did more: she remained faithful to his memory as well as to the ideas that he heroically championed in public and in his writings."[3] Michèle Bissière claims that in all of Duras's writing what shows just beneath the surface is a search for father, God, and King.[4]

As with Staël, devotion to paternal authority did not preclude an equally profound allegiance to liberal political views, including antislavery.[5] Duras rarely voiced those views directly. Bound to women's prescribed social roles, she never sought to enter the public sphere. But she was the "woman behind the scenes" for Chateaubriand's political career, and in her salon she was an influential voice who used her power to do what the American feminist bell hooks calls "talking back": "speaking as an equal to an authority figure." For hooks, speaking can be "an act of resistance, a political gesture that challenges politics of domination that would render us nameless and voiceless [...] It is that act of speech, of 'talking back' [...] that is the expression of moving from object to subject, that is the liberated voice."[6]

It is not surprising, then, that Duras chose not to relegate her black protagonist to silence. Ourika stands as an exemplar of a black woman who, having been nurtured in a world of women's talk—similar to the world of black women that hooks evokes—breaks the silence and gains her own voice. This chapter looks at what we can learn by listening to the voices of women and blacks, while also measuring the significant extent to which patriarchal authority remains intact in Duras's world.

We begin by listening to Duras's father to assess the degree to which his antislavery voice is echoed in *Ourika*. An analysis of *Ourika* follows. In order to amplify black women's voices, largely silenced in the historical record, another voice is introduced: that of the slave Judith, who was owned by Henriette de La Tour du Pin, the author of the memoir *Journal d'une femme de cinquante ans*.[7] La Tour du Pin, a friend of Duras's, wrote about Judith in her memoir and about the real Ourika in her correspondence. The chapter closes by moving from the nineteenth to the twentieth century and considering how Ourika's voice has been echoed or distorted in writings by the contemporary Francophone writers Aimé Césaire, Daniel Maximin, and Maryse Condé. This multiplicity of perspectives expands and enriches our understanding of *Ourika*, a now canonical work that until recently has often been viewed in a literary vacuum.[8]

* * *

The two works in which Kersaint discusses the French colonies—*Moyens proposés à l'Assemblée nationale pour rétablir la paix et l'ordre dans les colonies* and *Suite des Moyens*—suggest that he shared the attitudes of benevolent paternalism prevalent in the milieux in which French antislavery women writers were raised. Kersaint does not call patriarchal mastery into question per se. He admonishes the colonists, "Be masters in the colonies or their destruction is inevitable" and admits the role that he himself has played as a master: "I spent a great deal of time living in the colonies; I owned black slaves; part of my fortune is still in Saint-Domingue; I surely cannot thus want its destruction."[9] He points out to the colonists that he is not on the side of their enemies: "I do not belong to the Société des amis des noirs." (*Moyens* 3) But at the same time he voices an impassioned plea for the benevolent treatment of slaves:

> I have always felt that ameliorating the fate of Africans transported to the European colonies must inspire zealous outrage in the heart of anyone who cares about the suffering of his fellow men. My writings are not intended for those whose inhuman pride refuses to recognize the humanity of the wretched blacks, whose enslavement and mistreatment has lowered them to the level of our most poorly treated domestic animals. (*Moyens* 3)

His views correspond to those found in antislavery writings of his time: slaves are human beings, mistreatment of them will lead to revolts, free men of color should be granted the rights and privileges they deserve, reason rather than prejudice should guide plans for the future of the colonies, free labor should be the ultimate goal. Although he is not willing to consent to the abolition of the slave trade per se, he proposes changing the existing system to encourage the willing migration of African workers.

Kersaint expresses a number of points that have special relevance for *Ourika*. He asserts that it is not uncommon to find slaves who know how to read.[10] The intellectual capacity of blacks, a key argument among abolitionists and a key feature of Ourika's ability to have a voice, was thus a concern of both father and daughter. Another view expressed by Kersaint that brings us close to *Ourika* is that blacks should be conceived of as children in a family: "The colonies [...] can achieve independence through the same laws that within a family allow children to achieve emancipation from paternal authority." (*Suite* 19) Questions that we might pose today about Ourika's actual legal status probably would not have had the same meaning for Duras as for us. At the time, children were under the authority of their parents until they married: in one sense, they were no more "free" than is Ourika.[11] Moreover, according to the 1791 constitution, persons born outside of France could only become citizens if they acquired property or married a French person. The key plot component of Ourika finding an appropriate marriage prospect thus takes on added meaning. As Pratima Prasad states, "her social integration is predicated upon her marriageability."[12] In short, Ourika can never be truly "emancipated" but can only change from one authority figure to another: Boufflers, who rescued her in Africa; the family of her benefactress, Mme de B; a husband, were she able to find one; or, at the end of the novel, the Church. Kersaint also makes a point of distinguishing between slaves transported from Africa and those born in the colonies, creoles. In the system he proposes for reforming the status of the various racial groups in the future, he states that creoles should be able to aspire to "self-purchase"—emancipation which slaves achieved through reimbursing their owner for their worth as property—whereas Africans, who do not know the language or culture of the colonies, "will be honored with the name of minor children of the country under the guardianship of the law." (*Suite* 40) The authority exercised over Ourika would then have been all the more appropriate in his eyes because of her African birth.

Certainly, then, it is possible to read Duras as strongly influenced by and echoing the voice of her benevolent antislavery father, who stood as a liberal model for his daughter's politics at the time when she wrote *Ourika*. The importance that his model provided should not be underestimated. By upholding his political legacy, Duras exercised a moderating influence on the conservative views of other aristocrats in her milieu including Chateaubriand. As Steven Kale observes, "When the moderate royalists were in power, she encouraged him to display his independence and advertise the 'liberality' of his views [...] in April 1821, she advised him that his reputation as a liberal would harm him as the political winds shifted to the right."[13] Such vagaries of Restoration politics notwithstanding, Duras consistently had a voice in shaping attitudes toward slavery in her aristocratic world. As Pailhès explains, her salon, the most influential and prestigious during the Restoration, was frequented by writers, artists, intellectuals, diplomats, nobles, and persons of all political positions.

It was within the culture of this Restoration salon that *Ourika* was conceived, circulated, and exerted its extraordinary influence. But Duras was much more than "her father's daughter." Kersaint's writings are marked by the voice of authority that could have been expected of a naval officer involved in the political life of his times. As noted above, he was a master, and he supported his fellow colonists as masters, despite the fact that his views about the future direction of colonial politics diverged in many ways from theirs. When he speaks the language of benevolence—for example, seeking to provoke "outrage in the heart of anyone who cares about the suffering of his fellow men"—he is speaking as a man for his fellow men, not in the feminine, empathetic way that characterizes Duras as a writer. Nineteenth-century readers would have immediately recognized the difference, as did the reviewer of *Ourika* for *Le Diable Boiteux* in 1823: "You will guess right away that it is written by a woman [...] only a woman could penetrate the sanctuary where such delicate feelings reside."[14] Revealingly, Kersaint calls upon colonists to recognize that the men of color are "their sons, their brothers, their nephews." (*Suite* 39) His frequent appeals to reason are aimed at readers whose intellectual grounding is in the Enlightenment, not in sentimental literature. His concerns are money, property, order, and justice. They do not include the feminine perspective that enabled Duras as a woman and as a writer to find a voice enabling a slave woman to "talk back" to figures of authority such as her father.

This is not to say, of course, that an easy slippage from Claire the French woman to Ourika the African can or should occur. Regrettably, all too often it has. From Sainte-Beuve in the nineteenth century to the editor of the *des femmes* edition of *Ourika* in the twentieth century, Duras's lack of beauty, her unhappy marriage, her love for Chateaubriand, her rejection by her oldest daughter Félicie, her illnesses, and other biographical facts have been used to conflate the alienation that similarly afflicted the author and her black heroine. It says something about the condition of women that it has been so easy for critics to put an aristocratic woman such as Duras in the place of the slave! The conflation of the two women has had a number of especially unfortunate results. Claire, the white woman author, has tended to be foregrounded at the expense of Ourika, the black woman she wrote about. Furthermore, as with other women such as George Sand writing later in the nineteenth century, personal and sentimental details have tended to overshadow literary and intellectual accomplishments. Even John Fowles, who translated *Ourika* and acknowledges the impact it had on him as a writer, falls prey to this overvaluation of the personal when he states, "I am certain one reason Claire was able to enter a black mind was that she saw in that situation a symbolic correlative of whatever in her own psychology and beliefs had always prevented her from entering into a full relationship with Chateaubriand."[15] Along with the biographical slant of this statement, it is worth noting how Fowles patronizingly refers to Claire by her first name, whereas Chateaubriand is acknowledged with his proper name, suggesting his greater historical importance and stature. Even Pailhès names his biography of Duras *La Duchesse de Duras et Chateaubriand*, as if Duras were unable to sustain interest on her own.

* * *

In considering women's responses to paternal voices in *Ourika* I will roughly follow the linear order in which the story is presented. The first part of the analysis takes as its point of departure the frame narrative, which is set in a convent near the end of Ourika's life. In this section, I also digress to reflect upon the institutional authority of Church and medicine, not only in the frame narrative but in the novel as a whole. I then move on to the opening episode of the main narrative in which Ourika recounts how she was transported from Africa to France. In addition to discussing that opening episode, I also digress again, in this case to consider the novel as a whole in relation to colonial institutions. Finally I return to focusing directly on the main narrative and the way in which Ourika recounts her life raised in the aristocratic residence of Mme de B. This final part focuses on structures of authority within families and French *ancien régime* society.

The frame narrative—several pages at the beginning of the novel and a short paragraph at the end—is set in the convent where the protagonist chooses to end her life. We also learn the approximate date of the end of Ourika's life, since the emperor Napoléon allowed the re-establishment of convents in 1802. Authority is thus vested politically in Napoleon and in the Church, with which he signed the Concordat in 1801, restoring Catholicism as the majority church of France and re-establishing its civil rights. The final years of Ourika's story recounted in the frame occur under Napoleon's restored imperial authority of Church and state, just as Duras's story—the writing of the novel *Ourika*—occurs two decades later under the restored monarchical, religious society of the Restoration.

Yet, as presented at the beginning of the novel, the Church is feminized: the doctor/frame narrator is presumably summoned by a female inhabitant of the convent to care for Ourika; and it is the voice of nuns, Ourika and her fellow sisters, who speak about her condition and the past history of the convent in the opening pages. Although the doctor narrates, he repeatedly places emphasis on Ourika's voice: "le choix d'expressions dont elle se servait" ("the kinds of expressions she used"); "l'accent de sa voix était sincère" ("her tone of voice was sincere"); "cette douce voix" ("this sweet voice.") And although he initially proposes the "talking cure" to rid her of her past sorrows, she is the one who chooses to recount her story: "un jour, elle revint d'elle-même au sujet où je désirais la conduire" ("one day she came back on her own to the subject to which I wanted to lead her.") She decides when she will be ready and willing to recount her past sufferings: "je vous les confierai quand nous nous connaîtrons un peu davantage" ("I shall confide in you when we are better acquainted.")[16]

Although Ourika is not silenced or outweighed by the male authority of the doctor, either in the beginning frame or the novel as a whole, her voice and control over her story wane near the end of her life. Although Mme de B. summons a priest to the convent for the last rights, the priest's voice and the authority of God prevail as the end approaches. Using his power as the representative of the Church the priest tells Ourika to pray to God: "il est là, il vous tend les bras; il n'y a pour lui ni nègres ni blancs: tous les coeurs sont égaux devant ses yeux" (314) ("He is here; He is holding out his arms to you. For Him, there are no blacks and no whites; all hearts are equal before Him.") (215) Whereas nuns initially welcome Ourika into the convent,' and presumably comfort her during her illness, the priest as a representative of the ultimate authority of God assumes control near the end.

Yet overall it would be misleading simply to see religion as submission in *Ourika*. Although Ourika's voice is silenced when she is near death, religion was part of an empowered life for her while she lived, as it was for Claire de Duras and her avatar Mme de B.[17] Ourika's happiness in the woman-centered haven of the convent mirrors that which she found in the feminine world she was raised in by Mme. de B. From a feminist perspective, Ourika's choice of a conventual life represents a return to a pre-Oedipal phase in which the daughter is one with the mother.[18] Chantal Bertrand-Jennings calls attention to the description of the convent garden as a "berceau" which signifies not only "arbor" but "cradle" as well.[19] "Cradle" connotes an emotional and physical return to the comforting feminine refuge of childhood. Clearly, religious institutions provided psychological comfort for many women; according to Pailhès, Duras commented regarding her own life that when all hope of love was lost the convent would provide "a port in a storm." Moreover, religion served a positive social and humanitarian function in the minds of Duras and other women writers of the eighteenth and nineteenth centuries who wrote about slavery: Gouges, Staël, Sand, and Stowe are a few well-known examples. Christianity, for those who opposed the abuses of slavery, took various forms, from the socially oriented Protestant faith of Staël and Doin, to the radical Catholicism of Grégoire, to the traditional piety of Duras. Devotion to God for these religious and abolitionist figures was affirmation, not submission.

Medicine similarly functions both as authority and resistance in *Ourika*. If the male doctor/frame narrator leaves a space for women to speak, as noted above, it is still the case that as an educated, respected, male member of society, he functions to legitimize and provide the impetus for Ourika's recounting of her story. He exercises a masculine profession and possesses the kind of scientific knowledge that was crucial to the shift in the early nineteenth century from feminine sentimental fiction to the masculine realist novel, as Margaret Cohen was quoted earlier as observing. He also exercises power in his role as the focalizer: "the persona who sees the events of the story."[20] As focalizer, he describes the external appearance of the nun to the reader in the opening pages, including his shock in discovering that she was a black woman: "Elle se tourna vers moi, et je fus étrangement surpris en apercevant une négresse!" ("She turned towards me. I had a strange shock. I was looking at a negress.")[21] He then elaborates upon her physical appearance:

Son aspect ne confirmait que trop cette triste description de son état: sa maigreur était excessive, ses yeux brillants et fort grands, ses dents d'une blancheur éblouissante, éclairaient seuls sa physionomie; l'âme vivait encore, mais le corps était détruit, et elle portait toutes les marques d'un long et violent chagrin. (294)

(Her appearance only confirmed this sad description of her state of health: she was excessively thin, her large and shiny eyes, her brilliant white teeth were the only light in her face. Her soul was still alive, but her body was destroyed, and she showed all the marks of a long and acute grief.) (195)

With the presumably objective eye of the neutral observer and medical authority, the narrator dwells on Ourika's physical characteristics and describes them in the male medical discourse of feminine pathology. As Christine De Vinne observes, "The doctor embodies the empiricism of the Enlightenment and the iconoclasm of the revolution" with its "entrenched [...] anticlerical prejudices" against religion.[22]

Yet within her narrative Ourika competes with the doctor for control over her medical condition. True, he proposes that she adopt the "talking cure" of understanding her past in order to regain her health. But although he serves as facilitator by setting the process in motion, Ourika essentially serves as her own doctor for the rest of the novel. Ourika thus takes on the role vis-à-vis herself that French nuns in the nineteenth century typically assumed, not only within the convent but in society generally. According to Jacques Léonard, there was very little separation between science and religion at that time, enabling women, especially religious women, to play significant roles in both worlds.[23] As it turns out, neither the doctor nor Ourika is successful; but whereas Ourika gains in personal and spiritual empowerment by telling her story, the doctor never changes in his belief in the power of medicine. In the last lines of the narrative when he speaks, his voice seems weak and his powers depleted: "Je continuai à lui donner des soins: malheureusement ils furent inutiles; elle mourut à la fin d'octobre" (315) ("I kept on giving her medical care; unfortunately it was useless. She died at the end of October.") (216)

What we can conclude is that Ourika, like Duras herself, remained within the purview of patriarchal institutions, whether religion, restored monarchy, or medicine, but that those institutions were not forces of oppression against which the character or the author had no ability to resist. Duras was a religious woman, especially at the end of her life, and her commitment to the monarchy was firm, provided that it adhered to the principles of parliamentary government. Yet she had a lucid, progressive view of postrevolutionary French society. In 1822 she parted political ways with Chateaubriand and opposed France's attempts to restore the monarchy in Spain. Duras's lucidity is reflected in the ambivalent attitudes expressed in *Ourika*. Bissière insightfully observes that the black nun's ailing body, tortured by the past, corresponds to the crumbling ruins of the Church itself where she has taken refuge.[24] The novel suggests that institutions destroyed by the Revolution and rehabilitated by Napoleon—the Church and the monarchy—could not truly be restored. Duras suggests that traditional forms of authority had been weakened and rendered perhaps as ineffectual as the doctor sent to cure Ourika in the convent.

* * *

Ourika's narration of her story begins with the facts of her enslavement, her purchase by the governor of Senegal, her expedition to France, and her eventual designation as a gift to the governor's aunt, Mme de B.

> Je fus rapportée du Sénégal, à l'âge de deux ans, par M. le chevalier de B., qui en était gouverneur. Il eut pitié de moi, un jour qu'il voyait embarquer des esclaves sur un bâtiment négrier qui allait bientôt quitter le port: ma mère était morte, et on m'emportait dans le vaisseau, malgré mes cris. M. de B. m'acheta, et, à son arrivée en France, il me donna à Mme la maréchale de B., sa tante, la personne la plus aimable de son temps, et celle qui sut réunir, aux qualités les plus élevées, la bonté la plus touchante. Me sauver de l'esclavage, me choisir pour bienfaitrice Mme de B., c'était me donner deux fois la vie. (295)

> (I was brought back from Senegal, at the age of two, by monsieur le chevalier de B., the governor of that colony. He took pity on me one day when he saw slaves being taken aboard a slave ship which was about to leave the harbor: my mother was dead, and they were taking me away despite my cries. M. de B. bought me, and, upon his arrival in France, gave me to his aunt Mme la maréchale de B., the most amiable person of her time, and the person who was able to combine the most elevated qualities with the most touching kindness. My rescue from slavery, my being given Mme de B. as benefactress, were like two gifts of life.) (196)

M. le chevalier de B. would have been recognized by Duras's readers as Stanislas-Jean, chevalier de Boufflers, who was named by Louis XVI in 1785 as governor of Senegal, a function he fulfilled until the end of 1788. Boufflers brought the real-life Ourika to France on the *Rossignol*, which left Saint-Louis on June 14, 1786.[25] He gave her to la Maréchale de Beauvau, his aunt, the model for Mme de B. in the novel. The African girl died at 16 in 1799. Historical records even provide a trace of Ourika's own voice: Mme de Beauvau states in her memoirs that at the time of the girl's death a handwritten passage was found, bearing the words "my father and mother abandoned me, but the Lord took pity on me." The words are taken from Psalm 27, verse 10.[26]

Ourika's narration begins significantly with her own black voice, but one that is strongly inflected by a European perspective. She describes herself as "rapportée" ("brought back"), making the governor's home, France, seem to be hers. She also adopts the common topos of the "grateful negro": "Il eut pitié de moi, un jour qu'il voyait embarquer des esclaves sur un bâtiment négrier" ("He took pity on me when he saw slaves being taken aboard a slave ship.") Revealingly, this same construction of "taking pity" appears in the real Ourika's dying words. The governor and Mme de B. can thus be viewed as father and mother substitutes for the African parents. The governor's depiction is consistent with the benevolent attitudes toward slavery that his avatar, Boufflers, shared with Duras, Staël, and others of their social circle. As discussed in Chapter 2, Boufflers was known for his generosity and was honored by Senegalese inhabitants when he left Africa. As governor he had the authority to perform benevolent acts and he intervened in individual instances when an act of mercy seemed appropriate.

Ourika's voice seems far from African here and appears to differ little from the voice that one might attribute to the implied author of the novel: the person behind the narration whom we can imagine as linked to Duras herself. Neither Ourika nor the implied author seem to show an awareness of the wrenching separation from the native land that slavery entailed.[27] They view Boufflers as a kindly benefactor and liberator of slaves. But if we read between the lines, we can perhaps see what neither Ourika nor the implied author are willing to acknowledge. Bertrand-Jennings judges Boufflers harshly, calling what he has done to Ourika a "unique story of abduction and adoption."[28] Traces of Ourika's "authentic" voice exist in her cries in the opening passage, "ma mère était morte, et on m'emportait dans le vaisseau, malgré mes cris" ("my mother was dead, and they were taking me away despite my cries.") It is significant that these "authentic" African cries are voiced in connection with Ourika's African mother. As Bertrand-Jennings maintains, Boufflers eclipses the maternal function and substitutes himself for the biological mother: "It is a matter [...] of the appropriation of maternity by a character who incarnates the patriarchal system. This appropriation foreshadows the denial of Ourika's own potential maternity later in the novel."[29]

Elsewhere in the novel, Ourika has no African voice to "talk back" to colonial authority. When the slave insurrections occur in Saint-Domingue, she speaks in the same voice as Mme de B. or the implied author: "Les massacres de Saint-Domingue me causèrent une douleur nouvelle et déchirante: jusqu'ici je m'étais affligée d'appartenir à une race proscrite; maintenant j'avais honte d'appartenir à une race de barbares et d'assassins"

(302) ("The massacres in Saint-Domingue caused me a new, excruciating pain: Until then, I had been distressed at belonging to a proscribed race; now I was ashamed of belonging to a race of barbarians and murderers.") (203) These words echo Chateaubriand's reaction to the slave revolts— "who would still dare to plead the cause of blacks after the crimes they have committed?"[30] They contrast with statements by both Staël and Doin, who viewed the revolts as understandable responses to the cruelty that abusive white masters inflicted on slaves. Unquestionably, silence surrounds colonialism in *Ourika*. The novel leaves a great deal unsaid: that it was common practice to have decorative "poupées noires" ("black dolls") in salons and thus that Ourika was not unique; that white men desired black sexual partners so much that there existed a "bordel des négresses" ("Negress bordello") in Paris and thus that the idea of a white man desiring a woman like Ourika was less unthinkable than the novel suggests; that there were thousands of blacks in the major cities of France at the end of the eighteenth century, many of whom were free, trained as artisans, and thus potential marital partners for Ourika.[31] No mention is made either of the fact that there was an active slave market in Paris itself, contrary to the age-old concept that one was "free on French soil."[32]

Ourika is nonetheless a progressive work with respect to slavery. It may not directly tackle colonialism as a system, but such attacks were only developed later in the century. Although it does not overtly oppose slavery, arguments for emancipation began to gain momentum only in the 1840s. What *Ourika* does succeed in doing is presenting issues of oppression from the standpoint of daughters and slave women, as opposed to more masculine abolitionist perspectives. Consider, for example, the views of Grégoire, a Catholic voice against slavery for over forty years. The contrast between Grégoire and Duras is relevant to our discussion because of their contrasting views about interracial marriage. In *Ourika* Mme de B.'s friend the marquise presents the standard view that would have been held in the aristocratic society of her time: "Qui voudra jamais épouser une négresse? Et si, à force d'argent, vous trouvez quelqu'un qui consente à avoir des enfants nègres, ce sera un homme d'une condition inférieure" (298) ("What kind of man would marry a negress? Even supposing you could bribe some fellow to father mulatto children, he could only be of low birth.") (199) Writing in 1826, near the time of the publication of *Ourika*, Grégoire presents a far different, seemingly more radical view: "Laws in all countries can achieve the eradication of prejudice against color by favoring mixed marriages and assimilating those marriages into those of other citizens."[33] Grégoire's views are not necessarily more liberatory than those of Duras, however. Mixed marriage for Grégoire, who served as an advisor for Pétion's mulatto Haitian state, was an alternative to concubinage. Pétion's Haiti was mixed already;

as a man of the Church, Grégoire wanted marriage to curtail what he saw as the licentiousness and disregard for morality that was more the rule than the exception in colonial society. The persons he addresses and who are responsible for the moral degeneracy of Haitian society are men, "his brothers in Jesus Christ."[34] The use of "brothers" suggests the concept of fraternity central to republican government which both Grégoire and Pétion upheld. It is the concept illustrated in Guillon-Lethière's *Serment des ancêtres* discussed in Chapter 5.

Ultimately, as a priest, Grégoire speaks in the voice of authority and hierarchy. Liberatory views regarding slavery were thus not necessarily liberatory with respect to women. Grégoire strongly opposed divorce, which was abolished in France in 1816. Duras would have understood the negative impact that such opposition had for women. Her parents were separated and her marriage was not happy; indeed, conjugal disunity affected all of the women discussed in this book, either in the case of their parents, themselves, or both. They may not have wished to openly support divorce, but they surely did not join in Grégoire's chorus of vehement opposition to it or hold naive beliefs about the success of conjugal unions.

* * *

Ourika is without question a complex and ambiguous book. The well-intentioned beneficence of which the African girl is the recipient in the aristocratic salon can be read as both sexist and racist, as paternalistic and infantilizing, as alienating and destructive. In short, fathers win while daughters and slaves lose. There are other readings, however, that refuse to see Ourika as the victim and French society as the victor. Nathanael Wing observes that Ourika leaves her mark on the salon, just as it leaves its mark on her. He argues that although she participates in French society's denial of its cultural and economic interdependence with its colonies, that denial is ambivalent, "for her presence on French soil and within the intimate space of the family affirms a persistent need to include and domesticate the ethnic other." He sees in her "a powerful social dilemma and a profound source of cultural anxiety for the society that has embraced her seemingly without condition [...] Ourika serves as a figure of an unacknowledged Otherness within that society."[35] Wing offers an important reminder in calling our attention to the ambiguities surrounding *Ourika*. When it first appeared in 1823, Louis XVIII called it an "Atala for the salon," referring to Chateaubriand's widely read novel of that name published two decades earlier. Did he mean to compliment or insult Duras? That critics have answered this question in diametrically opposed ways indicates how widely interpretations vary according to historical period, ideological outlook, and interpretive approach. As Wing suggests, "to resolve these interpretive enigmas would be to efface the ambiguity that animates such stereotypes and reassemble that splitting that Bhabha has shown to underlie the demand placed upon representations of the black by colonial discourse."[36]

One such interpretive enigma concerns the resistance that slaves and daughters are able to voice within and against the *ancien régime* society which provides the setting of the novel. In the case of Ourika, resistance exists in the very fact that she stands as the narrator of her own story. Her narrative control gives her ownership and mastery of her past life, the tragic outcome of the story notwithstanding. Unlike Staël's largely silent, suffering Ourika, undoubtedly a model for Duras's choice of name, Duras's Ourika resembles Staël's Mirza: an African woman who not only has a voice but whose voice demonstrates her intelligence and ability to master the culture of European society. Duras thus affirms the intelligence of blacks, an important abolitionist objective for Grégoire and other antislavery writers. By granting Ourika a name—a real African name which, in the Peulh language, means "I have lived"—Duras grants her a degree of personhood and individuality.[37] Duras makes other moves toward acknowledging and valorizing Ourika's African identity: organizing a dance in which Ourika plays the part of Africa, and providing books to enable her to learn, albeit through European eyes, about her country of origin.

Regarding the white women in Duras's novel—Mme de B. and the young woman who becomes her daughter-in-law, Anaïs de Thémines—the matter of resistance is enigmatic: but, as Wing is quoted above as saying, the ambiguity that marks the text is essential to its meaning and needs to be preserved. On the one hand there is the power exercised by Mme de B. As the bearer of the family fortune, and as a strong, intelligent woman, Mme de B. possesses the considerable authority that eighteenth-century women held under the *ancien régime*. She is a mother: we learn that she had a daughter who died at a young age, leaving behind two sons. But her daughter's death, like the events of the French Revolution that form the backdrop of the novel, emblematizes a loss of feminine strength, private and public, that occurs over the course of the novel, as it did in the passage from the eighteenth to the nineteenth century. By the end, it is Charles, the grandson, who is ready to take over the reins of the family. He rescues Anaïs, an orphan, whose family went to the scaffold leaving only an elderly aunt who is approaching death. As feminist historians have convincingly demonstrated, the French Revolution considerably diminished women's role in the public sphere. And although by the time of the Restoration, when *Ourika* was written, salons led by women such as Duras flourished again, they were no more the same as before the revolution than were the restored monarchical and religious institutions. After the beheading of the king, French society, like Mme de B.'s family, was fatherless; Charles and his son will assume the paternal function, but not as they would have under the *ancien régime*.

A case can also be made for the resistant powers of a daughter like Ourika who escapes the chains, not only of slavery, but of marriage and thus submission to the authority of a husband.[38] Beneath the surface of *Ourika*, one could argue, lies a critique of the condition in society that affected Duras and her daughter Félicie: a fate that her slave protagonist escapes. As Michelle Chilcoat states,

> Duras's ambivalence regarding Félicie's marriage and marriage in general stayed with her throughout her life, as evidenced by her personal correspondence and, most powerfully, her novel *Ourika* [...] Duras's writings suggest that this 'natural' institution is the cause of woman's dis-ease in the confining and oppressive cultures of Revolutionary and Restoration France.[39]

We need not take at face value Ourika's dream of marriage and motherhood in Africa: "j'aurais un compagnon de ma vie, et des enfants de ma couleur, qui m'appelleraient: Ma mère! Ils appuieraient sans dégoût leur petite bouche sur mon front; ils reposeraient leur tête sur mon cou, et s'endormiraient dans mes bras!" (312) ("I would have had a companion to share my life and children of my color who would have called me 'Mother!' They would press their little lips on my forehead without disgust; they would rest their head on my shoulder, and they would fall asleep in my arms!") (212–13) As Wing has pointed out, that statement needs to be placed in the narrative arc of the character's growing desperation and possibly viewed as an "ironic repetition of a perversely self-serving colonialist stereotype." The author may well have considered motherhood to be fulfilling and empowering for women. But to the extent that motherhood was coterminous with marriage at the time, Duras undoubtedly also saw the limitations of women's prescribed domestic role. Upon this reading, *Ourika* functions as resisting the diminution of women's powers in postrevolutionary France and as "contributing to the efforts of women during the Restoration to regain the intellectual and social power and status enjoyed during the Enlightenment."[40]

* * *

A comparison between the author of *Ourika* and another aristocratic woman—Henriette de La Tour du Pin, author of *Journal d'une femme de cinquante ans*—illuminates Duras's attitude toward the black woman she depicted. On the surface, the two white women seem very similar. Both were daughters of aristocratic fathers who died on the scaffold. Both fled to the northern United States at a time of political upheaval and threats of economic and physical peril to themselves and their families. The two women knew each other and traveled in similar social circles. Like Guy-Armand Kersaint, La Tour du Pin's father, Arthur Dillon, had extensive familiarity with the colonies: he was governor of Saint-Christophe, deputy from Martinique, and governor of Tobago. La Tour du Pin and her husband were friends of Staël and shared the liberal views of the Staël and Necker families, La Fayette, Beauvau, and other enlightened members of the French social and political elite.

Did the two women share similar attitudes toward slavery? On the surface, La Tour du Pin would seem to be less sympathetic to blacks than Duras. Consider for example what she had to say about her slave Judith's physical appearance: "Judith avait trente-quatre ans et était excessivement laide, ce qui n'empêchait pas son mari d'en être fou" ("Judith was thirty-four and very ugly, but that did not prevent her husband being madly attached to her.")[41] One might take this comment at face value (perhaps the black woman was ugly) were it not for a related remark in La Tour du Pin's correspondence with la comtesse de la Rochejaquelein, Duras's daughter Félicie, concerning the African girl who served as the model for Ourika. La Tour du Pin reveals in a letter that when she was in the salon of Mme de Beauvau, who raised Ourika under the circumstances described in Duras's novel, "Mme de Beauvau ne se lassait pas de voir les bras noirs de cette petite autour de mon col; cela m'ennuyait à mort" (387) ("Mme de Beauvau couldn't get enough of seeing the black arms of this child wrapped around my neck; that bored me to tears.")[42] Did the physical presence of black women repulse Henriette de La Tour du Pin? Was she perhaps not only a slave owner but a racist as well?

Whatever the answers to such questions may be, *Journal d'une femme de cinquante ans* shows much of the same empathetic response to slaves found in the writings of Duras and the other women writers discussed in this book. In chapter 18 she describes how she came to acquire several slaves, including Judith, her husband, and their three-month-old daughter. (202–03) She chooses to purchase members of the same family, thereby performing an act that fulfilled one of the chief goals of the antislavery movement, preserving the integrity of the black family. The success of her action suggests to her that other slave owners would do well to pursue that same goal:

C'est ainsi que notre ménage noir se trouva formé. Nous eûmes véritablement beaucoup de bonheur. La femme comme l'homme étaient d'excellents sujets, actifs, laborieux, intelligents. Ils s'attachèrent à nous avec passion, parce que les nègres, quand ils sont bons, ne le sont pas à demi. On pourrait compter sur leur dévouement jusqu'à la mort. (205)

(And that is how our black household was formed. We were indeed extremely fortunate. The woman and her husband were both excellent servants: active, hard-working and intelligent. They were passionately devoted to us, because when blacks are good it is not by halves. You can count on their devotion to death itself.) (205)

La Tour du Pin also places great emphasis on American policies for ending or ameliorating the effects of slavery. She observes,

> un usage s'était établi auquel aucun maître n'aurait osé soustraire, sous peine d'encourir l'animadversion publique. Lorsqu'un nègre était mécontent de sa situation, il allait chez le juge de paix et adressait à son maître une prière officielle de le vendre. Celui-ci, conformément à la coutume, était tenu de lui permettre de chercher un maître qui consentît à la payer tant. (202)

> (a practice had been established that all masters felt obliged to respect for fear of incurring public blame. When blacks were unhappy with their situation, they went to a justice of the peace and addressed a formal request to be sold by their master who, according to the custom at the time, was expected to allow them to look for an owner that would pay a specified amount.) (251)

It is in such a manner that Judith and other slaves, having been abused and having heard of her kind treatment of workers, came to request that she purchase them. Unlike the slaves who are returned to their cruel master in *Paul et Virginie*, La Tour du Pin's slaves are able to benefit from the empathetic response of a new benevolent mistress.

In 1796, when the La Tour du Pin family returns to France, the author of *Journal d'une femme de cinquante ans* records a touching tableau of white and black mutual affection. The emotion experienced by the slaves intensifies when La Tour du Pin informs them that they are to receive their freedom.

> "Nous avons été si heureux avec vous qu'il est juste que vous soyez récompensés. Mon mari m'a chargée de vous dire qu'il vous donne la liberté." En entendant ce mot, nos braves serviteurs furent si stupéfaits qu'ils restèrent quelques secondes sans parole. Puis, se précipitant tous les quatre à genoux à mes pieds, ils s'écrièrent: "Is it possible? Do you mean that we are free?" Je répondis: "Yes, upon my honour, from this moment, as free as I am myself." (232)

> ("We have been so happy with you that it is only fair that you be compensated. My husband has authorized me to say to you that he grants you your freedom." Hearing these words, our worthy servants were so stupefied that they remained speechless for several moments. Then, all four knelt at my feet, crying: "Is it possible? Do you mean that we are

free?" I answered: "Yes, upon my honour, from this moment, as free as I am myself.") (282–83)[43]

The edifying spirit of this scene is striking. La Tour du Pin acknowledges how much whites owe to blacks for their labor and recognizes their identity as real persons, not just slaves. Their actual words are provided in English, a language that their mistress also employs in responding to them. It is thus apparent that actual communication exists between the black and white actors in this scene. The phrase "as free as I am" indicates the common condition of the black slave and white woman, who must receive authorization from her husband to dispose of his property. Like the slave, she exists within a system in which freedom is relative, not absolute.

Ultimately daughters and slaves engage in forms of resistance for Duras and La Tour du Pin, differences between their depictions of black women notwithstanding. Ourika has a voice and has an impact on *ancien régime* society. Judith is heard on only few occasions; but when she speaks, as in the assertion of her right to change owners, she resists in a meaningful and effective way. Ourika is wholly dependent on decisions made for her by benevolent whites about her rescue from slavery, her education in France, the inappropriateness of marrying beneath her station, her inability to integrate fully as an adult into French society. Judith, in contrast, exercises agency from within black slave culture. For the unhappily married Duras, marriage was the problem; for the happily wedded La Tour du Pin, it is presented as the solution, for herself as well as Judith. What matters in the final analysis is that both writers, Duras and La Tour du Pin, were empathetic women who called into question the injustice, the abuses, and the oppression to which women, black and white, were subjected in their time.

* * *

How should we evaluate the attempts of nineteenth-century white women to give voice to black women? Francophone writers provide a needed corrective to the tendency to overvalue the acts and attitudes of benevolent fathers and empathetic daughters from the past. Speaking of the French abolitionist Victor Schoelcher, whose name is celebrated throughout the French Caribbean, Patrick Chamoiseau says: "Schoelcher was as admirable and formidable as the maroons or unknown black rebels; but only Schoelcher has been remembered and exalted."[44] The same is true for the black women discussed in this chapter. *Journal d'une femme de cinquante ans* went through sixteen editions in a few years when it appeared in 1906, but only Henriette, not Judith, received attention. When contemporary Francophone writers complain about white authors eclipsing the black subjects who appear in their works, one of their favorite targets is *Ourika*

An example occurs in Aimé Césaire's *La Tragédie du roi Christophe*. The context is a salon setting that pits the opinions of frivolous black society women against the sober male voice of reason emanating from Christophe's secretary, Vastey. In response to the women's enthusiasm for *Ourika*, the latest craze from Paris, and their earlier criticism of Christophe's excesses, Vastey responds that Christophe acts "pour que désormais il n'y ait plus de par le monde une jeune fille noire qui ait honte de sa peau et trouve dans sa couleur un obstacle à la réalisation des voeux de son coeur" ("for the day when no little black girl, anywhere in the world, will be ashamed of her skin, when no little black girl's color will stand in the way of her dreams.")[45] On one level, by placing Christophe center stage, Césaire does what Chamoiseau recommends: he calls attention to black rather than white abolitionists. On another level, however, the discussion of *Ourika* constitutes a masculinist act of diminishing the reputation of a woman writer. For, as it turns out, it is not Duras's work at all that Césaire places under discussion. Instead, the lyrics to a poetic version of the novel by Ulric Guttinguer are presented in the text. This version retains little of the critical spirit of the novel and thus misrepresents its antislavery significance. Césaire also implicitly lessens the value of *Ourika* by presenting it as salon fare for unthinking women. He thereby pits the reasoned male voice of Vastey against that of the sentimental female writer Duras.[46]

Daniel Maximin's *L'Isolé soleil*, which was discussed in the Introduction, displays a different, more equivocal response to *Ourika* in "Jonathan's Notebook."

> Tandis que les livres de Paris nous apprenaient que la Négresse Ourika pleurait sur notre férocité, et qu'elle faisait rire les salons des colons par son affliction d'appartenir à une race de proscrits, de barbares et d'assassins, notre révolte s'étendait en douce, car nous étions les maîtres de la forêt et de la mort, avec la complicité de la terre, de l'eau et du feu.

> (While we read in the books from Paris how Ourika the Negress cried over our ferocity and made the colonists in their salons laugh at her affliction of belonging to a race of outlaws, barbarians, and murderers, our revolt spread quietly, with the complicity of land, water, and fire, because we were the masters of the forest and death.)[47]

Duras is indirectly blamed here for complicity with colonists and for taking the subject of slave revolts lightly and uncritically. Her Eurocentric, feminine literature is opposed to the Afrocentric, male action of bringing about an end to oppression. Jonathan's rejection of *Ourika* undoubtedly also stems from its promotion of the myth of the "grateful negro" that he abhors.

Maximin fully realizes that the divide between white and black voices is far from absolute. *L'Isolé soleil* suggests that Caribbean culture is "always already contaminated" by the works of nineteenth-century writers like Duras. Hence, while paying respectful attention to texts like *Ourika*, it rewrites them, at times with a parodic or sarcastic tone. In a revealing scene, the poet Léonard, considered the first French Caribbean writer for his *Lettre sur un voyage aux Antilles*, is depicted encountering a black rebel girl, whose name, Anaïs, recalls Charles's white fiancée in Duras's novel. Her "authentic" song inspires him. But of course there is no true authenticity for Maximin; and thus we recognize in the final line of her song the well-known poem "L'Isolement" by the romantic poet and abolitionist Lamartine.[48] An additional allusion occurs when Léonard offers to return Anaïs to her master, who, without the white man's intervention, would undoubtedly have inflicted on her the punishment of having her right leg crippled. The allusion to *Paul et Virginie* here is obvious. Maximin's presentation of Duras, Léonard, Lamartine, and Bernardin serves to highlight the complexities of cultural filiation and the impossibility of separating white and black sources.

As a woman writer, Maryse Condé responds to Duras in a different and I would say more sympathetic way than her male counterparts. Her response can be found in two different works and in two different forms. The first is a comment made in a text promoting the importance of French Caribbean women writers, *La Parole des femmes*. There Condé makes the following remark about the author of *Ourika*:

> Si l'on doit admirer Mme de Duras qui, en un temps où certains déclaraient que les Nègres ne valaient guère mieux que des bêtes, prend ouvertement leur défense, nous ne devons pas moins souligner les limites d'une pensée étroitement européocentriste—qui est aussi celle de Schoelcher et des abolitionnistes. Le nègre n'a ni vertus ni valeurs personnelles. Il doit les acquérir, c'est-à-dire mourir à lui-même afin d'avoir accès à la "civilisation de l'universel" définie par l'Europe. En réalité, la beauté intérieure d'Ourika n'est que mutilation.[49]

> (While we have to admire Mme de Duras for having openly risen to the defense of blacks at a time when some writers proclaimed that they had little more value than animals, we also have to underline the limitations of a narrowly Eurocentric outlook—which was shared by Schoelcher and other abolitionists. The negro had no virtues or personal value. He had to acquire them, that is, to die as himself in order to acquire the "universal civilization" defined by Europe. In reality, Ourika's interior beauty is a mutilation.)

It is important to acknowledge Condé's willingness to do more than dismiss or denigrate Duras as well as her reminder that, as a woman, she was no different or worse than men who are venerated such as Schoelcher. Whereas Césaire opposes frivolous salon women to serious thinkers like Vastey, and Maximin's Jonathan contrasts Ourika as a salon pet to efficacious black rebels, Condé takes Duras seriously enough to evaluate her strengths and limitations.

A far different response to Duras can be found in Condé's novel *La Migration des coeurs*. That work, a rewriting of Emily Brontë's *Wuthering Heights*, can be placed in the context of efforts by Caribbean women writers to re-evaluate and refashion the depiction of colonial women by canonized Western women writers. In transforming the white Cathy from Britain into a mulatto Cathy from Guadeloupe, Condé returns to the example of *Ourika*. Since Cathy suffers from feelings of alienation, what better model to evoke and problematize those feelings than Duras's heroine? It is in this spirit that Condé reprises the very words that Duras used in *Ourika*:

> lorsque je réfléchis à sa position, je la vois sans remède. Je la vois seule, pour toujours seule dans l'existence. Quel garçon de qualité voudra jamais se marier avec elle? [...] elle ne pourra même pas trouver un type de condition inférieure pour la faire madame. Elle ne peut vouloir que ceux qui ne voudraient pas d'elle

> (when I think about it, I see her situation as hopeless. I see her alone, forever alone in life. What boy of her class would ever want to marry her? [...] she'd never find anybody even in the lower classes to make her his wife. She can only desire those who will never want her.[50])

Differences in masculine and feminine perspectives concerning Duras and women writers like Condé are surprisingly enduring.[51] Regarding the similarities that exist between *Ourika* and *La Migration des coeurs*, Roger Little wants to make a case for plagiarism. Little contrasts Condé with the Cameroonian woman author Calixthe Beyala, who was convicted of a crime of plagiarism for similar copying. Condé is more culpable, to Little's mind, because she was schooled in Guadeloupe, where Western standards of literary practice prevail, as opposed to Africa, where repetition through oral tradition is commonplace.[52] One can contrast Little's evaluation with Mireille Rosello's more sympathetic interpretation:

> I am not even going to ask myself whether it would be judicious to seriously raise the serious question of a serious case of plagarism. Given the kind of novels that we are dealing with, such a concept would be theoretically inept: for to imagine a subject capable of asking, in good

faith, whether repetitions, echoes, resemblances cast a shadow of doubt, that subject would have to already be positioned in a particular way in relation to concepts of identity (of works, of the text) and origin.[53]

Rosello rightly understands that Condé's revoicing of a small but recognizable number of Duras's words in a new, Caribbean context engages in a meaningful dialogue between a nineteenth-century white woman from metropolitan France and a twentieth-century black writer from the French overseas departments. Neither adversarial nor congratulatory, this intertextual trace reaffirms Condé's premise in *La Parole des femmes* that filiations exist among women writers. One recalls Hélène Cixous's concept of the "propre" discussed earlier and Cixous's view that to claim what belongs to oneself as an individual is part of the masculine ethic that undergirds both propriety and property. Far different feminine concepts of identity and origin define women's lives and writings. Rather than rejecting or dismissing white writers from the past who chose to speak empathetically about blacks, women such as Condé can see the ties that bind white and black women writers along with the substantial distance in time, place, and ideology that divides them.

Notes

1 Armand Guy Kersaint, *Moyens proposés à l'assemblé nationale pour rétablir la paix et l'ordre dans les colonies* and *Suite de Moyens proposés à l'assemblé nationale pour rétablir la paix et l'ordre dans les colonies* (Paris: Imprimerie du cercle social, 1792). A note in *Suite des Moyens* written by the editor states that Kersaint's texts were written in November 1791 with no knowledge of the insurrections.

2 Heather Brady has shown that it is unlikely that Duras and her mother traveled to Martinique before or after their trip to Philadelphia as has long been assumed. Brady's argument is based on the family letters of Mme de Kersaint's sister and brother-in-law, *Une correspondance familiale au temps des troubles de Saint-Domingue: lettres du Marquis et de la Marquise de Rouvray à leur fille: Saint-Domingue-Etats-Unis (1791–1796)*; Heather Brady, "Recovering Claire de Duras's Creole Inheritance: Race and Gender in the Exile Correspondence of her Saint-Domingue Family," *L'Esprit créateur* 47, 4 (2007): 44–56. For a discussion of Duras's trip, see also Miller, *French Atlantic Triangle*, 160–61. In *Translating Slavery: Gender and Race in French Women's Writing* I followed the traditional assumption dating back to Sainte-Beuve that Duras did travel to Martinque.

3 Gabriel Pailhès, *La duchesse de Duras et Chateaubriand d'après des documents inédits* (Paris: Perrin, 1910), 33.

4 Michèle Bissière, "Union et disunion avec le père dans *Ourika* et *Edouard* de Claire de Duras," *Nineteenth-Century French Studies* 23, 3–4 (1995): 42–58.

5 Christopher Miller makes too much, to my mind, of the fact that Duras's family owned slaves. So did all wealthy colonial families: "The author of *Ourika* was [...] a slave trader: she had likely sold (or had others sell) human beings as chattel."

"Duras, Biography, and Slavery," in *Approaches to Teaching Duras's Ourika*, ed. Mary Ellen Birkett and Christopher Rivers (New York: MLA, 2008), 53.

6 bell hooks, *Talking Back* (Cambridge: South End Press, 1988), 5, 8, 9.

7 Parts of the comparison between La Tour du Pin and Duras as well as the analysis of *Ourika* appear in my article "Black Faces, White Voices in Women's Writing from the 1820s," in Birkett and Rivers, eds, *Approaches to Teaching Duras's Ourika*, 93–104. Other sections of this chapter appeared in modified form in "Rewriting Women's Stories: *Ourika* and *The French Lieutenant's Woman*," *South Atlantic Review* 62, 2 (1997): 74–87.

8 The MLA volume *Approaches to Teaching Duras's Ourika* places the novel in a useful, broad array of contexts. See also Doris Y. Kadish and Françoise Massardier-Kenney, eds, *Translating Slavery, vol. 2: Ourika's Progeny* (Kent: Kent State University Press, 2010).

9 Kersaint, *Moyens proposés à l'assemblé nationale*, 33 and *Suite des moyens*, 3.

10 *Suite*, 31. The editor of Kersaint's texts interjects that although matters may be different in the Windward Islands, in Saint-Domingue no more than one out 10,000 slaves can read. The editor, who identifies himself as "Reimond," may be the free person of color Jules Raimond, a planter and author, who tried to gain admission to the Constituent Assembly in the 1790s.

11 A father could lock up his children for not marrying the person chosen by the family; James F. Traer, *Marriage and the Family in Eighteenth-Century France* (Ithaca, NY: Cornell University Press, 1980), 41.

12 Pratima Prasad, *Colonialism, Race, and the French Romantic Imagination* (New York: Routledge, 2009), 116–17, 109. Prasad also notes that Ourika could not meet citizenship requirements for persons of color since they were confined to the daughters of freed blacks or membership in the class of gens de couleur.

13 Kale, *French Salons*, 139.

14 Pailhès, *La duchesse de Duras et Chateaubriand*, 314.

15 Claire de Duras, *Ourika*, trans. John Fowles (Austin: W.T. Taylor, 1977), 56–57.

16 Kadish and Massardier-Kenney, eds, *Translating Slavery: Gender and Race in French Women's Writing*, 294–95, 195–96. All page references are to this edition of *Translating Slavery* which contains the original French version and its translation into English. I have made certain minor modifications to the translation.

17 Christine De Vinne speaks of a "far-reaching feminization [...] a spike in membership for women's congregations, a plummet in male religious practice" after the French Revolution: "Religion under Revolution in *Ourika*," in Birkett and Rivers, eds, *Approaches to Teaching Duras's Ourika*, 41.

18 Julia Kristeva, "Stabat Mater," in *The Kristeva Reader*, ed. Toril Moi (New York: Columbia University Press, 1986), 160–86.

19 Chantal Bertrand-Jennings, "Problématique d'un sujet féminin en régime patriarcal: *Ourika* de Mme de Duras," *Nineteenth-Century French Studies* 23, 1–2 (1994–95): 51–52.

20 Following Gérard Genette, Susan Sniader Lanser distinguishes between voice (who speaks) and vision (who sees). She observes, "The persona who 'sees' the events of the story need not be the persona who speaks, because the narrator can cede to the perceptual sphere of a character without giving up phraseological control"; Susan Sniader Lanser, *The Narrative Act. Point of View in Prose Fiction* (Princeton: Princeton University Press, 1981), 37.

21 For an analysis of male authority exercised visually, see Thérèse De Raedt, "*Ourika* in Black and White: Textual and Visual Interplay," *Women in French Studies* 12 (2004): 45–69.

22 De Vinne, "Religion under Revolution in *Ourika*," 42.

23 Jacques Léonard, "Les Médecins et les soignants: Femmes, religion et médecine," *Annales* 5 (1977): 900.

24 Bissière, "Union et disunion," 319.

25 Chevalier de Boufflers wrote in his Journal intime on February 8, 1786, that he bought a little negress to give to the princesse de Beauvau. Roger Little identifies the date and the ship in "Le nom et les origines d'Ourika," *Revue d'histoire littéraire de la France* 98, 4 (1998): 633–37.

26 M. de Lescure, "Notice," in Claire de Duras, *Ourika* (Paris: Jouaust, 1878), xix; Thérèse De Raedt, "Representations of the Real Life Ourika," in Birkett and Rivers, eds, *Approaches to Teaching Duras's Ourika*, 61.

27 I disagree with Pratima Prasad's claim that Ourika has never been sold or owned. The text states that before le chevalier de B. rescued her, she had been captured, which indicates her insertion into the system of the slave trade, even if the details of her purchase or sale are not provided. Prasad, *Colonialism*, 45.

28 Bertrand-Jennings, "Problématique d'un sujet féminin," 45.

29 Bertrand-Jennings, "Problématique d'un sujet féminin," 46.

30 François-René de Chateaubriand, *Le Génie du christianisme*, II (Paris: Ernest Flammarion, 1948), 149–50.

31 Pierre Pluchon, *Nègres et Juifs au 18e siècle: le racisme au siècle des lumières* (Paris: Tallendier, 1984).

32 Although blacks did succeed in winning their freedom through the courts as early as the end of the seventeenth century, the concept of "free on French soil" was vitiated over the course of the eighteenth century and not fully restored until 1836. See Sue Peabody, *There are No Slaves in France: The Political Culture of Race and Slavery in the Ancien Régime* (Oxford: Oxford University Press, 1996).

33 Henri Grégoire, *De la Noblesse de la peau* (Paris: Millon, 1826), 247–48.

34 Henri Grégoire, *Considérations sur le mariage et sur le divorce adressées aux citoyens d'Haïti* (Paris: Baudouin 1823), 116, 132.

35 Nathanael Wing, *Between Genders: Narrating Difference in Early French Modernism* (Newark: University of Delaware Press, 2004), 93–94.

36 Wing, *Between Genders*, 107.

37 Little, "Le nom et les origines d'Ourika," 634–35.

38 Prasad interprets the marriage issue differently. She views the last lines of the novel, in which Ourika vows to think incessantly of Charles, as "a strong assertion of her own individual choices, and the right to her private experience of erotic love." *Colonialism*, 108.

39 Michelle Chilcoat, "Confinement, the Family Institution, and the Case of Claire de Duras's Ourika," *L'Esprit Créateur* 38, 3 (1998): 14.

40 Wing, *Between Genders*, 98, 80.

41 Henriette de La Tour du Pin, *Mémoires de la marquise de La Tour du Pin: journal d'une femme de cinquante ans, 1778–1815* (Paris: Mercure de France, 1989); *Memoirs of Madame de La Tour du Pin*, trans. Felice Harcourt (London: Century Publishing, 1985), 205, 255.

42 La Tour du Pin's correspondence, from which this quotation is drawn, does not appear in the English version of the text. This translation is my own.

43 I have been unable to find substantiation in the archival records of the state of New York that such an emancipation act occurred.

44 Patrick Chamoiseau, "De La Mémoire obscure à la mémoire consciente," in *De L'Esclavage aux réparations*, ed. Serge Chalons and Comité Devoir de mémoire (Martinique) (Paris: Karthala, 2000), 1.

45 Aimé Césaire, *La Tragédie du roi Christophe* (Paris: Présence africaine, 1970); *The Tragedy of King Christophe*, trans. Ralph Manheim (New York: Grove Press, 1969), Act 2, scene 2.

46 See Roger Little, "A Further Unacknowledged Quotation in Césaire: Echoes of *Ourika*," *French Studies Bulletin* 43 (1992): 13–16.

47 Maximin, *L'Isolé soleil*, 70–71; *Lone Sun*, 61–62.

48 "Un seul être me manque et tout est dépeuplé" ("One alone has left me and the whole world is empty.")

49 Maryse Condé, *La Parole des femmes* (Paris: L'Harmattan, 1979), 26.

50 Maryse Condé, *La Migration des coeurs* (Paris: Robert Laffont, 1995), 197; *Windward Heights*, trans. Richard Philcox (New York: Soho, 1998), 198.

51 Chris Bongie speaks in dismissive terms of Condé ("As someone who has never been wholly able to understand why my colleagues make such a fuss about Condé"), as he does of one of her most insightful feminist critics, Françoise Lionnet ("Lionnet's reading of Condé is modernist almost to the point of parody"); *Friends and Enemies*, 294, 297.

52 Roger Little, "Condé, Brontë, Duras, Beyala: Intertextuality or Plagiarism?" *French Studies Bulletin* 72 (1999): 11–15.

53 Mireille Rosello, "'Il faut comprendre quand on peut...'; L'art de désamorcer les stéréotypes chez Emile Ajar et Calixthe Beyala," in *L'Ecriture décentrée: la langue de l'Autre dans le roman contemporain*, ed. Michel Laronde (Paris: L'Harmattan, 1996), 177.

5

Uniting Black and White Families:
Sophie Doin

It is fitting to end with the example of Sophie Elisabeth Doin, née Mamy, who stands as undoubtedly the most fervent and committed abolitionist of the women considered in this book. Central to her abolitionist thought is a utopian vision of the harmonious roles of fathers, daughters, and slaves. Doin fashions a composite model—a man and a woman in some cases, a black and a white in others—which symbolizes the unity of divergent but complementary human traits. This model, which parallels and emblematizes the unity presumably achieved by France's recognition of Haiti in 1825, is the basis of Doin's abolitionism. It also provides the foundation of her views about women which, if not in the forefront of early nineteenth-century French thought about women, has significant feminist components.[1] Doin wants to believe that daughters and wives can be partners with fathers and husbands, just as she believes that whites and blacks can. These partners should work productively together, without a superior male authority. An independent woman and an active writer for over two decades of her short life—she was born in 1800 and died in 1846—Doin remained convinced of the possibility and desirability of harmonious gender and race models of justice and benevolence. Unity should provide the means through which women, like slaves, could best coexist in a society riddled with injustice and oppression. As we shall see later, Doin's vision doubles that of the important Haitian writer Juste Chanlatte in *L'Histoire de la catastrophe de Saint-Domingue*. Chanlatte's work exemplifies the harmonious relations between blacks and whites that is a central premise of Doin's abolitionist writing.

In the first part of this chapter, I refer to one of Doin's abolitionist stories, *Le Négrier*, as a springboard for understanding the personal and literary sentiments of partnership and unity found in her abolitionist writings. The second part focuses on other works: *Blanche et noir, Noire et blanc*, and *La*

Famille noire.[2] The third part of the chapter considers the painting *Serment des ancêtres* by the Guadeloupian artist Guillaume Guillon-Lethière and Chanlatte's *L'Histoire de la catastrophe de Saint-Domingue*. Both works date from the same period of the 1820s as Doin's antislavery texts. These examples illuminate through comparison and contrast Doin's constructions of fathers, daughters, and slaves.

* * *

Le Négrier contains elements that echo those found in Doin's own life. Léon, a twenty-year-old orphan seeking to make his way in the world, is convinced by a ship's captain to join forces with him and invest in the slave trade. Weak and easily influenced, Léon finds himself in the immoral situation of slave trading, from which he is unable to extricate himself. Léon and the captain visit the home of a wealthy slave trader whose daughter, Laure, deplores her father's inhumane business and has refused to marry any person connected with it. Although Léon and Laure fall in love, she resists his advances and her father's plans for them to marry. Ultimately *Le Négrier* has a happy ending. The couple are united when Laure promises to follow Léon if he will end his connection with the slave trade. Laure is indifferent to the wealth she risks losing by defying her father. When confronted with the fact that he would lose his only daughter as well as a future son-in-law whom he has come to value, Laure's father ultimately renounces his immoral trade and joins hands with his enlightened children.

Le Négrier undermines fathers and empowers daughters. Little is said about Laure's father other than that he is engaged in a business that she finds revolting and that he cares primarily about money. Problems are solved by daughters, not fathers: not only does Laure put an end to the evil existing within her own family, but she comes to the aid of a slave daughter who engages with Laure to actively help rescue the black girl's father, presented as merely a passive victim of slavery. Unlike Bernardin's ineffectual Virginie, Laure is an active force in helping to rescue slaves from oppression. Although the marriage at the end of the story is a partnership, Laure is the one who guides her father to accept it. She assumes power in educating him and in refusing to marry prospective husbands associated with the slave trade. Moreover, she is the dominant one in her relationship with Léon: "Léon obéit enfin aux ordres de sa maîtresse" ("Leon finally obeys the order of his mistress.")[3] Only in the future can one imagine Laure and Léon reclaiming the family's patronym and property. Significantly, neither the father's first nor last name is ever mentioned: he is not worthy of claiming or passing on his patronymic status. He is identified only as her father, as a rich businessman, and as an old man. Like Desbordes-Valmore at the end of *Sarah*, Doin eschews ownership or patriarchal names. The ideal couple—Léon and Laure, like Edwin and Sarah—will be better, more just stewards of colonial property than less worthy or prejudiced fathers.

Like *Le Négrier*, the story of Doin's life was largely one of empowered daughters resisting, guiding, and helping ineffectual male family members. Doin's story is based on three short autobiographical texts published shortly before her death: *Simple Mémoire* and its preface, *Avis au Public*, both published in 1842; and *Un Cri de mère*, which appeared in 1843. They relate how Doin was stripped of control of her money, property, and young son by an unjust legal system and by members of her family, including her husband, the abolitionist Guillaume Tell Doin. How accurate is the story she tells? It probably cannot be taken at face value; the "contamination between reality and literary fiction" that Henri Rossi identifies as widespread in postrevolutionary women's writing may well apply to Doin.[4] Such is the opinion of members of her family, according to her eighth-generation descendant, Marc Doin. He states that family oral tradition describes Sophie as "very romantic" and as having acted like a spoiled child. Her children took their father's side in the dispute betweeen the spouses.[5]

Like Laure in *Le Négrier*, Sophie Doin was the unhappy only child of a wealthy man. Christophe Mamy is presented as owing his success to a partnership with a woman. *Simple Mémoire* opens with the sentence "Mon père a fait sa fortune par son talent et son industrie" ("My father acquired his fortune through his talent and hard work.")[6] Interestingly, however, Doin proceeds to highlight less M. Mamy's success than the fact that it was due to the efforts of her maternal grandmother, Sophie Jublin (née Gillet), the daughter of the celebrated sculptor Nicolas-François Gillet.[7] Along with her sister Elisabeth, Sophie Gillet was admitted to study at the Academy of Art in Russia, became the Imperial Majesty's music instructor, and painted portraits that were singled out to be hung in the imperial chapel. After M. Gillet decided to return to France in 1778, Sophie Gillet remained in Russia where she built a successful business that produced costly silk and embroidered fabrics for the court. When a penniless sixteen-year-old painter appeared on her doorstep, she took him in and trained him as an associate. This young man was Doin's father. *Simple Mémoire* credits him with "de l'intelligence, de l'originalité, du génie" ("intelligence, originality, genius.") But Doin emphasizes that whatever he subsequently became in life he owed to a woman: "Excepté la peinture, mon père ne savait rien. Ma grand'mère dirigea ses études et lui prodigua toute l'instruction qui était compatible avec les exigences d'une industrie active" ("Except for painting, my father knew nothing. My grandmother took charge of his education and provided him with all that he needed to know to engage in a flourishing business.") Mme Jublin is thus the original source of the "fortune" that Doin

Figure 5. *Portrait de Sophie Doin* from Doin family archives.
Photo courtesy of Marc Doin.

attributes to her father in the first sentence of *Simple Mémoire*. When Mme Jublin eventually returned to France she left Mamy in charge, making a settlement with him for her portion of the worth of the business, which he subsequently expanded. Mme Jublin and M. Mamy form the first of many ideal or idealized female and male associations that function successfully, at least for a time, in Doin's life and her fiction.

Like Laure, daughters in Doin's world suffer from a lack of affection from masculine figures within the family. In her own case, she complains that her father was cold during her adolescent years, despite his attentions to her as a young child, and that he disregarded her financial interests later in life. She married at the young age of 20, she claims, to have someone to love, "à la place de mon père qui ne m'aimât pas" ("to take the place of my father who didn't love me.") She similarly presents other women in her family as deprived of emotional support. Her grandmother's husband, M. Jublin, "n'était pas un bon mari. Il n'était pas amoureux de sa femme […] il n'était pas son protecteur, il n'était pas son appui […] Malheureux tous deux, au bout de deux ans, leurs relations n'étaient plus que celles d'amis bien froids" ("he wasn't a good husband. He didn't love his wife […] he wasn't her protector, he wasn't her support […] After two years, the relationship between the unhappy spouses resembled that between two distant friends.") We also learn that Mme Mamy did not love her husband: "Ma mère n'aimait pas mon père" ("My mother didn't love my father.") Nor did Mme Jublin apparently care any longer for her former associate by the time of her daughter's death, when she was called upon to help look after her grand-daughter: "elle venait chez mon père, quoiqu'elle ne l'aimait pas" ("she came to my father's home although she didn't like him.")

Sophie Doin blames fathers per se less than traditional marriages in which the absence of love, and the preponderant concerns of money, prevent the couple from forming the effective and rewarding partnership that Laure and Léon presumably achieve at the end of *Le Négrier* and that other couples in Doin's fiction also enjoy. What she observed in her own family and her own life was that when marriage becomes entangled with concerns for money, property, and social position, as was the case with Laure's father, unhappy consequences can result for both men and women. Doin's father was not to blame for the feelings of antipathy that he inspired since "malheureusement les pauvres humains ne sont maîtres de rien, pas même de leur coeur" ("unfortunately poor humans are not masters of anything, not even their hearts.") Similarly she pities rather than blames her grandparents who were mismatched and consequently endured loneliness and alienation, the antithesis of the harmonious union that should exist between a man and woman in marriage. Doin's mother, we are told, was "sacrifiée à la fortune" ("sacrificed for money.") Like a slave of sorts, she was sold. Christophe

Mamy saw Mme Jublin's daughter grow up and eventually succeeded in gaining the young woman's hand in marriage. It is hard to believe that Mme Jublin desired this marriage since, as noted earlier, she came to dislike her business partner and future son-in-law. It seems plausible that, since fathers made the choice concerning appropriate marriage partners, it was M. Jublin who favored the marriage. Such a marriage would have had the financial advantage of keeping within the family the rest of the fortune generated by the business that Mme Jublin started in Russia and that M. Mamy successfully developed in the two years after her departure.

Ultimately Sophie Doin aspired to and remained resolutely committed to the kind of marriage that she depicts in *Le Négrier* and her other fictional works. Her sad story reveals that it was not meant to be. For some years, her marriage to Guillaume Tell appears to have been egalitarian and to have conformed to the model of shared authority and the union of different conditions or abilities that she promotes in her writings. Guillaume Tell and Sophie were committed to the same causes, most notably abolitionism. He assumed a public role largely inaccessible to women at the time. He belonged to the Société de la morale chrétienne, the chief abolitionist and benevolent society of the time.[8] Through the Société he had access to influential people and reading materials. He debated political and philosophical ideas in a public forum, writing about religious and philosophical topics. She pursued literary and humanitarian projects, undoubtedly financed by her inheritance. Although that inheritance would have been legally under her husband's control as the titular head of the household, he presumably granted her a considerable degree of independence. He had no objection to her signing contracts or, like other women discussed in this book, using his patronym on the cover of her books, a privilege that was often denied to women writers.[9] Her conception of her role was to put abolitionist ideas into literary forms that were accessible to average people. In the Preface to *La Famille noire* she notes the importance of popularizing awareness of the condition of enslaved Africans: "aucun ouvrage encore n'a fait connaître, à la masse de la nation, la véritable position des nègres; je le fais ici [...] sous cette forme légère, la vérité percera dans toutes les classes" ("no work has yet acquainted the whole nation with the true position of blacks; I do so here [...] through this light form, the truth will be apparent to all classes.")[10]

Even when her marriage deteriorated, Doin retained her belief in the union of man and woman and viewed her husband as the victim of the maleficent legal and financial advisors surrounding him.[11] True, she blames him for wasting money for years, dissipating her inheritance, and failing to take pity on her at the end when she was ill and even, according to her, starving and without the most basic necessities of life. But she persists in seeing him, as she did when she first married him, as a victim—of poor health, unfortunate circumstances, bad influences, and more—rather than as a perpetrator of injustice. Indeed, she describes her feelings at the time of their first separation in the 1830s as maternal: "Incapable de ressentiment, je me tournai vers ce pauvre homme avec toute ma sollicitude maternelle, et je sentis que s'il n'était plus mon mari, j'étais encore sa mère!" ("Incapable of resentment, I turned to this poor man with maternal solicitude, and I felt that if he was no longer my husband, I was still his mother!") Clearly she felt endowed with a special sense of love, maternity, and compassion—"cette corde qui devait vibrer" ("that nerve that quivers within us")—for all those, including her husband and slaves, whom she considered unfortunate and in need of her help.

Marriage thus remains an ideal and idealized construct in Doin's belief system, the failure of her own union notwithstanding. Her anger was directed not at Guillaume Tell but at males who exercised the privileges afforded to them under the Code Civil to strip her of her fortune, specifically her son-in-law M. Hugonet, the husband of her daughter Sophie Aline.[12] As with Doin's mother, this marriage was presumably authorized by a father, in this case Guillaume Tell, who would have had the power to override his wife's antipathy toward the prospective husband. As James Traer observes, what was lost from the French revolutionary period in the Code Civil was equality within marriage. "Almost every article concerned with family relationships reinforced the authority of the husband and father." Witnesses to marriage had to be male, and a wife had to live in the place designated by the husband.[13] Doin describes M. Hugonet in *Simple Mémoire* as a wily, unscrupulous lawyer who, in league with his wife and father-in-law, employed every means to gain control of her money and property in the final years of her life. As a woman Doin found herself with few means to thwart their plans. But in her autobiographical works she did exercise one of the options that Saint-Simoniennes encouraged women to elect: telling all, sullying the patronymic name, and pointing the finger at specific members of the male social network who exercised power over them.[14]

Only in Doin's last published work, *Un Cri de mère*, does she appear to have lost faith in the harmonious ideals promoted elsewhere in her writing. It is not only that she finally accedes to the demands placed on her by her family to relinquish all property rights from her inherited fortune. Like Laure in *Le Négrier*, possession never seems to have really mattered to Doin; in this sense, she prefigures modern feminists like Hélène Cixous who, as noted elsewhere in this book, denounces the values of property and profit as phallocentric and antithetical to a feminine ethical outlook. Rather, the loss of her eleven-year-old son appears to have broken Doin's spirit. That she was denied custody is not surprising; fathers alone had authority over children under the Code Civil.[15] And although Doin still does not directly connect her plight to women's loss of the freedoms they had gained during the French revolutionary period, as more militant women writers did, there is a distinctly feminist ring to the closing plea of *Un Cri de mère:* "Portez cet écrit au procureur du roi… il vous écoutera, car vous êtes un homme… moi, je suis une femme… et j'ai peur… Cependant, je veux mon fils… Oh! je veux mon fils!!!" ("Bring my words to the king's prosecutor… he will listen to you because you are a man… I am a woman… and I am afraid… But I want my son… Oh! I want my son!!!") Similar plaintive addresses to royal powers can be found in writings by slaves: for example, a letter written by a woman named Marie and addressed to the queen in 1846.[16] Although less overt in comparing women and slaves than feminist writers of the 1830s, Doin knew about the similarities between the two groups through the painful experiences of her own life.

* * *

Doin's antislavery works can be grouped into two categories. In the first are two short stories—*Le Négrier*, discussed above, and *Blanche et noir*—which highlight the agency of daughters in relation to fathers and slavery. It is through the intervention of daughters in these stories that the benevolence, tolerance, and harmony that Doin proposes as solutions to colonial problems are achieved. In the second category, which includes the short story *Noire et blanc* and the novel *La Famille noire*, the dyadic combination of father and daughter is less directly apparent. These works, in which events in Haiti play a prominent role, focus primarily on ways of promoting harmony between whites and blacks. The agency of women is not absent or insignificant, however. Indeed, Doin assigns to them an elevated moral mission within the family, which serves in these and her other antislavery writings as a microcosm of society at large.

Like *Le Négrier, Blanche et noir* undermines fathers and empowers daughters.[17] Pauline de Hauteville, of lofty birth as her name suggests, is raised in the colonies by a compassionate mother and a haughty, prejudiced father. Her mother takes pity on a young black orphan, Domingo, who grows up with Pauline and receives the same education as she does, much as Sarah and Edwin are raised together in *Sarah*. Despite his enslaved condition, Domingo loves Pauline. However, as signs of approaching revolution loom, Pauline's father, a rich plantation owner and slave master, arranges her marriage to a Frenchman, whom she respects but does not love. Domingo commits himself to the cause of freedom spreading throughout the island. He decides to flee, promising Pauline on the night of his departure to protect her and those she loves from the fury of the rebels. At a point in the ensuing battles, Domingo comes to the rescue of Pauline's father who is defending the property of the plantation owners and faces certain death. He expresses his thankfulness to Domingo on his deathbed: "tu méritais d'être blanc" ("you deserved to be white.") Pauline's expression of gratitude is even greater. She chooses a mixed-race relationship in a solitary forest retreat in Haiti with Domingo as her husband, in a manner reminiscent of Bernardin's mixed-class couple in *La Chaumière indienne*.[18] There, years later, her black neighbors, who admire the couple's happiness and devotion to one another, ironically echo her father's words when they observe that "elle méritait d'être noire" ("she deserved to be black.")[19]

The emphasis *Blanche et noir* places on women's role in antislavery is noteworthy. Daughters enlighten bad fathers. Men and women have complementary roles to play in solving colonial problems, including slavery. Pauline's mother educates the black child Domingo, whose later accomplishments depend in part on her, as M. Mamy's did on Doin's grandmother. Pauline plays the exemplary moral role of rising above common prejudices of color in choosing Domingo as her husband. Her moral authority can be appreciated through comparison with Bernardin's Virginie. Pauline's name recalls that of Virginie's beloved Paul, and the slave Domingue in Bernardin's novel reappears as Domingo in Doin's work. Salient differences can be noted, however. In contrast with Paul and Virginie, who attempt, ineffectually, to help a mistreated runaway slave, Pauline acts in a meaningful way, as did Laure, to combat prejudice and racism. Also, instead of following Virginie's example and sacrificing herself to an outmoded notion of feminine virtue, Pauline asserts her will to live and to choose her partner, a black man. She thus stands as a model of the will to liberate herself, non-violently, from the racist conventions of her society, to achieve a humanity free of prejudice and based on love, and to participate in the founding of a new multiracial Haitian society.

Blanche et noir also develops the notion of authority shared between whites and blacks. Domingo exerts moral authority throughout the story, both with blacks, as a participant in their fight for freedom, and whites, as the rescuer of Pauline's father. His actions thus go against two common pro-slavery views: first, that whites were responsible for giving blacks their freedom; and, second, that all blacks were savage and cruel in their treatment of whites during the uprisings.[20] Domingo also counters the widespread misconception that blacks were incapable of intelligent thought and meaningful discourse. The opening sentence of *Blanche et noir* is significant. Its very first words evoke Haiti as a "terre de liberté" ("land of freedom.") But freedom is not a mere gift that Domingo has received. By making him an active narrative participant who helped to gain that freedom and by highlighting his voice, Doin emphasizes the political agency of her black protagonist: "je te salue; je suis homme enfin, je suis libre! O soleil, sois plus brillant désormais; que tes feux bienfaisants réchauffent nos contrées glorieuses, qu'ils les fécondent, avec l'aide de Dieu et de nos bras indépendants" ("I salute you; finally I am a free man, I am free! O sun, be more brilliant henceforth, may your salutary rays warm our glorious country, may they make it fertile, with the help of God and our independent arms.")[21] Although "the help of God" is acknowledged, it is put on an equal level with the force of "our independent arms." After this opening section of the story, Doin establishes the kind of narrative partnership characteristic of her writing, with an omniscient narrator taking over the task of telling the story of how Domingo acquired his liberation from enslavement.

We now turn to *Noire et blanc* and *La Famille noire* in which the roles of fathers and daughters are assumed by other, closely related characters. In *Noire et blanc*, a rich uncle and a dissolute husband abuse the power typically exercised by fathers and stand in the way of the marriage between a white man and the slave who rescued him. A wealthy Frenchwoman, who enables the couple to overcome the obstacles placed in their path, plays the role of the benevolent, tolerant daughter found in the other short stories.

The story of *Noire et blanc* opens with the revolutionary events in Haiti:

Des tourbillons de flamme s'élevaient au-dessus de la ville du Cap, le sang humain bouillonnait dans les rues; partout des torrents vengeurs payaient le meurtre par le meurtre, des supplices par les supplices. L'indépendance des noirs venait d'être proclamée, et des êtres dégradés, des esclaves abrutis, accouraint de toutes parts, la haine dans le coeur et le fer à la main, demander compte à des maîtres barbares de leur intelligence détruite, de leur liberté anéantie.

A whirlwind of flames rose over the city of Le Cap. Human blood foamed in the streets. Everywhere torrents of vengeance paid for murder with murder, torture with torture. The independence of blacks had just been proclaimed, and degraded creatures, brutish slaves flocked from everywhere, with hatred in their hearts and weapons in their hands, asking that barbarous masters account for having destroyed their intelligence and crushed their freedom.[22]

In the midst of this scene of disorder, Nelzi rescues her master, Charles de Méricourt, thereby setting in motion a drama about relations between blacks and whites that corresponds closely to the drama of dealings between Haiti and France in the years leading up to the recognition of Haitian independence in 1825. Like those two countries, Nelzi and Charles, who live together in exile in America, experience but do not fully realize the depth of the lasting affective and moral bonds that unite them. A turning point in their personal relationship occurs, however, that parallels the public events of 1825. Charles is summoned to return to France where his uncle's fortune awaits him, under the condition that he marry his cousin. Ultimately, however, French society proves capable of tolerance and justice. Although Charles comes close to succumbing to the class expectations placed upon him and abandoning the woman to whom he owes his life, a benevolent Frenchwoman, Mme de Senneterre, intervenes to bring the couple back together and enable a repentant Charles to see the error of his ways. Charles's public recognition of his love for Nelzi emblematizes France's public recognition of Haiti's independence and the lasting bonds of friendship, filiation, mutual interest, and loyalty that unite the two countries.

In *Noire et blanc*, Doin attributes feminine authority to black and white women alike. Nelzi is not a mere passive recipient of Charles's love and gratitude for having rescued him. Like Boyer, who became president of a united Haiti in 1820 and who is implicitly praised in *La Famille noire*, Nelzi fights to forge and cement her ties with France in the person of her beloved Charles. Moreover, like the enlightened Haiti whose development Doin envisions, Nelzi is an apt and eager student, to whom Charles is able to teach the natural sciences, arts, religion, and other subjects that will make her an equal intellectual partner in the future. Mme de Senneterre, like Laure and Pauline, is a model of tolerance and compassion. Not content to merely embody benevolent attitudes, she actively exerts her influence in order to assist a black woman and to combat social inequality and injustice. *Noire et blanc* presents two individuals of different races, each contributing to the common good of their partnership, as abolitionists envisioned Haiti and France cooperating in the future. Nelzi demonstrates the heroism of the successful Haitian Revolution in her courageous rescue of Charles, whereas he embodies the civilizing factors of education and religion that Doin sees as the positive legacy of the French colonizing mission. Together these characters form the ideal combination of daughters and slaves working together to mitigate the negative effects of patriarchy. At the close of the novel, Charles and Nelzi will presumably marry. By locating shared authority between whites and blacks within the family unit, *Noire et blanc* identifies racial equality, commitment, and loyalty as the bases of the future moral and political ties between France and Haiti.

Interracial marriage would appear to be the answer for Doin, as it was for abolitionists such as Laisné de Villevêque and Grégoire, as noted in Chapter 4.[23] But Doin was less forthright about such a solution than her fiction might suggest. Revealingly, Doin reverses the pattern of intermarriage that existed in reality: on French soil, where Nelzi and Charles presumably marry, the issue was the marriage between white women and black men; in the colonies, where Pauline chooses Domingo as her partner, it was the union (legal or illegal) of white men and black women.[24] But the prospect of actual physical union is seemingly not what matters to Doin. Although she does not explicitly rule out the possibility of mixed-race children, as Duras does in *Ourika*, she chooses not to dwell on interracial marriage as a means of bringing forward a new non-white population in the colonies or elsewhere.[25] As the titles of her short stories indicate, black and white ultimately remain distinct and separate. But the separation in no way implies hostility or indifference. Daughters and slaves come together as a form of defiance against the patriarchal control of their lives. The solution that Doin proposes for women, for blacks, and for Haiti in relation to France is justice and freedom, without the nefarious dominance of one group over the other.

La Famille noire focuses on shared agency within the "black family" from which the story draws its title. Although relations between fathers and daughters are not foregrounded as such, substitute fathers are central to the development of the story. Evil slave traders and plantation owners assume the role and abuse the privileges of paternal authority. Sons and daughters display the compassion that in other stories is attributed to daughters alone. Benevolent, tolerant, antislavery men, both black and white, combine courage and heroism with virtues typically associated with women.

La Famille noire begins with the story of Phénor, a brave and compassionate young African, who has lived through the horror of seeing his compatriots and family members enslaved. Devoted to his mother, he surrenders himself to slave traders, believing that he is sacrificing his freedom for hers. From the start Phénor, as a son, thus displays the sentimental qualities attributed elsewhere to daughters. Indifferent to Phénor's sacrifice, however, the slave traders capture and mistreat his mother, prompting Néala, a stranger who shares Phénor's compassionate nature, to offer herself in exchange for his mother's freedom. She thereby demonstrates her profound respect for the value of motherhood, as well as the sentimental commonality between daughters and sons in the novel. Although her sacrifice too is in vain, the two young Africans, now slaves, fall in love, marry, and bear a son. If Doin chooses a son rather than a daughter to bear the family's legacy and provide hope for the future, it is because of the symbolic role that he will be called upon to play in the public sphere. And if he is born to two Africans, rather than persons of different races, it is because the harmony that he will be called upon to create results from a black partnership with whites, not through a mixing of races.

The white protagonist of the story is Merville, a French abolitionist traveler. When Néala spurns her master, who has tried to seduce her, she and her son are sold and sent away, causing Phénor to fall into a mood of deep despair. Merville vows to help him recover his lost family. The two men set off in search of Néala, glimpsing from afar beautiful Haiti, which has risen above its past under slavery and achieved the respect due to a free nation. Merville explains that God has forgiven the Haitian people for the violence of the slave revolts leading up to independence in 1804 "parce que sans doute il pensa que les blancs seuls devaient être responsables d'une fureur que leurs cruautés avaient si longtemps nourrie" ("because he undoubtedly felt that the whites alone should be held accountable for a rage that their cruelty had nurtured for so long.") (62) He emphasizes the agency exercised by blacks who "trouvèrent des héros au sein de leur ignomie. Ces héros leur rendirent la force, les menèrent à la gloire et brisèrent leurs liens" ("discovered heroes in the midst of ignominy. These heroes gave them strength, led them to glory and broke their chains.") (63) He explains how they declared themselves independent and created a country where "un homme sage préside maintenant aux destinées [...] des noirs régénérés. La sagesse, les talents et le génie éclairent toutes ses volontés, et assurent la gloire et la prospérité de l'heureuse Haïti [...] Salut, terre de justice et de liberté, tu ne porteras plus d'esclaves!" ("a wise leader now presides [...] over a regenerated black people. Wisdom, talent and genius illuminate all its efforts and assure the glory and prosperity of happy Haiti [...] Greetings Haiti, land of justice and freedom, you will bear the burden of slavery no longer.") (67)[26] The two travelers ultimately discover Néala on another island where slavery still prevails. But at the very moment when she rushes forward to embrace her long-lost husband, her cruel master strikes her with a fatal blow. Heartbroken, Phénor dies of grief. Merville chooses to raise and educate Néala's and Phénor's son as his own. No longer willing to remain on the island that witnessed Néala's tragic death, Merville chooses to live in Haiti, where the boy is able to receive a rigorous and distinguished education. The seeds planted in his young mind bear fruit. Merville leaves Haiti when the boy reaches manhood and can himself assume the responsibilities of educating and leading his people.

Shared black and white authority is the main message of *La Famille noire*. A privileged authorial voice makes statements at the beginning of the novel such as the following: "Ce livre n'est pas un roman, c'est l'histoire scrupuleusement fidèle des crimes qu'ont entraînés avec eux dès leur origine, et que perpétuent de nos jours la traite et l'esclavage des noirs" ("This book is not a novel, it is the scrupulously faithful story of the crimes that the slave trade and the enslavement of blacks caused and continue to perpetuate to this day).") (5) That voice, identifiable as belonging to a white abolitionist with access to a wide range of historical and political sources, later disappears, replaced by the closely related white, abolitionist voice of Merville. But with his entry into the story, there is a shift from a monologic to a dialogic narrative structure. Merville, unlike the omniscient authorial voice in the beginning, does not himself display his command of issues relating to slavery; instead, through long discussions with Phénor, he shares his information and learns from his African interlocutor, whose direct experience bears equal if not greater weight than Merville's purely second-hand knowledge as a European. And in the future, we learn, Phénor's son will "honorer sa nouvelle patrie par ses talents, l'illustrer par son éloquence, et, dans des écrits pleins d'énergie et de vérité, éclairer le monde et consoler ses frères affligés" ("honor his new country by his talents, will illustrate it by his eloquence, and, in works filled with energy and truth, will enlighten the world and console his afflicted brothers.") (67) The white abolitionist Merville, a stand-in for Doin, thus continues the pattern of sharing authority by extending it to his black pupil. Merville may have provided for the young man's education, as abolitionists aimed at facilitating the successful future of Haiti; but when the boy comes of age, as Haiti did in 1825, whites need to bow out as a sign that they fully recognize the intellectual and political independence of blacks. At the end of *La Famille noire*, the abolitionist effort will be fought on two fronts: by Phénor's son, a black writer in Haiti, and by Merville, a white abolitionist in France. Doin's novel thus actively promotes a strong component of black authority. Significantly, the son, whose lack of a name suggests in this case the non-specific, allegorical role that he is called upon to play, is presented as an author. The future of Haiti, for Doin, must ultimately lie to a significant extent in black hands and be articulated by black voices.

The pre-eminent role of sons in *La Famille noire* reveals a fault line in Doin's conception of the agency of daughters. As noted above, sons are the ones who function in the public sphere. Ideally, in doing so, they share women's sentimental qualities and form meaningful cooperative alliances with them. But Doin knew from her own experience that reality did not always live up to such ideal expectations and that marriage was often a form of slavery for women. In the journal *Le Christianisme*, which she edited from 1836 to 1838, she wrote:

> Je sais bien que l'esclavage de la femme dans le mariage produit d'effroyables malheurs et de profondes injustices, mais ces malheurs pèsent sur les hommes aussi, moins sans doute que sur leurs compagnes, mais aussi je le répète, ce sont les femmes, dans les masses, qui ont encore le plus besoin du mariage.

> (I know very well that women's slavery in marriage produces horrific misfortunes and profound injustice; but these misfortunes befall men as well: undoubtedly less so than their partners. But again I repeat, it is the masses of women who have the most need of marriage.)[27]

Ultimately Doin defends marriage for the social and economic benefits that it gives to the majority of women, especially poor women. She admits that "en général les malheurs, les misères, les douleurs qui pèsent sur les femmes doivent être imputés aux torts intolérables des maris" ("in general, the intolerable faults committed by husbands are the cause of the unhappiness, the misery, the suffering that weighs down women.") But she claims that she is the adversary neither of marriage nor of husbands.

> Je déclare au contraire que, dans l'état actuel de la civilisation, le mariage, en dépit de ses monstrueux abus, est tout l'avantage des femmes [...] Les femmes n'ont pas par elles-mêmes, dans notre société, assez de moyens d'existence pour pouvoir se passer du mariage, si elles n'ont pas [...] une fortune indépendante; enfin les femmes pauvres, tant pour elles que pour leurs enfants, ne sauraient se passer de la protection d'un mari.

> On the contrary, I proclaim that in the current state of civilization, marriage is to women's advantage, despite its monstrous abuses [...] Women in our society do not themselves have sufficient means of existence to do without marriage, unless they have [...] an independent fortune; in short, poor women need a husband's protection, for themselves and for their children.[28]

A shift occurs from Doin's optimism of the 1820s to a more resigned view in the 1830s in which daughters are more like slaves than their defenders. The revised version of *Le Négrier*, which appears as the last item in the last issue of *Le Christianisme*, is revealing in this regard.[29] The fact that Doin chooses to end the journal with this story clearly indicates that she did not abandon the cause of antislavery in the 1830s, even when it became a less popular topic. The treatment of the daughter changes in the revised version, however. No longer does she resist marriage with a slave trader, now named Pierre Delorme. She passively accedes to her father's wishes. She is not named, nor does she play any role in modifying or mitigating the inhumane practices of her husband, who dies during the slave uprising while fighting on the side of the colonists. The narrator boldly articulates antislavery rhetoric in this revised story, but the daughter plays a diminished role.

For the most part, however, Doin continued in the 1830s to uphold the moral exemplarity and humanitarian mission of women. In the short story "Petites cruautés des gens du monde" in *Le Christianisme*, she revealingly compares the condition of women and slaves at the same time that she argues for the harmony between genders and races that is at the heart of her social worldview:

> Souvenez-vous que le Christ en émancipant les esclaves a donné la liberté aux femmes, ces nobles esclaves de toutes les sociétés humaines! Il les a émancipées non pas pour régner sur les hommes, mais pour régner avec eux; car il savait, le Christ, qu'aux femmes il est donné par le ciel une grande puissance d'intelligence et d'amour! [...] Quand les hommes

d'autrefois disaient aux femmes: nous vous adorons, vous régnez sur nous; ils les trompaient, c'était une chaîne de fleurs, en apparence, qu'ils rivaient à leur corps pour les asservir, c'était un hochet doré qu'ils tendaient à l'enfant dont ils voulaient faire un esclave; maintenant l'homme ne dira pas à la femme *je vous adore comme mon Dieu*, mais comme mon égale, comme mon frère!

(Remember that in emancipating slaves Christ gave freedom to women, those noble slaves of all human societies! He emancipated them not to reign over men but to reign with them; for Christ knew that heaven gave women a great power of intelligence and love! [...] Men deceived women when they used to say "we adore you, you reign over us"; the men's words were like a garland of flowers attached to the women's bodies in order to enslave them, a rattle that they held out to make a child into a slave. Now men will not say to women "I love you like my God," but like my equal, like my brother.)[30]

Although women's enslavement is placed in the past and set in a religious context, Doin is more willing than in her earlier writings to acknowledge the similarity between the condition of women and slaves. Moreover, she openly confronts men's deceptive discourse in seeming to put women on a pedestal while in fact seeking to make them subservient. Ultimately, however, her goal is not a divisive or separatist one. Instead, as in all of her abolitionist and other writings, she seeks to promote fraternity and harmony: between the male and female sexes and between blacks and whites.

* * *

Sophie Doin's rejection of the authority of fathers and the construction of a model of shared authority can be productively compared to that found in the works of the Guadeloupian painter Guillaume Guillon-Lethière and the Haitian writer Juste Chanlatte. In the works of both of these men, women are excluded. Unlike modern Francophone writers such as Maximin discussed elsewhere, nineteenth-century men did not acknowledge the importance of women in constructing new postcolonial societies. To some extent, then, they reinforced the patriarchal nature of those societies.[31] Both Lethière and Chanlatte shared Doin's belief in shared authority between races, however.

Shared authority is central to an understanding of Guillon-Lethière's *Serment des ancêtres* (1822, Figure 6).[32] The painting, which depicts two leaders of the Haitian Revolution and founders of the nation—the mulatto officer Alexandre Pétion and the black slave leader Jean-Jacques Dessalines—harks back to Haiti's revolutionary past. Its subject matter represents a departure

Figure 6. Guillaume Guillon-Lethière, *Serment des ancêtres* (1822).
Reproduction courtesy of Art Resource.

in Lethière's artistic career. A member of the elite class of mixed-race persons living in France, he was a successful, respected painter during the Restoration, holding prestigious appointments as director of the Academy in Rome, member of the Legion of Honor, and professor at the Ecole des Beaux-Arts. Unlike Doin, who was wealthy but marginalized by her Protestant religion and female gender, Lethière belonged to the fashionable salon culture during the Restoration in which hostile feelings about the slave uprisings in Haiti were the order of the day. Lethière clearly did not share those feelings. Drawing on his positive feelings toward Haiti's revolutionary past and his commitment to the Haitian cause, Lethière chose to paint *Oath of the Ancestors* and have it personally delivered to the Haitian people covertly by his son. He thus paid tribute to Haiti's heroic past and anticipated the Restoration government's act of recognizing Haiti's legitimacy three years later. As Darcy Grimaldo Grigsby notes,

> *Oath of the Ancestors* was therefore a surreptitious revolutionary picture made in honor of another revolution won at France's expense. In this painting Lethière aligned himself with [...] the black and mulatto men who rebelled as soldiers [...] Lethière's painting bravely refuses to repress the war—the conflict—that brought Haiti into existence.[33]

Significant limits mark Lethière's allegiance to Haiti's revolutionary past, however, which are symptomatic of his allegiance to fathers, and to racially superior fathers. Despite the Haitian audience for whom this work was destined, Lethière ultimately subordinated both the black and mulatto figures in the dark foreground of the painting to the white God who hovers over and sheds light on them.[34] As Grigsby notes,

> he thereby reinscribed the ultimate authority of the white patriarch [...] Recognition is a gift, not an accomplishment; recognition represents benevolence toward a subordinate rather than surrender to a victor. Moreover, the Haitian revolution, this picture implies, remains incomplete without the recognition of the white French father.[35]

Grigsby observes moreover that Lethière visually privileges the mulatto Pétion over the black Dessalines by indicating a diagonal line descending from God, the father, toward Pétion, not toward Dessalines. That privileging corresponds to the painter's persistent attempt to obtain legitimacy from his white father. It also reflects the glorification of Pétion that surrounded his regime following his death on March 29, 1818.

Matters are far different in the abolitionist rendering of similar dramatic scenes involving men of two races that occur in the final pages of Doin's works. At the end of *Blanche et noir*, Léopold and Domingo stand before

Pauline, presenting her with the choice between returning to France with a white man or living in Haiti with a black man. As Léopold promises to join with her "aux pieds des autels" ("at the foot of the altar"), Pauline interrupts him to announce her choice to remain in Haiti. Instead of bowing to the white, religious authority evoked in Lethière's painting, it is before his wife Pauline that Domingo bows down: "Domingo resta longtemps devant sa divinité" ("For a long time Domingo remained prostrate before his divinity.") At the end of the story, twelve years later, he is living happily with Pauline, "lorsque la république d'Haïti fut assise glorieusement sur de solides bases" ("when the republic of Haiti was gloriously established on a solid basis.")[36] The degree to which both black men and white women are empowered in this scene contrasts sharply with the privileging of the white father and his elite mulatto son in *Oath of the Ancestors*.

In *La Famille noire*, the by now familiar beach scene occurs when Merville's ship leaves Haiti. As Phénor's son kneels, with arms outstretched toward his protector, both men look upward toward the sun shining down benevolently upon them. "Mon Dieu! s'écria le noir, progégez mon père! Mon Dieu! dit Merveille, répandez vos bénédictions sur cet être régénéré! Veillez sur ses destins et sur les destins d'Haïti!" ("My God! exclaimed the black, protect my father! My God! spoke Merville, grant your benediction to this regenerated being! Watch over his destiny and the destiny of Haiti!") The last sentence of the novel—"et toi, Haïti! Ô que ta splendeur ne soit pas un brillant météore, mais un phare immortel de salut et de liberté!!!" ("And you, Haiti! may your splendor be not a brilliant meteor, but an immortal beacon of salvation and freedom!!!")—is followed by a lengthy footnote praising the Christian king who, by recognizing Haiti's independence, sanctifies the regeneration of this oppressed race of men. It ends, "Puisse sa main protectrice s'étende également sur les nègres qui souffrent encore!" ("May his protective hand stretch out equally over all blacks who still suffer!") (68) As in *Oath of the Ancestors*, two men of different races appear beneath the benevolent eye of a God whose transcendent powers parallel those possessed on earth by fathers and kings. Lethière's and Doin's works are ultimately very dissimilar, however. Lethière aspires to be recognized by and be a part of the patriarchal system he evokes. Doin, in contrast, calls into question its oppression of the downtrodden. Although she respectfully acknowledges the powers of God and the white king, she places greater emphasis on human agency, and especially the shared strength that educated black Haitians and enlightened white Europeans can derive from relationships of respect and reciprocity.

Ironically, the Lethière family history comes closer to the novelist's vision than to that of the painter. Lethière's son Lucien, who brought *Oath of the Ancestors* to Haiti in 1822, chose to define himself as a "man of color" and to remain in Haiti, where he married a Haitian woman.[37] Like Domingo and Phénor's son, Lucien Lethière, whose untimely death occurred several years after his return to Haiti, had faith in the future of the former French colony. Like Pauline he made a conscious choice to marry a Haitian and to pick an uncertain but hopeful future in Haiti over a secure but traditional life in France. And like Phénor's son, he presumably believed that his place was on Haitian, not French, soil. Those choices, whether real or fictional, are indicative of how much the kind of black agency that abolitionists sought to promote differed from the recognition passively received from white fathers that *Oath of the Ancestors* implies.

* * *

A second Haitian example is Juste Chanlatte's *L'Histoire de la catastrophe de Saint-Domingue*. Chanlatte, a mulatto poet and playwright, was educated in France and served as secretary to Dessalines, Henry Christophe, and Boyer. By adding Chanlatte to her list of authorities, Doin reconfigures mastery as deriving from sources that were both black and white, European and Haitian. Her writing thereby expresses in literary form her concept of Haiti as a locus of freedom and black empowerment.

As in many nineteenth-century works such as *Ourika*, in which a white European introduces the voice of a black, *L'Histoire de la catastrophe de Saint-Domingue* begins with the words of the French naval officer Bouvet de Cressé. He then passes on narrative responsibility to Chanlatte. Why Bouvet de Cressé chooses to identify Chanlatte only in a footnote as "M. J. C.," or why Chanlatte opts to identify himself in the Author's preface only as "J...E CH......E" is unclear. One recalls Doin's reticence in naming Phénor's son, as if the act of black authorship needs to be protected from the white enmity that a too public declaration might incur. Hostility on the part of former white colonists would have been especially strong in 1824 when *L'Histoire de la catastrophe de Saint-Domingue* was published. At that time, hopes for blocking the recognition of Haiti's independence were still being fueled by ultraconservative political forces and former colonists in France.

A benevolent attitude toward whites is displayed by the white and black narrative voices in *L'Histoire de la catastrophe de Saint-Domingue*. In an attempt to placate whites, the opening sentences of Bouvet de Cressé's preface hasten to make clear that negative references to Frenchmen, colonists, and Europeans in this work do not refer to those whose "traces honorables" ("honorable traces") marked their passage on the island of Saint-Domingue.[38] To draw an analogy with the characters in Doin's texts, it would be Néala's cruel master, not Merville, who is targeted in *L'Histoire de la catastrophe de Saint-Domingue*. Moreover, Chanlatte's narrative refrains from stigmatizing all whites. As "catastrophe" in the title of the work indicates, what happened to whites after the French left was horrific. But Chanlatte emphasizes that Christophe did all he could to protect white property owners in Haiti. Acknowledgment is given to whites who fought for the black cause, especially Englishmen like the "immortal Wilberforce": "nous regarderons comme des divinités ces créatures bien-faisantes qui ont consacré leurs veilles et leurs écrits à l'amélioration du sort de l'espèce humaine" ("we will always look upon as divinities these benevolent creatures who devoted their nights and their writings to the amelioration of the fate of mankind.") (77, 90) The similarity between Chanlatte's designation of benevolent whites as divinities and Domingo's language in describing his feelings for Pauline is apparent.

Chanlatte's narrative illustrates what Doin and other abolitionists considered the unique contribution that blacks could make in their partnership with whites. Only a black could provide an eye-witness, first-hand account, as Chanlatte does, in the collective voice of all formerly enslaved Haitians: "Interrogez les malheureux que vous avez voués aux tourments de l'enfer; voici ce qu'ils répondent par mon organe: 'De quels bienfaits voulez-vous nous parler? Quelle reconnaissance vous devons-nous? Ou plutôt, quels reproches mérités n'avons-nous pas à vous faire'" ("Go speak to the unhappy victims whom you have condemned to the torments of hell; here is what they say through my mouth: 'What good things have you done for us? What gratitude do we owe you? Rather, what well-justified injustices are we not entitled to reproach you with?'") (15–16) What follows is page upon page refuting white attempts to occupy a moral and intellectual high ground by claiming that they acted in a civilized way toward blacks. The litany of horrors perpetrated by whites serves as the basis for Chanlatte's conclusion, which Doin endorses, that the violence during the Haitian Revolution had as its root cause the culpable conduct of whites: "Sur qui doit tomber le blâme, la responsabilité de ces fléaux, si ce n'est sur ceux qui les ont provoqués?" ("On whom should the blame fall, the responsibility for these disasters, if not on those who provoked them?") (82–83)

The emphasis on intellectual achievement as the solution to Haiti's future is another common thread in the writings of Doin and Chanlatte. Doin emphasizes black intelligence by giving Domingo voice and agency in *Blanche et noir*, by bringing out Nelzi's intellectual capacities in *Noire et blanc*, and by designating Phénor's son as a future writer at the end of *La Famille noire*. Chanlatte dwells on blacks' intellectual capacity at great length, providing a catalogue of arguments which abolitionists could use to make the case for Haiti's future. His plea to the French to provide "de zélés instituteurs" ("zealous teachers") to guide them on the path to enlightenment prefigures the pedagogical function assumed by Merville. His praise for those Haitians who succeed in manifesting "quelques étincelles de génie et d'érudition" ("sparks of genius and erudition") recalls Phénor's son. His faith in the intellectual and artistic future of Haiti, like Doin's, is unshakable: indeed, he envisions the moment when true civilization and creativity will stem less from Europe than from "une énergie vierge, jointe au mérite de l'expérience et de l'instruction" ("the virgin energy, joined with the merit of experience and instruction") of the New World. (10, 19–20, 29)

In the spirit of cooperation to which Doin subscribes, Bouvet de Cressé and Chanlatte complement each other's role in promoting acceptance of Haiti. Bouvet de Cressé explains at the beginning that by coordinating the publication of the work, polishing it, and writing footnotes, he has merely helped to further the important goal that he and Chanlatte share:

> apprendre à nos rêveurs politiques qui comptent l'argent pour tout, et pour rien le sang de leur compatriotes, qu'il y a impossibilité physique de reprendre Saint-Domingue par la force des armes, et stupidité morale à vouloir exposer encore une fois en pure perte des armées françaises sur ce climat brûlant.

> (to teach our political dreamers who count money for everything and the blood of their compatriots for nothing that it is physically impossible to take back Saint-Domingue through the force of arms, and morally stupid to thus pointlessly expose the French army to danger once more in this torrid climate.)

He also states that he is fulfilling a promise made some twenty years earlier "au plus jeune des fils de Toussaint Louverture, mon ami, dans une île de l'Océan occidental" ("the youngest of the sons of Toussaint Louverture, my friend, on an island in the western ocean.") (70) In his official role in colonial affairs, Bouvet de Cressé undoubtedly had a broad network of connections, including with the Louverture family. Like the partnership between Guillaume Tell and Sophie, the two abolitionist partners made different contributions based on their public roles and personal experiences.

The fact of the black authorship of *L'Histoire de la catastrophe de Saint-Domingue* clearly matters to Doin. In a footnote to *La Famille noire* she recommends that readers consult this "ouvrage admirable d'un noir" ("admirable book by a black.") (20) What is more, the style, tone, themes, and arguments of *La Famille noire* resemble those found in Chanlatte's writing. Her justification for the violence that occurred during the Haitian Revolution echoes his, as does the central place she assigns to arguments in support of the humanity and intelligence of blacks. Of course many of the similar features of the two works occur throughout the body of abolitionist writing of the time. But justifying Haiti for the writers in question had little to do with originality. It had to do with disseminating information, especially that derived from reliable sources and from first-hand accounts such as Chanlatte's. Doin was an intermediary, someone who could reach out to the French people, including women, translating abolitionist writings into touching stories.

What distinguishes Doin from her male contemporaries in the final analysis is her awareness of the gender implications of creating harmonious relations for the future of Haiti and France. Lethière and Chanlatte sidestep the issue of where women fit into plans for social amelioration. Bouvet de Cressé even goes so far as to purposely exclude women from the discussion of issues affecting Haiti and its revolutionary past. In his preface he asserts that women should not read the work: "leur âme serait trop péniblement affectée; il y aurait trop de danger pour elles à seulement parcourir cette longue série de crimes de lèse-humanité" ("they would be too painfully affected; there would be too much danger for them even in glancing at this long series of crimes against humanity.") (vi) Doin ignored such admonitions for women to stay out of affairs taking place in the public sphere. Instead, she chose with courage and commitment to play the role that daughters play in her fictional works: shedding light on forms of injustice, and telling abolitionist stories to a wide spectrum of readers, including women and especially prejudiced fathers, oppressive masters, and other figures of male authority.

Notes

1 Claire Goldberg Moses explains the difference between revolutionary-period "equality" feminism and Saint-Simonian "difference" feminism in "'Equality' and 'Difference.'" Doin conforms more to the Saint-Simonian outlook, especially in her writings of the 1830s, but differs from it in numerous ways: for example, she shows no interest in separatism, communal living, or the abolition of private property. An important commonality that does exist, however, is the belief in harmony between the sexes.

2 All French quotations from these works refer to *La Famille noire suivie de trois nouvelles blanches et noires*, ed. Doris Y. Kadish (Paris: L'Harmattan, 2002). English translations of the short stories come from Kadish and Massardier-Kenney, eds, *Translating Slavery, vol. 1: Gender and Race in French Abolitionist Writing*. Translations from parts of *La Famille noire* that have not been published are my own.

3 *La Famille noire*, 81; *Translating Slavery, vol. 1*, 218.

4 Rossi, *Mémoires aristocratiques féminins*, 110.

5 Email message from Marc Doin dated April 7, 2007. I am grateful to M. Doin for the copy of the portrait of Sophie Doin included in this book. To my knowledge, it is the only known likeness of her.

6 Sophie Doin, *Simple Mémoire* (Paris: Vassal frères, 1842), 1–24. Because of the brevity of the autobiographical texts, I refer to them in the following pages without specific page references.

7 Marc Doin's article about Nicolas-François Gillet, "La Sculpture française à Saint-Petersbourg," provides valuable biographical information about Sophie Doin and her family.

8 He belonged to the Société's subcommittees in favor of Greeks, charity, religious books, and improving the condition of the blind. See Assemblée Générale Annuelle de la Société de la morale chrétienne 1824–1826.

9 Carla Alison Hesse, "Reading Signatures: Female Authorship and Revolutionary Law in France, 1750–1850," *Eighteenth-Century French Studies* 22 (1989): 467–89.

10 *La Famille noire,* 5–6.

11 The autobiographical texts include many recriminations against Guillaume Tell Doin but they do not explain the exact reasons for the breakdown of the marriage.

12 The names of Sophie Doin's children are found in the Acte de décès de Sophie Doin, Archives Nationales, DQ18/332: Sophie Aline, Guillaume Amédée, and Guillaume Tell.

13 Traer, *Marriage and the Family,* 190. The Code Civil was formally promulgated on March 1, 1804; in 1807 its name was officially changed to the Code Napoléon

14 For these Saint-Simonian principles, see Leslie Wahl Rabine, "Feminist Texts and Feminist Subjects," in *Feminism, Socialism, and French Romanticism,* ed. Claire Goldberg Moses and Leslie Wahl Rabine (Bloomington: Indiana University Press, 1993), 124, 133.

15 *Code Napoléon* (Paris: Collin, 1807), Article 373.

16 http://slavery.uga.edu/texts/works_color/MARIE.pdf (accessed March 2, 2012).

17 The analyses that appear in the remainder of this chapter draw in part on material found in my article "Haiti and Abolitionism in 1825: The Example of Sophie Doin," *Yale French Studies* 107 (2005): 108–30.

18 Although the geographical context of Doin's story remains vague, it is the case that in Haiti, white women were granted citizenship according to the proclamation of April 1804 and article 13 of the constitution of May 1805.

19 *La Famille noire,* 93, 94; *Translating Slavery, vol. 1,* 210, 211.

20 Doin conforms here to the agenda that Haitian memoir writers consistently promoted at the time: "the refutation of the popular notion that the Haitian revolutionists, both slave and free, were the perpetrators of violence and betrayal and the French planters and colonists the unfortunate victims." Marlene L. Daut, "Un-Silencing the Past: Boisrond-Tonnerre, Vastey, and Re-Writing of the Haitian Revolution, 1804–1817," *South Atlantic Review* 74, 1 (2009): 41.

21 *La Famille noire,* 85 (translation amended).

22 *La Famille noire,* 97; *Translating Slavery, vol. 1,* 196.

23 Jennifer Heuer, "One-Drop Rule in Reverse? Interracial Marriages in Napoleonic and Restoration France," *Law and History Review* 27, 3 (2009): 542.

24 Heuer, "One-Drop Rule," 525, 526. The union of Pauline and Domingo would have been forbidden under Napoleon, who ordered Leclerc to deport any woman who had relations with a black man; Cohen, *French Encounter with Africans,* 119. Dessalines allowed white women married to blacks to stay after independence; Joan Dayan, *Haiti, History, and the Gods* (Berkeley: University of California Press, 1995), 24.

25 In 1844, two decades after Doin's writing, a mixed-race author from Réunion published *Les Marrons,* which depicts an interracial couple who give birth to a

son as the solution to the problems of colonial society; see Vergès, *Monsters and Revolutionaries*, 24.

26 After Henry Christophe became paralyzed on August 15, 1820, his control of the northern part of Haiti waned and insurgents increasingly gained the upper hand, conspiring to unite the part controlled by Christophe with the southern part under the control of the mulatto President Boyer. On October 8, Christophe took his own life, after which Boyer declared himself president of a united Haiti on October 28. He is the "wise" leader to whom Doin refers.

27 *Le Christianisme*, II, No. 1 (October–November 1837). Doin opposed divorce to protect women, unlike conservative thinkers such as Bonald who considered it a threat to paternal authority; see Claudie Bernard, *Penser la famille au dix-neuvième siècle* (Saint-Etienne: Publications de l'université de Saint-Etienne, 2007), 211.

28 *Le Christianisme*, I (1836), 102.

29 http://www.slavery.uga.edu/texts/literary_works/NegrierChristianisme.pdf contains my transcription of this text (accessed March 3, 2012).

30 *Le Christianisme*, III (October–November 1838), 3–5.

31 For political and ideological qualifications regarding blacks in the postrevolutionary period, see Buck-Morss, *Hegel, Haiti, and Universal History*, 96, 143.

32 My analysis of this painting draws substantially on Darcy Grimaldo Grigsby's illuminating essay "Revolutionary Sons, White Fathers, and Creole Difference: Guillaume-Lethière's *Oath of the Ancestors* (1822)," *Yale French Studies* 101 (2002): 201–26. The painting was damaged during the earthquake of January 12, 2010. As of February 12, 2010, plans were underway for its restoration: http://haitirectoverso.blogspot.com/2010/02/haiti-restauration-du-tableau-serment.html (accessed September 28, 2011).

33 Grigsby, "Revolutionary Sons," 212.

34 Baron de Vastey, writing in 1816, wrongly claimed "our Haitian painters depict the Deity and angels black." Quoted in Buck-Morss, *Hegel, Haiti, and Universal History*, 143.

35 Grigsby, "Revolutionary Sons," 216.

36 *La Famille noire*, 94; *Translating Slavery*, vol. *1*, 211.

37 Grigsby, "Revolutionary Sons," 224.

38 Auguste Jean-Baptiste Bouvet de Cressé, ed., *L'Histoire de la catastrophe de Saint-Domingue* (Paris: Librairie de Peytieux, 1824), i.

Postscript

A closing pictorial example can help weave together the diverse constructions of fathers, daughters, and slaves considered in this book. The example is Anne-Louis Girodet's *Portrait du citoyen Belley, ex-représentant des colonies* (Figure 7). Jean-Baptiste Belley, the first black deputy to the National Convention during the French Revolution, is depicted standing alongside a bust of Guillaume-Thomas Raynal, the author of *Histoire des deux Indes*, which famously predicted that a black Spartacus would arise to avenge the rights of the oppressed.[1] Although the painting itself and the two persons it portrays predate the chronological framework of this book, the issues raised in Girodet's painting remained as urgent and timely in the first decades of the nineteenth century as at the time of its exhibition in 1797. The painting also has special relevance here because of its striking similarity to Firmin Massot's *Mme de Staël à côté du buste de son père Jacques Necker* discussed briefly in Chapter 1 (Figure 2). Massot's painting, presumed to have been commissioned by Staël shortly after her father's death in 1804, was undoubtedly modeled after Girodet's work. That Staël would have chosen a white-and-black dyad to model her relationship with her father supports the premise that women abolitionists (the "daughters" of this book) perceived deep-seated bonds between themselves and people who were black, mixed-race, or of African descent (this book's "slaves").[2]

Our closing overview begins with the category of fathers. In this category, Necker stands as a prototype of benevolence and fatherly love, as Massot's portrayal of him reveals. Massot brings Necker and Staël together in art as they were in life. In contrast, Girodet sharply contrasts Raynal, a celebrated, native-born Frenchman, and Belley, an African-born inhabitant of the colonies, who had just newly acquired the right to French citizenship. Massot conveys the bond between father and daughter by placing Necker in close proximity to Staël. His attire is simple, and whereas the marble statue

Figure 7. Anne-Louis Girodet, *Portrait du citoyen Belley, ex-représentant des colonies* (1797). Reproduction courtesy of Art Resource.

of Raynal presents an inert abstraction, the bust of Necker seems to place a living human being on display.[3] While the sightless Raynal faces away from Belley, Necker looks down fondly at his daughter. Father and daughter are both clothed, as opposed to the classical nude bust of Raynal which contrasts starkly with Belley's elaborate contemporary attire. Moreover, Necker and Staël gaze in the same direction, with the same slight smile on their faces and the same kindly expression in their eyes. Massot's painting can be viewed as a feminine rewriting of Girodet's work in which women's agency replaces male power, and the more overt abolitionist agenda of the revolutionary period gives way to a more feminized, familial spirit. Although Necker stemmed from the same Enlightenment milieu as Raynal and Diderot (reported to be the true author of the abolitionist parts of *Histoire des deux Indes*), he valued his accomplished only child greatly. His respect for his daughter undoubtedly tempered the masculinist perspective of his time found, for example, in Guillon-Lethière's *Serment des ancêtres* (Figure 6), where the very existence of women is erased; or in Géricault's *Radeau de la Méduse* (Figure 4), where women were removed from the final version.

Numerous avatars of paternal authority have been considered in this book. If few of them measure up to Necker, either objectively or in the eyes of their daughters, it would be unfair to rush to pass judgment on them, to overlook the particularities of time and place, or to fail to take seriously the complex social, personal, and political conditions of their lives. Often uncles, sons, or husbands played the role of a father, with varying results. In some cases they provided inspiration, as with Desbordes-Valmore's uncle Constant; in others they carried forward a woman's legacy, as with Auguste de Staël; in still others they assumed oppressive and exploitative legal control, as with Guillaume Tell Doin. Substitute fathers were also often ambivalent figures: the prototype in this regard, who appears on several occasions in this book, is the chevalier de Boufflers, seen in Chapter 1 as the model colonialist in *Mirza*, in Chapter 2 as a collaborator with if not exploiter of African *signares*, and in Chapter 4 as either a benevolent rescuer of slaves or, as some critics argue, an abductor who separated an African child from her mother and her culture. Similar ambivalence surrounds Rousseau and Bernardin, the creators of the fathers who reappear so often in the pages of this book. Rousseau's *Julie* stands as a key intertext for works such as Staël's *Histoire de Pauline* and Desbordes-Valmore's *Sarah*. Julie's patriarchal father, M. d'Etange, is presented as the problem; her benevolent husband, M. de Wolmar, as the solution. But even with a benevolent father such as Wolmar, women continue to remain firmly in the control of men for a largely masculinist author such as Rousseau.

Turning to the category of daughters, and looking again at the paintings by Girodet and Massot, one notes that Staël stands lower than her father, a reflection of her position "beneath" him with respect to her sex, her role in the family, and her literary rather than historical importance. But does that position suggest that women are by nature or in the specific instances of their lives inferior to men? Not at all. By fashioning Corinne as a substitute Napoleon, by constructing Mirza as an African woman poet, and by viewing herself as carrying on Necker's legacy after his death, Staël demonstrated repeatedly her belief in women's intelligence and empowerment. So too did Duras, as evidenced by her political agency behind the scenes in her salon, her attribution of voice to an African woman, and her questioning the institution of marriage. Dard, Desbordes-Valmore, and Doin would have known from their own experience that they owed their accomplishments to themselves, not to their ineffectual fathers or husbands, and thus that they were not inferior. All five writers emerge from the pages of their books as strong, resolute, intelligent, accomplished women and noteworthy writers.

Ironically, Massot's painting of Staël itself emblematizes the relegation of women to a less visible or valued position: it remains unknown, displayed privately in the château de Coppet, and of limited availability for public viewing. It also belongs to the lesser genre of portraiture, which Girodet's work transcends by its imposing size, public display, and historical subject matter. Massot's painting of Staël typifies the portrait's association with the family and femininity. In contrast, the most elevated and prestigious genre, historical painting, was associated with history and masculinity.[4] One is reminded of Dard's account of the shipwreck of the *Medusa*, often dismissed or denigrated by historians and critics. Focused on her father and her family, Dard produced a work that contrasts sharply with Géricault's. His painting depicts the same event as her story, but in an imposing and historical mode. For similar reasons, Guillon-Lethière's rendering of Haitian history stands above Vernet's sentimental landscape peopled by black and female literary characters. Yet, like Massot's portrait of Staël, its location in Haiti makes it inaccessible to most viewers.

Where, one might ask, is the "slave" component of Massot's painting, which is being analyzed here as emblematic of the relationship among fathers, daughters, and slaves? Hints can be found in the upper half of the painting, although clearly no overt representation of slavery exists. Dark, stormy clouds in the landscape, when viewed through the lens of slavery, announce revolutionary events. Another noteworthy component concerns color. Staël is white, although not in the stark way in which white is used in Girodet's painting to heighten racial dichotomies. Her skin, reddish and shaded, stands on a color spectrum composed of objects, people, and the natural scene. Necker's face, brightened in the upper half, highlights his intelligence. But his face, his minimally coiffed hair, and his simple clothing are brownish. One is reminded of Géricault's blurring of color distinctions for abolitionist purposes in *Le Radeau de la Méduse*. Did Massot in painting the portrait or Staël in commissioning it intentionally seek to evoke Necker's abolitionism through this use of color? Was Staël's unruly black hair, unfettered by the turban with which she was depicted in other portraits, meant to emphasize freedom from constraint?[5] Upon my interpretation, the painting displays two different modes, which correspond to Staël's ambivalent adherence to both classicism and romanticism. The top half is romantic in theme, coloration, and character depiction. Empathy for the objects of oppression, the missing slaves in this portrait, belongs to this upper half. The lower half moves toward a more conventional mode in the fashionable empire clothing, the rich fabric of the shawl, the simple objects and dark, neutral colors. This half evokes Staël's moderate Enlightenment outlook and adherence to the rule of God and father.

An analysis of the category of slaves requires a careful consideration of Girodet's Belley and a comparison between him and Staël, his non-hegemonic counterpart in Massot's painting. Belley stands tall, with his head at the same level as Raynal's. Equality of stature and historical importance between the two men is part of Girodet's abolitionist message. On a number of other hierarchies, Raynal occupies a superior position. The starkly white Raynal holds an enduring place in universal history, as the proud inscription of his name on the marble bust proclaims. Belley is clothed, as befits his insertion into the mundane political vicissitudes of life. Raynal stands above all that is earthly and transitory. Most importantly, he enjoys the superiority of mind over body. Nude, blind, and truncated as a classical bust, he embodies his intellectual legacy. Having transmitted his thought and his influence, he remains inaccessible. As Darcy Grimaldo Grigsby observes,

> He is above all a public man, a man in public. Head hurned away and eyes raised as though not looking on the things and persons of the world, he appears in thought but his is not a consciousness to which we are privy. His solemn face conveys the seriousness of a reflective intelligence without disclosing its contents. Rather his gravity is signaled by his withholding, his self-absorption, his refusal to meet our eye.[6]

As a black man, Belley cannot yet enjoy the purely intellectual identity that Raynal possesses. To prove his humanity he must display distinctive, human qualities that render him individual and contemporary. Grigsby notes that his individuality is the basis of the abolitionist implication of the painting. For to achieve personhood was the goal of emancipation: "the picture's emphatic empiricism enhances our sense of the personal autonomy and psychological independence of a specific black man."[7]

An accent on the physical, an important component of Girodet's depiction of Belley, functions ironically both to accentuate and to diminish his identity as a man. The black deputy's hand pointing toward the upper region of his pants suggests strength and virility but also the hypersexualization common in racist conceptions of black men. As Grigsby observes, "it is a narrative of the body's freedom but also, or course, its precedence over the mind."[8] Along with masculinity, however, Belley's depiction bears subtle traces of the feminine: daughters may seem to be totally absent from this painting, but in fact they seep in through the non-hegemonic figure of the black man, with whom they have been seen so often to be associated. The multitudinous folds of fabric in Belley's elaborate clothing evoke not only the sartorial but the bodily modality of women. The hand reaching toward his pronounced genital area seems soft and feminine. His earring and hair also mark his head as vaguely feminine, especially in contrast with Raynal's stark masculinity. It is worth mentioning that Girodet similarly inscribed femininity into masculine figures in relation to contemporary historical and political situations in *Le Sommeil d'Endymion* (1793) and *Atala au tombeau* (1808).[9]

Girodet falls into line with the treatment of slaves in works by men at the time, even those who held abolitionist sentiments. In such texts as Hugo's *Bug Jargal*, Rémusat's *L'Habitation de Saint-Domingue*, and Mérimée's *Tamango*, male sexuality, sexual rivalry, and stereotypical feminine roles related to blacks drive the plot. In contrast, the women writers considered in this book followed Staël's example in placing value on the life of the mind, which they considered available to blacks and whites, women and men. In this they followed the lead of Grégoire who, as early as 1808, identified the intelligence of blacks as a key component of the abolitionist agenda.[10] Staël's Mirza is a poet, Duras's Ourika is a narrator, Dard and her husband focused on education in Africa. And the ability to acquire an education is common to Doin's Nelzi and the son of her slave character Phénor in *La Famille noire*.

* * *

The categories of fathers, daughters, and slaves are admittedly porous.[11] Males like Desbordes-Valmore's father and Sophie Doin's husband behaved more like daughters or wives than patriarchs. Conversely, Staël was often mocked in her appearance, lifestyle, and intellectual pursuits as masculine, a fact that Massot perhaps tried to address in his feminized portrayal of her. Black men like Belley aspired to adopt France as their fatherland and leave the disempowered role of "slave" behind them. Like Toussaint Louverture, and like Dessalines and Pétion depicted in Lethière's *Oath of the Ancestors*, Belley was a military man and public personage. He published books, commanded men in the army, owned property and even, as David Geggus confirms, owned slaves. Geggus also notes, "It is broadly true that non-white slave owners generally acted according to their class interests during the struggles of the 1790s."[12] However, the fact that definitive boundaries cannot be drawn around the categories of fathers, daughters, and slaves does not change the importance of paying attention to each of them separately. To do so is to acknowledge the considerable differential that exists between those who possess power and those who have been relegated to a lesser status. Like Toussaint Louverture, Belley's authorship and command of the French language were questioned, and ultimately he too was imprisoned and left to die in France. Other blacks encountered in the pages of this book—Ourika, Minette, Dard's Etienne, the *signares*, La Tour du Pin's slave Judith—similarly died at a young age or barely appear, if at all, in the historical record.

The same is true of women. Even Staël, the only one of our five authors to have achieved something approaching canonical status, was often mocked and is still often neglected in literary and historical accounts. Historians often pay more attention to Auguste than Germaine as an active force in abolition. Moreover, it is irksome to observe the extent to which many of the otherwise enlightened and important male critics cited in this book—Hoffmann, Debbasch, Mercier, Fanoudh-Siefer, Miller, and others—have had occasion to treat the women considered here dismissively. Such dismissals limit and diminish our understanding of literature and history. Women's writings of the past may not always conform to accepted standards of aesthetic merit and may not gain canonical status. But it is a disservice to them and to us when their merits are ignored in favor of their perceived defects. Gayatri Spivak calls attention to "stylistically noncompetitive" texts which, as Chris Bongie notes, "will allow us to encounter a diversity of writerly worlds." Bongie also emphasizes the fact that the writings of lesser known or valued women writers function "as a way of subverting gendered hierarchies that have been central to the creation of 'literature' as an autonomous field of cultural production."[13]

A closing remark concerns the eyes depicted in Girodet's and Massot's paintings. Raynal's are blank. His Enlightenment vision is fixed for all time; he no longer sees or needs to see the particular suffering or injustice of the world. Belley occupies a place in time and space in which he views the world but without inviting engagement or intimacy with the viewer of the painting. His distant gaze and serious demeanor suggest the elevated, unapproachable status of a military commander. Although his head is erect, his eyes—most specifically his left eye—look upward, subtly acknowledging his allegiance to God and his fatherland, France. In contrast Necker and Staël convey the message of sentimentalism, benevolence, and empathy that this book has sought to illustrate. An abolitionist father casts his eyes downward at his beloved daughter. Although no longer among the living,

Necker lives on in his progeny, with eyes lucid and engaged, as if eager to see the unfolding of history in which his daughter and her children will play a part. Staël emblematizes the antislavery woman. With the blessing of her benevolent father, and in dutiful obeisance to his wishes, she looks slightly downward toward those who stand beneath her in social condition. Her gaze is kindly and empathetic. Her exposed breasts suggest fecundity and a commitment to nurture a new generation of compassionate Frenchmen.[14] She is a mother and defender of those below her including slaves. Above all, she is a daughter.

Notes

1 Guillaume Thomas Raynal, *Histoire philosophique et politique des établissemens et du commerce des européens dans les deux Indes* (Geneva: Libraires associés, 1783).

2 In "Staël, Corinne, and the Women Collectors of Napoleonic Europe," Heather Belnap Jensen states her conviction that Massot's portrait has Girodet's painting of Belley and Raynal as its antecedent: "If this connection were indeed cultivated by the artist and/or his sitter, this portrait gives yet another indication of Staël's commitment to the abolitionist movement and her commitment to freedom of the individual." Heather Belnap Jensen, "Staël, Corinne, and the Women Collectors of Napoleonic Europe," in *Sensibility, Society and the Sister Arts: Germaine de Staël's Historical Revisionism*, ed. Tilli Boon Cuillé and Karyna Szmurlo, forthcoming.

3 In "The Many Faces of Germaine de Staël," Mary Sheriff explains that Massot remade a 1793 portrait by Joseph Siffred Duplessis, and that the use of a portrait heightens the affective bond between Necker and Staël. Mary Sheriff, "The Many Faces of Germaine de Staël," in Cuillé and Szmurlo, eds, *Sensibility, Society and the Sister Art*, forthcoming.

4 In Desbordes-Valmore's "Le Nid d'hirondelles," Ondine notes the pattern of privileging fathers and subordinating women in the work of Girodet, who was the friend and neighbor of Desbordes-Valmore's uncle Constant; and she associates this pattern with male painters' access to the more prestigious genre of historical painting; Wettlaufer, *Portraits of the Artist as a Young Woman*, 89.

5 Sheriff considers that the hair calls attention to Staël's mental activity. I see its wildness more in keeping with representations of non-hegemonic figures like Chactas in Girodet's *Atala au tombeau*.

6 Grigsby, *Extremities*, 48.

7 Grigsby, *Extremities*, 49.

8 Grigsby, *Extremities*, 55.

9 See Doris Y. Kadish, *Politicizing Gender: Narrative Strategies in the Aftermath of the French Revolution* (New Brunswick: Rutgers University Press, 1991), 81–88.

10 Henri Grégoire, *De la littérature des Nègres* (Paris: Maradan, 1808).

11 For a discussion of the theoretical issues surrounding the notion of porosity, see Buck-Morss, *Hegel, Haiti, and Universal History*, 126.

12 Geggus, "Racial Equality, Slavery, and Colonial Secession," 1305, 1300.

13 Gayatri Spivak, "Teaching for the Times," in *Dangerous Liaisons: Gender, Nation, and Postcolonial Perspectives*, ed. Anne McClintock, Aamir Mufti, and Ella Shohat

(Minneapolis: University of Minnesota Press, 1997), 479, 483; Bongie, *Friends and Enemies*, 8, 319.

14 For a discussion of the symbolism of breasts in the revolutionary period, see Kadish, *Politicizing Gender*, 163.

Bibliography

Primary Texts

Ardouin, Coriolan. *Poésies*. Port-au-Prince: R. Ethéart, 1881.

Boilat, David. *Esquisses sénégalaises*. Paris: P. Bertand, 1853.

———. *Esquisses sénégalaises, Atlas*. Paris: P. Bertand, 1853.

Bouvet de Cressé, Auguste Jean-Baptiste, ed. *L'Histoire de la catastrophe de Saint-Domingue*. Paris: Librairie de Peytieux, 1824.

Césaire, Aimé. *La Tragédie du roi Christophe*. Paris: Présence africaine, 1970.

———. *The Tragedy of King Christophe*. Trans. Ralph Manheim. New York: Grove Press, 1969.

Chateaubriand, François-René de. *Le Génie du christianisme*, vol. II. Paris: Ernest Flammarion, 1948.

Chauvet, Marie. *Dance on the Volcano*. Trans. Salvator Attanasio. New York: William Sloane, 1959.

———. *La Danse sur le volcan*. Paris: Plon, 1957.

Clarkson, Thomas. *Cries of Africa, to the Inhabitants of Europe*. London: Harvey and Darton, 1822.

Collet de Messine, Jean-Baptiste. *Sara, ou la fermière écossaise*. Paris: Durand Dufrenoy, 1774.

Condé, Maryse. *La Migration des coeurs*. Paris: Robert Laffont, 1995.

———. *La Parole des femmes*. Paris: L'Harmattan, 1979.

———. *Ségou: les murailles de terre*. Paris: Robert Laffont, 1984.

———. *Windward Heights*. Trans. Richard Philcox. New York: Soho, 1998.

Corréard, Alexandre, and Jean-Baptiste Savigny. *Naufrage de la frégate la Méduse*. Paris: Eymery, 1818.

Dard, Charlotte Adélaïde. *La Chaumière africaine, ou histoire d'une famille française jetée sur la Côte occidentale de l'Afrique à la suite du naufrage de la frégate La Méduse*. Dijon: Noellat, 1824.

———. *La Chaumière africaine, ou histoire d'une famille française jetée sur la Côte occidentale de l'Afrique à la suite du naufrage de la frégate La Méduse*. Ed. Doris Y. Kadish. Paris: L'Harmattan, 2005.

————. *The Sufferings of the Picard Family after the Shipwreck of the Medusa in the Year 1816.* Trans. P. Maxwell. Edinburgh: Constable, 1827.

Dard, Jean. *Dictionnaire français-wolof et français-bambara, suivi du Dictionnaire wolof-français.* Paris: Imprimerie royale, 1825.

————. *Grammaire wolof ou méthode pour étudier la langue des Noirs qui habitent en Sénégambie.* Paris: Imprimerie royale, 1826.

Desbordes-Valmore, Marceline. *Huit Femmes.* Paris: Chlendowski, 1845.

————. *Huit Femmes.* Ed. Marc Bertrand. Geneva: Droz, 1999.

————. "La Jambe De Damis. " In *Contes.* Ed. Marc Bertrand. Lyon: Presses Universitaires de Lyon, 1989. 71–72.

————. *La Jeunesse de Marceline ou l'Atelier d'un peintre.* Paris: Editions de la Nouvelle Revue Française, 1922.

————. *Les Oeuvres poétiques de Marceline Desbordes-Valmore.* Ed. Marc Bertrand. Grenoble: Presses Universitaires de Grenoble, 1973.

————. *Sarah: An English Translation.* Ed. Deborah Jenson and Doris Y. Kadish. New York: MLA, 2008.

————. *Sarah: The Original French Text.* Ed. Deborah Jenson and Doris Y. Kadish. New York: MLA, 2008.

————. *Les Veillées des Antilles.* Paris: François Louis, 1821.

————. *Les Veillées des Antilles.* Ed. Aimée Boutin. Paris: L'Harmattan, 2006.

Doin, Sophie. *Avis au public.* Paris: Vassal frères, 1842.

————. *Un Cri de mère.* Paris: Vassal frères, 1843.

————. *La Famille noire suivie de trois nouvelles blanches et noires.* Ed. Doris Y. Kadish. Paris: L'Harmattan, 2002.

————. *Simple Mémoire.* Paris: Vassal frères, 1842.

Duras, Claire de. *Ourika.* Paris: Jouaust, 1878.

————. *Ourika.* Trans. John Fowles. Austin: W.T. Taylor, 1977.

Favart, Charles Simon, and Pierre-Alexandre Monsigny. *La Belle Arsène.* 1775.

Grégoire, Henri. *Considérations sur le mariage et sur le divorce adressées aux citoyens d'Haïti.* Paris: Baudouin frères, 1823.

————. *De La littérature des Nègres.* Paris: Maradan, 1808.

————. *De La Noblesse de la peau.* Paris: Badouin frères, 1826.

Kadish, Doris Y., and Françoise Massardier-Kenney, eds. *Translating Slavery: Gender and Race in French Women's Writing, 1783–1823.* Kent: Kent State University Press, 1994.

————. *Translating Slavery, vol. 1: Gender and Race in French Abolitionist Writing, 1780–1830.* Kent: Kent State University Press, 2009.

————. *Translating Slavery, vol. 2: Ourika's Progeny.* Kent: Kent State University Press, 2010.

Kersaint, Armand Guy. *Moyens proposés à l'assemblé nationale pour rétablir la paix et l'ordre dans les colonies* and *Suite de Moyens proposés à l'assemblé nationale pour rétablir la paix et l'ordre dans les colonies.* Paris: Imprimerie du cercle social, 1792.

La Tour du Pin, Henriette, marquise de. *Mémoires de la marquise de La Tour du*

Pin: journal d'une femme de cinquante ans, 1778–1815. Paris: Mercure de France, 1989.

———. *Memoirs of Madame de La Tour du Pin.* Trans. Felice Harcourt. London: Century Publishing, 1985.

Louverture, Isaac. *Mémoires d'Isaac, fils de Toussaint Louverture, sur l'expédition des Français sous le Consulat de Bonaparte.* In *Histoire de l'expédition des Français à Saint-Domingue.* Ed. Antoine Marie Thérèse Métral. Paris: Fanjat aîné 1825. 227–339.

Louverture, Toussaint. *Mémoires du Général Toussaint Louverture écrits par lui-même.* Ed. Joseph Saint-Rémy. Paris: Pagnerre, 1853.

Mandeleau, Tita. *Signare Anna.* Dakar: Nouvelles Éditions africaines du Sénégal, 1991.

Marmontel, Jean-François. "Silvain." (1770). In *Oeuvres complètes*, vol. V. Geneva: Slatkine Reprints, 1968. 678–700.

Maximin, Daniel. *L'Isolé soleil.* Paris: Seuil, 1981.

———. *Lone Sun.* Charlottesville: University Press of Virginia, 1989.

Park, Mungo. *Travels in the Interior Districts of Africa.* Ed. Kate Ferguson Marsters. Durham, NC: Duke University Press, 2000.

Raynal, Guillaume Thomas. *Histoire philosophique et politique des* établissements *et du commerce des Européens dans les deux Indes.* Genève: Libraires associés, 1783.

Rémusat, Charles de. *The Saint-Domingue Plantation, or, the Insurrection.* Ed. Doris Y. Kadish. Trans. Norman R. Shapiro. Baton Rouge: Louisiana State University Press, 2008.

Saint-Pierre, Bernardin de. *La Chaumière indienne.* In *Oeuvres choisies.* Paris: Firmin Didot, 1848.

———. *Paul et Virginie.* In *Oeuvres choisies.* Paris: Didot, 1848.

———. *Voyage à l'île de France.* Paris: Ledentu, 1840.

———. *Voyage à l'île de France.* New York: Interlink Books, 2003.

Senghor, Léopold Sédar. *The Collected Poetry.* Charlottesville: University Press of Virginia, 1991.

Smith, Adam. *The Theory of Moral Sentiments.* Cambridge: Cambridge University Press, 2002.

Staël, Germaine de. *Caractère de M. Necker.* In *Oeuvres complètes de Mme la Baronne de Staël*, vol. XVII. Paris: Treuttel et Wurtz, 1820.

———. *Considérations sur la révolution française.* Ed. Jacques Godechot. Paris: Tallendier, 2000.

———. *Corinne, ou, l'Italie.* Paris: Gallimard, 1985.

———. *Correspondance générale de Madame de Staël.* Ed. Béatrice Jasinski. Paris: Jean-Jacques Pauvert, 1962.

———. *De L'Influence des passions.* In *Oeuvres complètes de Mme la Baronne de Staël*, vol. III. Paris: Treuttel et Wurtz, 1820.

———. *De La Littérature dans ses rapports avec les institutions sociales.* Paris: Garnier, 1998.

————. *Dix Années d'exil*. Paris: Fayard, 1996.

————. *Oeuvres de jeunesse*. Ed. John Isbell and Simone Balayé. Paris: Desjon-quiers, 1997.

————. "Quelques Réflexions sur le but moral de *Delphine*." In *Oeuvres complètes de Mme la baronne de Staël*, vol. V. Paris: Treuttel et Wurtz, 1820.

Secondary Texts

Allen, James Smith. *Poignant Relations: Three Modern French Women*. Baltimore: Johns Hopkins University Press, 2000.

Alliston, April. "Transnational Sympathies, Imaginary Communities." In *The Literary Channel: The Inter-National Invention of the Novel*. Ed. Margaret Cohen and Carolyn Dever. Princeton: Princeton University Press, 2002. 133–48.

Ambrière, Francis. *Le Siècle des Valmore: Marceline Desbordes-Valmore et les siens*. Paris: Seuil, 1987.

Anderson, Benedict. *Imagined Communities: Reflections on the Origin and Spread of Nationalism*. London: Verso, 1983.

Angrand, Jean-Luc. *Céleste ou le temps des signares*. Sarcelles: Edition Anne Pépin, 2006.

Appiah, Anthony. *The Ethics of Identity*. Princeton: Princeton University Press, 2005.

Bell, Susan G., and Karen M. Offen. *Women, the Family, and Freedom*. Stanford: Stanford University Press, 1983.

Berchtold, Alfred. "Sismondi et le groupe de Coppet face à l'esclavage et au colonialisme." In *Sismondi Européen*. Ed. Sven Stelling-Michaud. Geneva: Slatkine, 1976. 169–221.

Bernard, Claudie. *Penser la famille au dix-neuvième siècle*. Saint-Etienne: Publications de l'université de Saint-Etienne, 2007.

Bertrand-Jennings, Chantal. "Problématique d'un sujet féminin en régime patriarcal: *Ourika* de Mme de Duras." *Nineteenth-Century French Studies* 23, 1–2 (1994–95): 42–58.

Bertrand, Marc. *Une Femme à l'écoute de son temps*. Lyon: La Cicogne, 1997.

————. "Introduction." In *Les Oeuvres poétiques de Marceline Desbordes-Valmore*. Ed. Marc Bertrand. Grenoble: Presses universitaires de Grenoble, 1973. 5–10.

Birkett, Mary Ellen, and Christopher Rivers, eds. *Approaches to Teaching Duras's Ourika*. New York: MLA, 2008.

Bissière, Michèle. "Union et disunion avec le père dans *Ourika* et *Edouard* de Claire de Duras." *Nineteenth-Century French Studies* 23, 3–4 (1995): 316–23.

Blennerhassett, Charlotte. *Madame de Staël, her friends and her influence in politics and literature*, vol. III. London: Chapman and Hall, 1889.

Blot, Jean-Yves. *La Méduse, chronique d'un naufrage ordinaire*. Paris: Arthaud, 1982.

Boime, Albert. *The Art of Exclusion: Representing Blacks in the Nineteenth Century.* Washington, DC: Smithsonian Institution Press, 1990.

Bongie, Chris. *Friends and Enemies: The Scribal Politics of Post/Colonial Literature.* Liverpool: Liverpool University Press, 2008.

———. *Islands and Exiles: The Creole Identities of Post/Colonial Literature.* Stanford: Stanford University Press, 1998.

Bonin, Kathrine. "*Paul et Virginie* in the Marketplace." Paper delivered at the Nineteenth Century French Studies colloquium, Mobile, Alabama, 2007.

Bordonove, Georges. *Le Naufrage de la Méduse.* Paris: Laffont, 1973.

Boutin, Aimeé. "Colonial Memory, Narrative, and Sentimentalism in Desbordes-Valmore's *Les Veillées Des Antilles.*" *L'Esprit créateur* 47, 4 (2007): 57–67.

———. "Introduction." In Marceline Desbordes-Valmore, *Les Veillées des Antilles.* Ed. Aimée Boutin. Paris: L'Harmattan, 2006.

———. *Maternal Echoes: The Poetry of Marceline Desbordes-Valmore and Alphonse de Lamartine.* Newark: University of Delaware Press, 2001.

Boyer d'Agen, Auguste Jean. "Préface." In Marceline Desbordes-Valmore, *La Jeunesse de Marceline ou L'Atelier d'un peintre.* Paris: Editions de la Nouvelle Revue Française, 1922, i–xxiii.

Brady, Heather. "Recovering Claire de Duras's Creole Inheritance: Race and Gender in the Exile Correspondence of her Saint-Domingue Family." *L'Esprit créateur* 47, 4 (2007): 44–56.

Brooks, George E. "Artists' depictions of Senegalese signares: insights concerning French racist and sexist attitudes in the nineteenth century." *Genève-Afrique* 18, 1 (1980): 75–89.

———. "The *Signares* of Saint-Louis and Gorée: Women Entrepreneurs in Eighteenth-Century Senegal." In *Women in Africa: Studies in Social and Economic Change.* Ed. Nancy J. Hafkin and Edna G. Bray. Stanford: Stanford University Press, 1976. 19–44.

Buck-Morss, Susan. *Hegel, Haiti, and Universal History.* Pittsburgh: University of Pittsburgh Press, 2009.

Camier, Bernard. "Musique coloniale et sociale à Saint-Domingue dans la seconde moitié du 18e siècle." unpublished dissertation, Université des Antilles et de la Guyane, 2004.

Chamoiseau, Patrick. "De La Mémoire obscure à la mémoire consciente." In *De L'Esclavage aux réparations.* Ed. Serge Chalons and Comité Devoir de mémoire (Martinique). Paris: Karthala, 2000.

Cheyne, Michelle. "Introduction. " In Jacques-Louis Lacour, *Pyracmond, ou les Créoles.* Paris: L'Harmattan, 2012.

———. "Pyracmond, ou les Créoles: L'Articulation d'une hiérarchie des rôles raciaux sur la scène française sous la Restauration." *French Colonial History* 6 (2005): 79–102.

Chilcoat, Michelle. "Confinement, the Family Institution, and the Case of Claire de Duras's Ourika." *L'Esprit Créateur* 38, 3 (1998): 6–16.

Cixous, Hélène. *Prénoms de personne.* Paris: Seuil, 1974.

Cixous, Hélène, and Annette Kuhn. "Castration or Decapitation?" *Signs* 7, 1 (1981): 41–55.

Cohen, Margaret. *The Sentimental Education of the Novel*. Princeton: Princeton University Press, 1999.

Cohen, William B. *The French Encounter with Africans: White Response to Blacks, 1530–1880*. Bloomington: Indiana University Press, 2003.

Collins, Patricia Hill. *Black Sexual Politics*. New York: Routledge, 2004.

Colwill, Elizabeth. "Epistolary Passions: Friendship and the Literary Public of Constance de Salm, 1767–1845." *Journal of Women's History* 12, 3 (2000): 39–68.

Cornevin, Robert, "Précurseurs de la négritude au XIXe siècle: Edward W. Blyden ou Jean Dard?" *Journal of African History* 9, 2 (1968): 315–17.

Coursil, Jacques, and Delphine Perret. "The Francophone Postcolonial Field." In *Postcolonial Theory and Francophone Literary Studies*. Ed. H. Adlai Murdoch and Anne Donadey. Gainesville: University Press of Florida, 2005. 193–207.

Cuillé, Tilli Boon, and Karyna Szmurlo, eds. *Germaine de Staël: Forging a Politics of Mediation*. Oxford: Voltaire Foundation, 2011.

Dakar-Matin. "L'Ecole sénégalaise a aujourd'hui 150 ans." 7 mars 1967.

Dauphin, Cécile. "Women's Culture and Women's Power: Issues in French Women's History." In *Writing Women's History: International Perspectives*. Ed. Karen M. Offen, Ruth Roach Pierson, and Jane Rendall. Bloomington: Indiana University Press, 1991. 107–31.

Daut, Marlene L. "Un-Silencing the Past: Boisrond-Tonnerre, Vastey, and Re-Writing of the Haitian Revolution, 1804–1817." *South Atlantic Review* 74, 1 (2009): 35–64.

Davidson, Denise Z. *France after Revolution: Urban Life, Gender, and the New Social Order*. Cambridge, MA: Harvard University Press, 2007.

Dayan, Joan. *Haiti, History, and the Gods*. Berkeley: University of California Press, 1995.

Debbasch, Yvan. "Poésie et traite: l'opinion française sur le commerce négrier au début du 19e siècle." *Revue française d'histoire d'outre-mer* 48 (1961): 311–52.

Denby, David J. *Sentimental Narrative and the Social Order in France, 1760–1820*. Cambridge: Cambridge University Press, 1994.

De Raedt, Thérèse. "*Ourika* in Black and White: Textual and Visual Interplay." *Women in French Studies* 12 (2004): 45–69.

———. "Representations of the Real Life Ourika." In *Approaches to Teaching Duras's Ourika*. Ed. Mary Ellen Birkett and Christopher Rivers. New York: MLA, 2008. 86–103.

De Vinne, Christine. "Religion under Revolution in *Ourika*." In *Approaches to Teaching Duras's Ourika*. Ed. Mary Ellen Birkett and Christopher Rivers. New York: MLA, 2008. 104–18.

Erickson, John D. "Maximin's *L'Isolé soleil* and Caliban's Curse." *Callaloo* 15, 1 (1992): 119–30.

Fabre, Jean. *Lumières et romantisme.* Paris, Klinckseick, 1963.

Fanoudh-Siefer, Léon. *Le Mythe du nègre et de l'Afrique noire dans la littérature française.* Paris: Klincksieck, 1968.

Ferguson, Moira. *Subject to Others: British Women Writers and Colonial Slavery, 1670–1834.* New York: Routledge, 1992.

Fouchard, Jean. *Le Théâtre à Saint-Domingue.* Port-au-Prince, Haïti: H. Deschamps, 1988.

Garraway, Doris. *The Libertine Colony: Creolization in the Early French Caribbean.* Durham, NC: Duke University Press, 2005.

Gaucher, Joseph. *Les Débuts de l'enseignement en Afrique francophone: Jean Dard et l'école mutuelle Saint-Louis du Sénégal.* Paris: Le Livre africain, 1968.

Geggus, David. "Racial Equality, Slavery, and Colonial Secession during the Constituent Assembly." *American Historical Review* 94, 5 (1990): 1290–1308.

Grigsby, Darcy Grimaldo. *Extremities: Painting Empire in Post-Revolutionary France.* New Haven: Yale University Press, 2002.

_____. "Revolutionary Sons, White Fathers, and Creole Differences: Guillaume Guillon-Lethière's *Oath of the Ancestors* (1822)." *Yale French Studies* 101 (2002): 201–26.

Guerlac, Suzanne. "Writing the Nation (Mme de Staël)." *French Forum* 30, 3 (2005): 43–56.

Gutwirth, Madelyn. *Madame De Staël, Novelist: The Emergence of the Artist as Woman.* Urbana: University of Illinois Press, 1978.

Hanniet, Michel. *Le Naufrage de la Méduse, Paroles de rescapés.* Louviers: Franck Martin, 2006.

_____. *La Vérédique Histoire des naufragés de la Méduse.* Paris: Actes Sud, 1991.

Hesse, Carla Alison. *The Other Enlightenment: How French Women Became Modern.* Princeton: Princeton University Press, 2001.

———. "Reading Signatures: Female Authorship and Revolutionary Law in France, 1750–1850." *Eighteenth-Century French Studies* 22 (1989): 467–89.

Heuer, Jennifer. "One-Drop Rule in Reverse? Interracial Marriages in Napoleonic and Restoration France." *Law and History Review* 27, 33 (2009): 515–48.

Hoffmann, Léon-François. *Le Nègre romantique: Personnage littéraire et obsession collective.* Paris: Payot, 1973.

hooks, bell. *Talking Back.* Cambridge: South End Press, 1988.

Hunt, Lynn. *Inventing Human Rights: A History.* New York: Norton 2007.

Isbell, John. "Voices Lost? Staël and Slavery, 1786–1830." In *Slavery in the Caribbean Francophone World: Distant Voices, Forgotten Acts, Forged Identities.* Ed. Doris Y. Kadish. Athens: University of Georgia Press, 2000. 39–52.

Jenson, Deborah. *Beyond Slave Narratives: Sex, Politics, and Manuscripts the Haitian Revolution.* Liverpool: Liverpool University Press, 2011.

Jordan, Winthrop D. *White over Black: American Attitudes Toward the Negro, 1550–1812.* New York: Norton, 1977.

Jore, Léonce, and Gabriel Debien. "Autour de *La Chaumière africaine*." *Bulletin de l'institut français d'Afrique noire* 27, 1–2 (1965): 287–318.

Kadish, Doris Y. "Black Faces, White Voices in Women's Writing from the 1820s." In *Approaches to Teaching Duras's Ourika*. Ed. Mary Ellen Birkett and Christopher Rivers. New York: MLA, 2008. 93–104.

_____. "Haiti and Abolitionism in 1825: The Example of Sophie Doin." *Yale French Studies* 107 (2004): 108–30.

_____. *The Literature of Images: Narrative Landscape from Julie to Jane Eyre*. New Brunswick: Rutgers University Press, 1986.

———. "Narrating the French Revolution: The Example of Corinne." In *Germaine De Staël: Crossing the Borders*. Ed. Madelyn Gutwirth. New Brunswick: Rutgers University Press, 1991. 113–21.

_____. *Politicizing Gender: Narrative Strategies in the Aftermath of the French Revolution*. New Brunswick: Rutgers University Press, 1991.

_____. "Rewriting Women's Stories: Ourika and the French Lieutenant's Woman." *South Atlantic Review* 62, 2 (1997): 74–87.

———. "*Sarah* and Antislavery." *L'Esprit créateur* 47, 4 (2007): 93–104.

Kale, Steven D. *French Salons: High Society and Political Sociability from the Old Regime to the Revolution of 1848*. Baltimore: Johns Hopkins University Press, 2004.

Keen, Suzanne. "A Theory of Narrative Empathy." *Narrative* 14, 3 (2006): 207–36.

Kent, Sherman. *The Election of 1827 in France*. Cambridge, MA: Harvard University Press, 1975.

Kitson, Peter J. "'Bales of Living Anguish': Representations of Race and the Slave in Romantic Writing." *English Literary History* 67, 2 (2000): 515–37.

Kristeva, Julia. "Stabat Mater." In *The Kristeva Reader*. Ed. Toril Moi. New York: Columbia University Press, 1986. 160–86.

Lanser, Susan Sniader. *The Narrative Act. Point of View in Prose Fiction*. Princeton: Princeton University Press, 1981.

Le Hir, Marie-Pierre. "Feminism, Theater, Race: *L'Esclavage des noirs*." In *Translating Slavery, vol. 1: Gender and Race in French Abolitionist Writing, 1780–1830*. Ed. Doris Y. Kadish and Françoise Massardier-Kenney. Kent: Kent State University Press, 2009. 65–88.

Léonard, Jacques. "Les Médecins et les soignants: Femmes, religion et médecine." *Annales* 5 (1977): 887–907.

Lerner, Gerda. *The Creation of Patriarchy*. New York: Oxford University Press, 1986.

Lescure, M. de. "Notice." In Claire de Duras, *Ourika*. Paris: Jouaust, 1878.

Lionnet, Françoise. "Francophonie, Postcolonial Studies, and Transnational Feminisms." In *Postcolonial Theory and Francophone Literary Studies*. Ed. H. Adlai Murdoch and Anne Donadey. Gainesville: University Press of Florida, 2005. 258–69.

Little, Roger. "A Further Unacknowledged Quotation in Césaire: Echoes of Ourika." *French Studies Bulletin* 43 (1992): 13–16.

————. "Condé, Brontë, Duras, Beyala: Intertextuality or Plagiarism?" *French Studies Bulletin* 72 (1999): 11–15.

————. "Le nom et les origines d'Ourika." *Revue d'histoire littéraire de la France* 98, 4 (1998): 633–37.

Masson, Philippe, *L'Affaire de la Méduse*. Paris: Tallendier, 1989.

Melzer, Sara E., and Leslie W Rabine, eds. *Rebel Daughters: Women and the French Revolution*. New York: Oxford University Press, 1992.

Memmi, Albert. *The Colonizer and the Colonized*. Trans. Howard Greefield. New York: Orion Press, 1965.

Mercier, Roger. *L'Afrique noire dans la littérature française; les premières images, XVIIe–XVIIIe siècles*. Dakar: Université de Dakar, 1962.

————. "Le Naufrage de 'La Méduse': réalité et imagination romanesque." *Revue des sciences humaines* 125 (1967): 53–66.

Midgley, Clare. *Women against Slavery: The British Campaigns, 1780–1870*. London: Routledge, 1992.

Miller, Christopher L. "Duras, Biography, and Slavery." In *Approaches to Teaching Duras's Ourika*. Ed. Mary Ellen Birkett and Christopher Rivers. New York: MLA, 2008. 51–56.

————. *The French Atlantic Triangle: Literature and Culture of the Slave Trade*. Durham, NC: Duke University Press, 2008.

Morgan, Philip D. *Slave Counterpoint: Black Culture in the Eighteenth-Century Chesapeake and Lowcountry*. Chapel Hill: University of North Carolina Press, 1998.

Moses, Claire Goldberg. "'Equality' and 'Difference' in Historical Perspective: Saint-Simonian Feminism." In *Feminism, Socialism, and French Romanticism*. Ed. Claire Goldberg Moses and Leslie Wahl Rabine. Bloomington: Indiana University Press, 1993. 17–84.

Nochlin, Linda. "Géricault, or the Absence of Woman." In *Géricault, Louvre conférences et colloques*, vol. I. Ed. Michel Régis. Paris: La Documentation française, 1996. 405–18.

Nussbaum, Martha C. *Upheavals of Thought: The Intelligence of Emotions*. New York: Routledge, 2001.

Pailhès, Gabriel. *La duchesse de Duras et Chateaubriand d'après des documents inédits*. Paris: Perrin, 1910.

Pajou, Jean-Charles. *Esclaves des îles françaises*. Paris: Les Editeurs libres, 2006.

Pange, Comtesse Jean de. "Madame de Staël et les nègres." *Revue de France* 5 (1934): 425–34.

Patterson, Orlando. *Slavery and Social Death: A Comparative Study*. Cambridge, MA: Harvard University Press, 1982.

Peabody, Sue. *There are No Slaves in France: The Political Culture of Race and Slavery in the Ancien Régime*. Oxford: Oxford University Press, 1996.

Pluchon, Pierre. *Nègres et Juifs au 18e siècle: le racisme au siècle des lumières.* Paris: Tallendier, 1984.

Prasad, Pratima. *Colonialism, Race, and the French Romantic Imagination.* New York: Routledge, 2009.

Rabine, Leslie Wahl. "Feminist Texts and Feminist Subjects." In *Feminism, Socialism, and French Romanticism.* Ed. Claire Goldberg Moses and Leslie Wahl Rabine. Bloomington: Indiana University Press, 1993. 85–144.

Reddy, William M. *The Navigation of Feeling: A Framework for the History of Emotions.* New York: Cambridge University Press, 2001.

Reinhardt, Catherine A. *Claims to Memory: Beyond Slavery and Emancipation in the French Caribbean.* New York: Berghahn Books, 2006.

Rosello, Mireille. "'Il faut comprendre quand on peut…'; L'art de désamorcer les stéréotypes chez Emile Ajar et Calixthe Beyala." In *L'Ecriture décentrée: la langue de l'Autre dans le roman contemporain.* Ed. Michel Laronde. Paris: L'Harmattan, 1996. 161–84.

Rossi, Henri. *Mémoires aristocratiques féminins: 1789–1848.* Paris: Champion, 1998.

Ryan, Maureen. "Liberal Ironies, Colonial Narratives and the Rhetoric of Art: Reconsidering Géricault's *Radeau de la Méduse.*" In *Théodore Géricault: The Alien Body: Tradition in Chaos.* Ed. Serge Guilbaut, Maureen Ryan, and Scott Watson. Vancouver: University of British Columbia, 1997. 18–51.

Sartre, Jean-Paul. "Orphée noir." In *Anthologie de la nouvelle poésie nègre et malgache de langue française.* Ed. Léopold Sedar Senghor. Paris: Presses universitaires de France, 1948.

Said, Edward W. *Culture and Imperialism.* New York: Knopf, 1993.

Schor, Naomi. *George Sand and Idealism.* New York: Columbia University Press, 1993.

Sepinwall, Alyssa. *Abbé Grégoire and the French Revolution.* Berkeley: University of California Press, 2005.

Sharpley-Whiting, T. Denean. *Black Venus: Sexualized Savages, Primal Fears, and Primitive Narratives in French.* Durham, NC: Duke University Press, 1999.

Spitzer, Alan B. *The French Generation of 1820.* Princeton: Princeton University Press, 1987.

Spivak, Gayatri. "Teaching for the Times." In *Dangerous Liaisons: Gender, Nation, and Postcolonial Perspectives.* Ed. Anne McClintock, Aamir Mufti, and Ella Shohat. Minneapolis: University of Minnesota Press, 1997. 468–90.

Sussman, Charlotte. *Consuming Anxieties: Consumer Protest, Gender, and British Slavery, 1713–1833.* Stanford: Stanford University Press, 2000.

Traer, James F. *Marriage and the Family in Eighteenth-Century France.* Ithaca, NY: Cornell University Press, 1980.

Trouillot, Michel-Rolph. *Silencing the Past: Power and the Production of History.* Boston: Beacon Press, 1995.

Vergès, Françoise. *Monsters and Revolutionaries. Colonial Family Romance and Métissage*. Durham, NC: Duke University Press, 1999.

Volet, Jean-Marie."Mme Dard, le naufrage de la Méduse en 1816 et le début de l'expansion coloniale au Sénégal. Africa and Women Writers" (2007). http://aflit.arts.uwa.edu.au/colonie_19e_dard_fr.html. Accessed May 1, 2011.

Wettlaufer, Alexandria. *Portraits of the Artist as a Young Woman: Painting and the Novel in France and Britain, 1800–1860*. Columbus: Ohio State University Press, 2011.

Wing, Nathanael. *Between Genders: Narrating Difference in Early French Modernism*. Newark: University of Delaware Press, 2004.

Index

abolition of slave trade *see Appel aux souverains réunis à Paris, Préface pour la traduction d'un ouvrage de M. Wilberforce:* Staël
  opposition to 71, 105
  threats to in 1820s: 1, 45–46, 58, 148
  violation of ban on 56
  see also abolitionists, antislavery, Congress of Vienna, antislavery: Dard, Desbordes-Valmore, Doin, Duras
abolition of slavery in French colonies in 1848: 88
  freedom gained 19, 98–99, 105–06, 139 *see Blanche et noir*
  freedom granted 38, 93, 118–19, 135, 144
  French Revolution, during 35
  Napoleon, reinstitution of slavery 32, 41, 48
  see also antislavery, abolitionists
abolitionists
  black 146 *see* Chanlatte, *L'Isolé soleil*, Vastey
  British 20–21, 28n26, 40, 91, 92 *see* Clarkson, Fox, Macaulay, Wilberforce
  fictional *see* Merville: *Famille Noire*, Alliot: *L'Isolé soleil*

French *see* Broglie, Brissot, Diderot, Grégoire, Necker, Schoelcher, Auguste de Staël
  see also shipwreck of Medusa, Amis des noirs, Société de la morale chrétienne
Africa *see* Moors, Britain, control of Senegal
  commerce 34, 35, 54, 59–60, 67, 72, 77n12
  culture 66, 70–73, 76
  education in 2, 18, 69–70, 78n41
  free labor 14, 27n8, 34–36, 51n7, 60, 70
  governors of Senegal *see* Blanchot, Boufflers, Roger, Schmaltz
  history 22, 54, 60, 72–73, 75
  interactions between blacks and whites 72, 74 *see* Senghor
  language 69, 70–71, 115
  Richard Toll 74, 78n38
  Western coast: figure 3, 55
  see also Charlotte Dard, Jean Dard, Mungo Park, Picard
Africans
  character 38, 71
  commitment to freedom 37
  devotion to family 38–39, 46, 68–69, 138–40
  intelligence 40, 71, 105

as slave owners 74, 157–58 *see signares*
women 20, 73, 91
see also Baartman, Boilat, Moors, real-life model of Ourika: Duras, Senghor, *signares*
Allen, James Smith viii, 9
Ambrière, Francis 80
American slave narratives 90 *see* neo-slave narratives
lack of French equivalents 17, 29n55
Amis des noirs 19, 40, 105
Anderson, Benedict 8, 20
Angrand, Jean-Luc vii, 75–76, 79n58
antislavery *see* antislavery: Dard, Desbordes-Valmore, Doin, Duras, Staël
American policies of 118–19
arguments for 3, 49, 71, 90, 93, 105
inhuman conditions 68, 87, 90, 105, 139, 147
preserving families 117–18
summary of 105
and education 71, 91, 93 *see La Famille noire, Noir et blanc*
eye-witness accounts 17, 19, 21, 34, 90, 140, 147, 149
French societies of *see* Amis des noirs, Société de la morale chrétienne
and literature 2, 20–21
refuting pro-slavery views 135, 147, 150n20
and social class 2, 58
and universalism 66, 71, 77–78n29
and women 159
key themes 5
political importance of 6, 7, 25–26
popularizing 3, 9, 87, 132, 149
Appiah, Anthony 8–9, 20
Appel aux souverains réunis à Paris: Staël 49
Ardouin, Coriolan 91

Atala 35, 114
Atelier d'un peintre L': Desbordes-Valmore 81, 84–85, 85, 100n5
Avis au public: Doin 129

Baartman, Saartje 91, 101n25 *see* Hottentot Venus
Balzac, Honoré de 11, 12
Baudelaire, Charles 14
Beauvau, Maréchale de 111–12, 117
Belley, Jean-Baptiste 25, 157–58 *see* Girodet, *Portrait du citoyen Belley*
benevolence *see* empathy, paternalism, sentimentalism
Bernardin de Saint-Pierre *see Paul et Virginie*
and Dard 66–67
Chaumière indienne, La 14, 66–67
and Desbordes-Valmore 85–87
and antislavery 4, 13–14
Chaumière indienne, La 14, 66–67, 86–87, 135 *see* pariahs
Empsaël et Zoraïde 14
as precursor of romanticism 13
Voeux d'un solitaire 14
Voyage à l'île de France 14
see also Charlotte Dard, Vernet
Bertrand, Marc 82, 92, 100n17
Bertrand-Jennings, Chantal 109, 112
Beyala, Calixthe 122–23
Bhabha, Homi 115
Bildungsroman 12
Bissière, Michèle 104, 111
Blanche et noir: Doin
antislavery 135, 144–45, 150n20
daughter's role 134–36
freedom gained 135–36
shared authority 135, 137, 145
Blanchot, François: governor of Senegal 73
Boilat, abbé 76, 79n58
Boime, Albert 64

Bonaparte, Napoleon *see* Napoleon
  Bonaparte
Bongie, Chris 27n13, 126n51, 158
Bordonove, George 61
Boufflers, chevalier de 154
  and Anne Pépin 22, 73, 74
  as governor of Senegal 59, 111–12
  and Ourika 22, 73, 106, 111–12,
    125n25, 154
  and slavery 35, 40, 73, 112
Boutin, Aimée viii, 92–94, 100n11,
    101n27, 101n31
Bouvet de Cressé, Auguste
    Jean-Baptiste 25, 146–49
Boyer, Jean-Pierre 137, 139, 146, 151n26
Brady, Heather viii, 123n2
Brissot, Pierre 40
Britain *see* abolitionists
  admiration for 59–60, 91–92, 147
  control of Senegal 54, 59, 60, 73, 75
Broglie, duc de 32, 50, 103–04
Brontë, Emily 122
Buck-Morss, Susan 26n4, 27n15, 51n7,
    77–78n29, 78n43
Butler, Octavia 17

Camier, Bernard 99, 102n37
Canning, George 49
Caractère de M. Necker, Le: Staël
    44–48
  exile 45
  meaning of "character" 45
  Mémoires d'Isaac, compared to 34,
    44–47
  and Napoleon 45
  reason for writing 34, 44–45, 84
  virtues of Necker 21, 44–45, 47
censorship 2, 34
Césaire, Aimé 24, 104, 120, 122
Chamoiseau, Patrick 119, 120
Chanlatte, Juste Histoire de la
    catastrophe de Saint-
    Domingue, L' 146–49
  antislavery 127–28, 147–48

attitude toward whites 146–47
authorship of 25, 146–48
title 147
women's role 142, 149
Charles X 6, 145
Charte 6
Chateaubriand, François-René
  Atala 35, 114
  and Duras 104, 106, 107, 110–11
  and Paul et Virginie 13–14
  and slavery 113, 114
Chaumière africaine, La see Charlotte
  Dard
Chaumière indienne, La see Bernardin
  de Saint-Pierre
Chauvet, Marie 99
Chilcoat, Michelle 116
Christianisme, Le: Doin 2, 140, 141
Christophe, Henry 24, 120, 146, 147,
    151n26
citizenship *see* Jews, theatrical world
  in Haiti 150n18
  non-French born 105
  and persons of color 124n12, 152
  and women 3, 6, 8, 27–28n18
Cixous, Hélène 39, 93–94, 123, 133
Clarkson, Thomas 21, 49, 50
classicism 13, 155
Code Civil 133, 150n13
Cohen, Margaret 12–13, 109
Cohen, William B. 72
Collet de Messine, Jean-Baptiste 98
colonialism
  defense of 32, 34, 36, 64, 105, 137
  French policies of 59, 70, 74
  privileges of 15
  vision of future 60, 64, 66, 74, 93,
    94, 135, 137–38
  see also Kersaint, Picard
Compagnie de la Guyane 73
Compagnie des Indes 39
Concordat 108
Condé, Maryse
  and *Ourika* 24, 104, 121–22

Migration des coeurs 122–23
Parole des femmes, La 121, 123
and *signares* 23, 74
Congress of Vienna 49, 56
*Considérations sur la révolution
    française*: Staël 47, 50
constitutional monarchy 6
contrapuntal analysis 5, 20, 22, 25,
    27n15, 56
Cooper, William 69
Corinne: Staël 42–44
    agent of resistance 44, 155
    men chained to tradition in 37,
        39, 43
    oppression by fathers in 34, 43
    Oswald and Necker 43
    Toussaint Louverture, comparison
        with 21, 42–44
    as victim 43–44
Cornevin, Robert 72
Corréard, Alexandre 54, 56, 63–64,
    67, 74
Correspondance: Staël 38, 41, 43
creole identity 106
Créole language 94, 99
Cri de mère, Un: Doin 129, 133–34
crowds 46
Czar Alexander I 36, 49

Dard, Charlotte, *La Chaumière
    africaine* 53–79
    antislavery 62, 64, 66–71, 73
    and Bernardin de Saint-Pierre
        66–67
    biography 56–57, 70, 75–76, 78n36
    daughter's role 61–64, 73, 155
        reasons for writing 22, 53, 54,
            57, 76
    education 53, 69–70
    family members 22, 72, 77n14,
        77n16
        children 60–61, 67, 69–70,
            75–76, 79n56, 79n58
        stepmother 57, 60–61, 76n6

maternal grandfather 56–57, 70
mother 56–57, 70
sister Caroline 56, 60–61, 68,
    70, 78n38 75–76, 76n6, 78n36,
    78n38
father 56–62, 70, 73, 76 *see* Picard
Francophone perspective,
    comparison with 73–75
Géricault, comparison with 64–66
male writers, comparison with
    63–64, 67, 74
life in Africa 53, 67–70
persecutors 57–60, 76, 76n9
poetry 70, 78n37
slave identity 67–70
title of 67
translation 53, 59–60, 69, 78n33
see also Picard, shipwreck of
    Medusa, *signares*
Dard, Jean 22, 70–72, 78n41
**DAUGHTERS for overview
    see Introduction, 1–30;
    Postscript, 152–60;
    daughter's role: Dard,
    Desbordes-Valmore, Doin,
    Duras, Staël**
affirmation of paternal authority,
    examples 2–3, 23, 25, 76, 110
and class 2, 9, 13, 141
control of, examples 2, 6, 31–32, 82,
    110, 133
denunciation of slave trade *see Le
    Négrier*
male versions of 157 *see* Guillaume
    Tell Doin, Phénor: *La
    Famille noire*, Picard
as rebels 2, 26n5
resistance to paternal authority 48,
    70, 76, 119
use of term 1–2, 152, 157, 158
see also empathy, empowerment of
    women, marriage, sentimen-
    talism, women's roles, women
    writers

David, Jacques-Louis 85
De La Littérature: Staël 32
De Vinne, Christine 110, 124n17
Debbasch, Yvan 7, 158
Debien, Gabriel 69, 75
Delphine: Staël 37
Desbordes-Valmore, Constant 81, 84,
    85, 154
Desbordes-Valmore, Marceline
    80–102 *see L'Atelier d'un*
    peintre, Sarah
    antislavery 19, 81–83, 89, 90–93
    and Bernardin de Saint-Pierre
        85–87
    biography 23, 80–83, 85, 89, 94–95,
        98, 100n8, 100n10
    champion of downtrodden 13, 23,
        82, 94
    daughter's role 23, 80–84, 94–96,
        98–99, 155
    father 23, 80–84 *see* maternal man
    language 94, 99
    Marie 86
    Minette, comparison with
        94–99
    poems by 81, 84, 94, 99–100n3
    slave identity 7, 23, 83, 89–92,
        96
    theatrical career 80, 95–99
    uncle 81, 84–85
Dessalines, Jean-Jacques 25, 142, 144,
    146, 157
Diderot, Denis 154
discovery
    and Africa 60
    definition of 53
    see also Mungo Park, Picard
divorce 48, 114, 151n27
Dix Années d'exil: Staël 49
Doin, Guillaume Tell 10, 129, 132–33,
    148, 150n11, 154
    and antislavery 131, 150n8
Doin, Marc vii, 129, 130, 149n5,
    150n7

Doin, Sophie 127–51
    and antislavery 2, 24–25, 127,
        131–32, 141, 147–49 *see*
        Blanche et noir, Famille noire,
        Le Négrier, Noir et blanc
    biography of 10, 24, 127–34, 150n7,
        150n12 *see Avis au public, Cri*
        de mère, Simple mémoire
    champion of downtrodden 2, 24,
        131–33, 141–42, 145
    Chanlatte, comparison with
        146–49
    Christianisme, Le 2, 140, 141
    daughter's role 128–34, 149, 155
        see Blanche et noir, Famille
        noire, Le Négrier, Noir et
        blanc
        assumed by Phénor in *La*
            Famille noire 138
        diminished in revised version
            of *Le Négrier* 141
    defense of slave revolts 113
    father 129, 131–32
    and feminism 127, 133–34, 141–42,
        149n1
    Guillon-Lethière, comparison
        with 25, 128, 142–46
    mother 131–32
    portrait of: figure 5, 130, 149n5
    shared authority 10, 19, 24, 127,
        131–34, 142, 145–46, 148 *see*
        Blanche et noir, Famille noire,
        Le Négrier, Noir et blanc
    and slave identity 131–32, 134,
        140–42
    see also Guillaume Tell Doin,
        Marc Doin, marriage
Dupont de Nemours, Pierre Samuel
    14
Duras, Claire de 103–26 *see Ourika*
    antislavery 24, 104, 112–13, 115,
        120–21
    biography of 24, 103–104, 107, 114,
        119, 123n2

and Chateaubriand 104, 106, 107, 110–11

daughter's role 103–07, 155

Grégoire, comparison with 113–14

politics 104, 106, 110–11

real-life model of Ourika 22, 73, 104, 117

father 24, 103–07 *see* Kersaint

religion 109–11

slave identity 107

and Staël 103–04

La Tour du Pin, comparison with 24, 116–19

and voice 104–105

Duroy de Chaumareys, Hugues 54, 58

Emancipation 19, 88, 105, 106, 118–19, 142

empathy *see* Adam Smith, slaves and white women, sentimentalism

and Britain 59–60

examples of 14–15, 35–36, 84–87, 137

limits of 4, 26

and male writers 4–5, 15, 17 *see* Necker, Wilberforce

meaning of 3, 27n7

models of 45, 92

empowerment of women 155

ancien régime 86, 115, 116

artists 84–85, 129

clothing 66, 85

economic 82, 115, 127, 129, 131–32 *see signares*

education 9, 82, 95, 137

maternal ethic of caring 93–94

medicine 110

narrative agency 37–38, 89

rejection of marriage 97, 116

religion 108–109

theater 23, 82, 96

travel 2, 16–17, 53, 67, 103, 116, 123n2

and Virginie: *Paul et Virginie* 85–86, 135

voice 44, 61–64, 133–34

Enlightenment

Kersaint 107

patriarchy 8, 20, 87, 110, 116

Staël 32, 49, 154, 156

see also Diderot, Raynal

Erickson, John 17

exile 2, 3 *see* Necker, Staël

Famille noir, La: Doin 138–40

antislavery 138–40

dialogic structure 25, 139–40

Merville as abolitionist 138–40

Phénor as "daughter" 138

slave family 138–39

shared authority 139–40, 145

symbolic role of son 138–40

vision of Haiti 138–40

Fanoudh-Siefer, Léon 62, 158

FATHERS: for overview see Introduction, 1–30; Postscript, 152–60; *see also* fathers: Dard, Desbordes-Valmore, Doin, Duras, Staël

as abolitionists 2 *see Kersaint, Necker, Picard*

bad fathers, examples of 14, 23, 35–39, 86, 131

death in French Revolution 24, 103, 115, 116

economic struggles 57–58, 62, 80, 82 *see* Desbordes-Valmore, Picard

model *see Caractère de M. Necker*

use of term 2, 157–158

substitute 2, 15, 23, 35, 38–39, 49–50, 56–57, 84–87, 112, 154

weakened authority 2–4, 6, 8, 35, 42, 89, 101n27, 115–16

see also Histoire de Pauline, patriarchy

Favart, Charles Simon 95, 96–97, 102n42

feminism 1, 8, 9, 49, 133 *see* Cixous, hooks, Lerner, Schor, Spivak
  and antislavery 9, 13
  Condé 74
  co-option 8
  ethic of caring 94, 132–33
  gender equality 5, 10, 19–20
  informal feminism 10–11, 20
  nineteenth-century 2, 9–10, 20, 28n32, 115, 127, 134–35, 149n1
  see also Saint-Simonian
  postcolonial 20, 29–30n57
  race, class, and gender 5, 9, 13, 20, 24, 26–27n6, 66, 91
  social complementarity 9, 10, 20
  "talking back" 104, 107, 112
  women's history 6–7, 20, 26n5, 115
  see also Gouges

Flaubert, Gustave 11, 14

focalizer 109, 124n20

Fouchard, Jean 95, 99

Fowles, John 107

Fox, William 49

frame narratives
  Mirza: Staël 35, 38
  "Mon Retour en Europe": Desbordes-Valmore 89
  Ourika: Duras 89, 107–11, 146
  Paul et Virginie: Bernardin de Saint-Pierre 15, 86
  Sarah: Desbordes-Valmore 89–90

Francophone
  definition of 5, 27n13
  exclusion of women 142
  masculinism 18–19, 29–30n57, 120
  nineteenth-century writers 19, 142 *see* Chanlatte, Isaac Louverture
  rewriting Western canon 122–23

twentieth-century writers *see* Césaire, Condé, Mandeleau, Chamoiseau, Chauvet, Maximin, Senghor

French Revolution
  anticlerical outlook 110
  effects of 1–3, 6, 8, 115
  ideology of 12, 103
  National Convention 25, 35
  Terror 24, 85, 103
  and women 3–4, 26n5, 115, 133–34
  see also Kersaint

Garraway, Doris 7

Geggus, David 157–58

gens de couleur *see* Chanlatte, Minette, Pépin, Vastey

Géricault, Théodore: *Le Radeau de la Méduse* 22, figure 4, 65
  antislavery 54, 6, 64–66
  blurring 64, 66, 155–56
  Dard, comparison with 64, 66, 155
  gender 66, 154
  and the Medusa affair 54, 56, 64–66
  race 64, 66, 77n27

Gillet, Nicolas-François 129, 150n7

Girodet, Anne Louis
  Atala au tombeau 157
  historical painting 159n4
  Portrait du citoyen Belley 25, 152–60; figure 7, 153
  antislavery 156
  depiction of Belley 156–59
  and Massot 152–60
  patriarchal authority 158
  and Raynal 152, 154, 156–59
  Sommeil d'Endymion 157

Goldsmith, Oliver 91

Gouges, Olympe de 2, 26n5, 109

"grateful negro" *see* slaves

Grégoire, Henri 66, 71, 109, 113–15, 137, 157

Grigsby, Darcy Grimaldo 64, 144,
    151n32, 156, 157
Guadeloupe 2, 17, 23, 25, 122
    Desbordes-Valmore's voyage to 2,
        23, 80, 81, 83, 89, 90
    and Guillon-Lethière 25, 142
    and Maximin 17
Guerlac, Suzanne 46
Guillon-Lethière, Guillaume 25, 114,
    155
    biography 144–46
    Doin, comparison with 25,
        142–46
    exclusion of women 142, 154
    fraternity 114
    Haitian revolution 142, 144
    historical painting 155
    Oath of the Ancestors (Serment des
        ancêtres): figure 6, 143;
        142–46, 151n32
    patriarchy 25, 144
    shared authority 142, 145
    son Lucien 144–45
Guttinguer, Ulric 120
Gutwirth, Madelyn 43, 45

Haiti
    France's recognition of 13, 21, 25,
        44, 81, 127, 136
    future of 146, 148 see colonialism:
        vision of future, La Famille
        noire
    political leaders see Boyer,
        Christophe, Dessalines,
        Pétion, Toussaint
        Louverture
    and race 113–14, 135
    symbolic political representations
        of 25, 46, 127, 136–38
    threats to independence in 1820s
        45–46, 58, 146, 148
    see also Grégoire, Guillon-Lethière,
        Minette, theatrical world:
        colonial plays

Haitian revolution 98–99, 103
    and Doin 136–38, 141, 147–49
    echoes of in Corinne 42–43
    honored see Guillon-Lethière
    Leclerc's mission 41
    Ourika and 112–13
    responsibility for 113, 139, 147,
        149
    violence 42, 136–39, 147
    see also Blanche et noir, L'Histoire
        de la catastrophe de Saint-
        Domingue, Minette,
        political leaders, Noir et
        blanc, slavery: revolts
Hanniet, Michel viii, 57, 61, 75, 76,
    76n9, 77n16, 79n56
Hegel, Georg Wilhelm Friedrich
    71
Histoire de la catastrophe de Saint-
    Domingue, L' see Chanlatte
Histoire de Pauline: Staël 38–39
    bad fathers 21, 32
    relation to slavery 35, 38
    women's agency 32
    see also patriarchy
historical painting 155, 159n4
Hoffmann, Léon-François 7, 158
honor 48
hooks, bell 104 see feminism:
    "talking back"
Hottentot Venus 91, 101n25 see
    Baartman
Hugo, Victor 4, 11, 157
Huit Femmes: Desbordes-Valmore
    81, 88, 89
Hundred Days 54, 59

individual slaves, fictional
    see Arsène: Sarah, Domingo:
        Blanche et noir, Jonathan:
        L'Isolé soleil, Néala: La
        Famille noire, Nelzi: Noire
        et blanc, Phénor: La
        Famille noire

individual slaves, historical
  see Etienne: *La Chaumière africaine*, Judith: *Journal d'une femme de cinquante ans*, Néali: *Voyage to the Interior of Africa*, Ourika: *Ourika see* Marie: slave
implied author 112
Isbell, John 40, 51n9
Isolé soleil, L': Maximin
  Alliot as abolitionist in 19
  antislavery 18–19
  deconstruction of male accounts 17–19
  narrative style 17, 19
  as neo-slave narrative 17
  and *Ourika* 24, 104, 120–21
  perspective "from below" 17–20
  and women 1, 18, 19, 29n57

Jambe de Damis, La: Desbordes-Valmore 81, 93
Jefferson, Thomas 50
Jensen, Heather Belnap viii, 159n2
Jenson, Deborah viii, 52n22, 52n27
Jews, emancipation of 43, 95, 101n36
Jones, Edward 17
Jordan, Winthrop 26
Jore, Léonce 69, 75
Journal d'une femme de cinquante ans see La Tour du Pin
Julie, ou la Nouvelle Héloise: Rousseau
  Clarens as name 98
  marriage in 39
  Saint-Preux as maternal man 83, 93–94
  M. d'Etange as imperfect father 35, 39, 86, 87, 154
  Mme d'Etange as imperfect mother 39
  M. de Wolmar as model 39, 44, 86, 87, 154
July Monarchy 12

Kale, Steven 106
Keen, Suzanne 3
Kersaint
  and antislavery 24, 103–107, 123n1
  as colonialist 105, 117
  and French Revolution 103
  masculine outlook 106–07
  Moyens proposés à l'Assemblée nationale 104–07
  Ourika, relation to 104–07
  as slave owner 105, 106
  Suite des Moyens proposés à l'Assemblée nationale 104–07
Kitson, Peter 69

La Fayette, marquis de 50, 59, 117
La Tour du Pin, Henriette de:
  Journal d'une femme de cinquante ans 116–19
  Duras, comparison with 24, 104, 116–19
  empathy toward slaves 117–19
  Ourika, attitude toward 117
  as slave owner 117–19, 126n43
Lacan, Jacques 43–44
Lamartine, Alphonse de 4, 5, 121, 126n48
Leclerc, général Charles 41, 42
Léonard, Jacques 110, 121
Lerner, Gerda 6–8, 32
Lionnet, Françoise 126n51
Little, Roger viii, 122, 125n25
Louis XVI 3, 42, 103, 111, 115
Louis XVIII 6, 114
Louverture, Isaac *see Caractère de M. Necker*
  Mémoires d'Isaac 22, 45–47, 52 n27
  mothers 47–48
  reason for writing 34, 45
  sentimental discourse 22, 46–47
  and Toussaint Louverture 22, 34, 45–47

Louverture, Toussaint *see* Isaac
  Louverture, *Caractère de*
  M. Necker
and Belley 157–58
and *Histoire de la catastrophe de*
  Saint-Domingue (Chanlatte)
  148
historical role 34, 41, 42
honor as principle 45, 48
as literary model 4
memoirs 22, 43, 48
and Napoleon 22, 34, 41–43, 48
Necker, comparison with 45–48
Oswald in *Corinne*, comparison
  with 42–43
relation to France 41–43, 48
rescue of white owners 43
Staël's criticism of 41

Macaulay, Zachary 49
male writers compared to women
  writers
  antislavery 1, 4–5, 113–14, 149, 157
  Dard 61–64, 67
  erotic elements 62–64, 74
  Ourika 106–07
  realist tradition 11–13
  signares 22–25, 74
  Staël 48–49
Mandeleau, Tita 23, 75
Marat, Jean-Paul 103
Marie: Desbordes-Valmore 86
Marie: slave 134
Marmontel, Jean-François 95, 97–98
maroons 19, 119
marriage
  in Africa 22, 72–73, 78–80n49
  arranged 131, 133, 137
  authority of father 39, 86, 97–98,
    105, 132, 134
  class prohibitions against 12, 17, 39,
    86, 91, 97–98
  Doin's views 131–34, 140–41, 150n11
  and Germaine Necker 40

Grégoire's views 113–14, 137
interracial 73, 75–76, 79n58, 113–14,
  135–38, 150n24, 150–51n25
and slavery 7, 97, 116, 140–41
unhappy unions 114, 116, 119 *see also*
  Desbordes-Valmore, Doin,
  Duras: biography
Martinique 75, 103, 117, 123n2
Masson, Philippe 56
Massot, Firmin 25, 31, 48, 49, 152, 155
  see Girodet, *Portrait du citoyen*
  Belley 152–60
  Mme de Staël à côté du buste de son
    père Jacques Necker: cover and
    figure 2, 33
  antislavery 154–56
  gender 154, 158–59
  slaves 155–56
  Necker 152, 154–55, 158–59, 159n3
  pictorial mode of 156
  Staël's commission of 155, 159n2
maternal men 83, 93–94
Maximin, Daniel *see Isolé soleil*
Maxwell, Patrick 59, 60, 69
Medusa Affair 22, 56 *see* shipwreck of
  Medusa
Memmi, Albert 15
Mercier, Roger 61–62, 158
Mérimée, Prosper 4, 157
Miller, Christopher 39–40, 51n15,
  77n13, 123n2, 123–24n5, 158
Minette 23, 95–99, 102n37
Mirza 21, 34–38
  antislavery 34–38
  black agency in 34–38, 115
  father figures in 35–37
  influence of 40
  Ourika character in 35, 115
  women's agency in 32, 37–38, 155
Mme de Staël à côté du buste de son père
  Jacques Necker see Massot
Mon Retour en Europe: Desbordes-
  Valmore 89
Moore, Hannah 69

Moors 59, 60, 63–64, 67, 74
Morgan, Philip 92
Morrison, Toni 17, 83–84
La Mort de Virginie, La see Vernet
mothers
    bad mothers 43, 83, 84, 93
    exclusion of 10–11, 66, 74
    importance of 82
    and Isaac Louverture 47–48
    loss of 23, 56, 70, 80, 89, 90, 112
    in *Paul et Virginie* 15–16, 86
    and Rousseau 11
    and slaves 88, 96, 99
    and Staël 47–48
    substitutes for 23, 57, 88, 89, 94,
        112
    see also Cri de mère: Doin
Moyens proposés à l'Assemblée nationale
    see Kersaint

names
    British 91
    first name only 90–91, 96, 98,
        107
    lack of 44, 94, 128, 140, 141, 146
    mixed-race children 73
    nom du père 43–44
    Ourika 35, 115
    Paul et Virginie 14, 135
    patronym 94, 96, 98, 128–29, 132,
        133
    right to use for publication 10, 132,
        150n9
    slaves 90–92
Napoleon Bonaparte
    bad father 6, 40–41, 44, 48
    fall of 6, 49, 54
    persecution of Staël 32, 34, 44,
        48
    reinstitution of religion 108, 111,
        124n17
    reinstitution of slavery 32, 41, 48
    Staël, opposition to 22, 41, 48
    and Toussaint Louverture 41, 45

Necker, Jacques 43, 59 *see Caractère de
    M. Necker*
    antislavery 21, 31–35, 40
    colonial ties 39–40
    colonization 59
    exile of 34, 47
    see also Massot, Staël
Necker, Suzanne Churchod 40
Négrier, Le: Doin
    antislavery 128, 134
    daughter's role in 127–29, 134–35
    involvement in slave trade 128, 141
    marriage 128, 134–35
    later version 141, 151n29
négritude 72
neo-slave narrative 17–20, 83–84
Nochlin, Linda 66
Noir et blanc: Doin
    Haitian politics, symbolic
        representation of 136–38
    interracial marriage 137–38
    revolution 136
    role of daughters 136–38
    shared authority 137

*Oath of the Ancestors (Serment des
    Ancêtres) see* Guillon-Lethière
Ourika: Duras 23–24, 107–23
    authority figures 24, 107–11
    description of 109–110
    feminine perspective 106–07
    frame narration 107–11
    Francophone perspectives on 24,
        119–23
    interpretations of 24, 113, 114–16,
        125n27, 125n38
    legal status of 105
    life story 111–12
    marriage 105–06, 113, 116, 122
    narrative structure 89, 109
    religion 107–11
    slave revolts 112–13, 120–21
    voice 24, 104, 108–09, 111–15, 119,
        155

Pailhès, Gabriel 104, 106, 107, 109
painters *see* David, Desbordes,
    Géricault, Girodet, Guillon-
    Lethière, Massot, Vernet
Pange, comtesse Jean de 40
pariahs 14, 66–67, 86
Park, Mungo 21, 60, 69
patriarchy 6–8, 37
    abuses 15, 23, 48, 87, 90, 92, 112,
        124n11, 136
    definition 8, 92
    and family 7, 8, 32, 43, 62,
        124n11
    and home of father 31, 42–44
    institutions 24, 32, 35, 106–11, 114,
        145
    legal status under 8, 105, 119, 132
    liberation from 1, 8, 18, 42–43, 138
    oldest son 81–82, 97–98, 116
    and paternalism 92–93
        definition 37, 55
    responsibilities of 8, 35, 46, 87,
        92–93
    see also fathers, Gerda Lerner,
        Guillon-Lethière
Paul et Virginie: Bernardin de
    Saint-Pierre
    and Charlotte Dard 66–67
    and Desbordes-Valmore 85–86
    influence of 13–15
    narrative structure 15
    paternal authority 17, 39
    return of slaves to owner 66, 118,
        121, 128, 135
    shipwreck 66
    versions 13
    Virginie as slave 85–86
    virginity as motif 66, 85–86
Pépin, Anne 22, 73–76
Pépin, Nicolas 73
Pétion, Alexandre 25, 113–14, 142, 144,
    157
philanthropists 10, 14, 93
Phillips, Caryl 7

Picard, Charles 77n19 *see* Charlotte
    Dard, Jean Dard, shipwreck
    of Medusa, *signares*
    antislavery 58–59, 68–69, 70, 73
    biography 54, 59, 76n2
    colonialism 53–54, 57, 59
    commercial failings 22, 57–58, 61,
        62
    as sentimental figure 62, 68–69
Pitt, William 40, 49
plagiarism 122–23
Poivre, Pierre 14, 15
Portrait du citoyen Belley see Girodet
portraiture 129, 155, 159n3
postcolonial 20, 27n13, 142
Prasad, Pratima viii, 105–06, 124n12,
    125n27, 125n38
*Préface pour la traduction d'un ouvrage
    de M. Wilberforce*: Staël 36, 49
pre-romanticism 13
propre 39, 93–94, 123
psychoanalytic concepts
    talking cure 108, 110
    pre-Oedipal phase 109, 124n18

racial prejudice 40, 42, 63–64, 71,
    78n43, 86–87, 114, 117, 120,
    134–35
Radeau de la Méduse, Le see Géricault
Raynal, Guillaume-Thomas 15 see
    Girodet, *Portrait du citoyen
    Belley* 25, 152–60
realism 11–12, 109
religion
    and antislavery 109, 141–42
    Concordat 108
    and Duras 109
    in *Ourika* 107–11
    Protestant 43, 109, 144
    re-establishment of convents 108
    and Staël 21, 31, 50
    see also Grégoire, Wilberforce
Rémusat, Charles de 4, 101n29, 157
Rémusat, Claire de 4

Richardson, Samuel 31
Roger, baron: governor of Senegal
  60, 74, 77n13
romanticism 13–14, 37, 83, 94, 155
Rosello, Mireille 122–23
Rossi, Henri 129
Rousseau, Jean-Jacques see Julie, ou la
  Nouvelle Héloïse
  influence of 86, 154
  as masculinist author 154
  reproductive role of women 11
  theater 95, 99

Sabran, comtesse de 73, 74
Safal 61, 67, 69
Said, Edward 3, 5, 10, 20, 72, 94, 98
Saint-Barthélemy 40, 89, 94
Saint-Domingue see Haiti
Saint-Lambert, Jean-François 98
Saint-Louis 59, 60, 61
Saint-Simonian 2, 133, 149n1, 150n14
Sainte-Beuve 107, 123n2
salon 6, 144
  of Beauvau 117
  Tragédie du roi Christophe, La:
    Césaire 120, 122
  of Duras 104, 106, 114, 115, 155
  "poupées noires" 113, 122
  of Staël 41
Sand, George 11, 14, 107, 109
Sarah: Desbordes-Valmore 87–94
  abuses of overseers 87, 88, 93, 94
  antislavery 87–94
  editions 88, 89, 100n17, 100n23
  fathers 87, 91–93
  irresponsible owners 87, 88, 93
  names 90–94
  narrative structure 89–90
  sentimentalism 87–89
Sartre, Jean-Paul 15
Savigny, Jean-Baptiste 54, 56, 63–64,
  67, 74
Schmaltz, Julien-Désiré: governor of
  Senegal 58–59, 61

Schoelcher, Victor 119, 121–22
Schor, Naomi 11–13
Senghor, Léopold Sédar 74
sentimentalism
  discourse of 7, 12–14, 17, 20–21,
    87, 95,158–59 see Sarah, Staël:
    Louverture, Isaac
  limits of 26, 69
  literary values 11, 41
  thematic elements of 12
    Atlantic crossing 15–17, 67, 80,
      81, 85, 91
    beach scenes 16, 17, 85, 145 see
      Vernet
    huts 14, 17, 67
    Néali motif 21
    shipwrecks 62, 66, 85 see Vernet
  see also Bernardin de Saint-Pierre,
    empathy, paternalism
Serment des ancêtres (Oath of the
  Ancestors) see Guillon-
  Lethière
shipwreck of Medusa 22
  antislavery 53, 56, 64
  archival record of 53, 56
  criticism of 54, 56
  race 63–66, 77n27
  raft 54, 64–66
  responsibility for 54, 56, 58, 70
  social class 58, 64, 66
  summary of events of 53–56
  see also Charlotte Dard, Géricault,
    Picard
signares see Angrand, Anne Pépin
  and Condé 23, 74
  hybrid identity 73
  and Mandeleau 23, 75
  "marriage à la mode du pays"
    72–73, 78–79n49
  and Picard family 22, 69–70,
    72–76
  roles of 72–75
  and Senghor 22–23, 74
  as slave owners 73

Simple mémoire: Doin 129
slave agency
    drowning 43, 85–86, 90
    education 18, 91, 93, 95, 134, 135,
        137, 139–40, 147, 157
    literacy 105, 124n10
    killing children 19, 83–84
    maroons 19, 119
    perspective 92 *see Isolé soleil,*
        Chanlatte
    rescuing whites 43, 88 *see Blanche et
        noir, Noir et blanc*
    "self-purchase" 106
    voices 37, 68–69, 89–90, 99, 118–19,
        121, 147 *see Isolé soleil, Blanche
        et noir, Ourika*
    writing 18, 134, 140, 146–49, 150n16,
        157 *see Isolé soleil,* Chanlatte
slavery
    markets 32
    owners 15, 38, 123–24n5 *see Blanche
        et noir,* Kersaint, La Tour du
        Pin, *Sarah, signares*
    revolts 19, 41–42,105 *see* Chanlatte,
        *Blanche et noir, Noir et blanc,
        Ourika*
        Desbordes-Valmore 2, 23, 80,
        89, 94
    traders 35–36, 67, 138 *see Le Négrier*
        association with 39–40, 64, 70,
        73, 123–24n5
    subsidy to 40
SLAVES; for overview see
        **Introduction, 1–30;
        Postscript, 152–60; see also
        antislavery, slave identity:
        Dard, Desbordes-Valmore,
        Doin, Duras, Staël**
    and birds 83, 84, 85–86, 100n12
    black owners 157–58
    in France 113, 125n32
    "grateful negro" motif 36, 112,
        117–19, 121
    and pariahs 14, 66–67, 86–87

regenerated 66, 71, 121, 145
and serfs 49
sexuality 18, 91, 113, 157
use of term 3, 26n2,92, 49, 92, 152,
    157, 158
*see also Blanche et noir, Noir et blanc,
    Ourika, Sarah*
slaves and white women 157 *see* slave
    identity: Dard, Desbordes-
    Valmore, Doin, Duras, Staël
    empathy 3–4
    La Tour du Pin 118–19
    patriarchy 7, 10
    Virginie 85
Smith, Adam 3, 27n8
social complentarity 9
social death 86
social sentimental novel 12–13
Société de la morale chrétienne 10,
    28–29n37, 70, 132, 150n8
Spivak, Gyatri 158
Staël, August de 32, 50, 154, 158
Staël, Germaine de 31–52 *see Corinne,
    Histoire de Pauline, Mirza*
    antislavery 21, 31–32, 34–40, 48–50,
        109, 112, 113, 117 *see Appel
        aux souverains réunis à Paris,
        Préface pour la traduction d'un
        ouvrage de M. Wilberforce*
    evolution of views on 21, 32, 34,
        45, 48–50, 159
    conflicting values 21, 31–32, 49–50,
        155
    daughter's role 154–55, 158–59 *see
        Caractère de M. Necker*
    exile 34, 42, 44, 45
    father 25, 31, 35, 37, 47–50, 158–59
        see Caractère de M. Necker
    influence of 4, 40
    family members 32, 40, 47–48, 49
    legacy 4, 31, 32, 49–50, 155, 159
    and Louverture, Isaac 22, 34,
        45–47
    and Louverture, Toussaint 41

mother 47–48, 52n31
resistance to paternal authority
   31–32, 49
slave identity 35, 38–40, 44, 45
and women 45, 48, 50
see also Massot, Napoleon, Necker,
   Wilberforce
Stendhal 11, 12
Stowe, Harriet Beecher 109
subordination of women 6–9, 13, 15,
   3   2
Suite des Moyens proposés à l'Assemblée
   nationale see Kersaint
Sussman, Charlotte 20–21

theatrical world
   careers in 23, 82, 95–97
   citizenship 95, 101n36
   colonial plays 95–99
Traités de Paris 60
Traer, James 133
Trouillot, Michel-Rolph 61

universalist 66, 71, 77–78n29, 121
Unsworth, Barry
utopian 11, 78n31, 127

Vastey, baron de 120, 122
Veillées des Antilles: Desbordes-
   Valmore 87
Vernet, Joseph: *La Mort de Virginie*
   figure 1, 16; 17, 85, 155
Villevêque, Laisné de 137
Volet, Jean-Marie 77n19, 78n31
Voltaire 95
Voyage to the Interior of Africa see
   Mungo Park

Wilberforce, William
   abolition of slave trade 40, 49, 50
   father figure for Staël 49–50
   praise for Chanlatte 50, 147
   religion 50
   see also Préface pour la traduction
      d'un ouvrage de M. Wilberforce
Wing, Nathanial 114–16
women's roles 6–8, 15, 17, 61, 66 *see*
   daughters
   in commerce 72, 74 *see signares*
   in political arenas 2, 6, 12,
      27–28n18, 49, 104, 138, 149
   preserving slave legacy 18
   in publishing 6, 10 *see* Doin
   in revolution *see* Minette
   survival 22, 53, 62, 82, 85, 86, 95
   see also empowerment of women,
      salons
women writers 11–13 *see* daughters
   and black writers 5, 19–20, 25
   class replacing race in 1830s 13, 141
   dismissed from canon 1, 5, 7, 9,
      11–12, 158
   idealism 11
   importance of 1–2, 4, 5, 7–9, 25–26,
      40
   lesser-known 2, 5, 7, 158, *see* Dard,
      Doin
   motivations for writing by 2–3
   poetry 18, 70 *see* Desbordes-
      Valmore, poems
   treatment by male critics 7, 39–40,
      61–62, 107, 120–23, 126n51, 155,
      157–58

Zola, Emile 11

Printed and bound by CPI Group (UK) Ltd, Croydon, CR0 4YY

09/06/2025

14685809-0002